T0302146

'Wong and Chau present a wonderful historical ethnography of a Hong Kong jewellery company, charting out its transformation from a one-man entrepreneurial show into a large company with multiple branches and marketing campaigns. Interwoven into this depiction is a very skilful analysis and deconstruction of the idea of traditional "Chinese management methods" or "Chinese companies" in the context of contemporary capitalism. Well-written, empirically rich, and full of insights, it represents a true contribution to studies of current-day models of management.'

—**Eyal Ben-Ari**, *Senior Research Fellow, The Kinneret Center on Peace, Security and Society in Memory of Dan Shomron*

'In their examination of a Hong Kong family jewellery business, Heung Wah Wong and Karin Ling-Fung Chau's extraordinary book provides a devastating critique of contemporary management theory and its politics, whilst making a compelling case for the decisive importance of culture in business. As it does so, it also provides a brilliant anthropological study that has revolutionary implications for business and management studies.'

—**Wayne Cristaudo**, *Professor of Political Science, Charles Darwin University*

'This book makes an important contribution to the literature by combining business, entrepreneurship, anthropology, and comparative cultural traditions of Hong Kong, Mainland China, Taiwan, and Japan. It is significant to note that the authors offer a different perspective not often heard from the business and management field. It will be of great interest to scholars to see how the book melds cultural family traditions (e.g. tribal and patrilineal, among others) with the usual narrative on business, entrepreneurship, and cultural elements. The book's use of the case study method is also notable, especially how the authors morph it into an academic tome. Business schools should take note of this book. It will reinforce their drive for a multidisciplinary perspective. Very useful in this era of never-felt-before challenges.'

—**Reuben Mondejar**, *Emeritus Associate Professor, City University of Hong Kong*

Tradition and Transformation in a Chinese Family Business

Family businesses have been an important part of the economy in Hong Kong, Taiwan, Singapore, and in the Chinese diaspora, and, since the reforms, in mainland China itself. Some people have argued that the success of Chinese family businesses occurs because of the special characteristics and approach of such businesses. This book examines the nature of Chinese family business and the key issues involved by exploring in detail the case of a leading Hong Kong jewellery company which was established in the early 1960s and which has grown to become one of the biggest jewellery manufacturers, exporters, and retailers in post-war Hong Kong. The book considers the motivations of Chinese people to set up their own businesses, outlining the strategies adopted, including the strategies for raising capital, and the qualities of successful Chinese entrepreneurs. It discusses the management of the company, including relations between family members, profit sharing and succession planning, and assesses how conflict and crises are coped with and overcome. It also charts the evolution of the company, looking at how it has been transformed into a listed corporation and modernized. The book concludes by arguing for the importance of studying Chinese family businesses culturally.

Heung Wah Wong is an Associate Professor in the School of Modern Languages and Cultures at the University of Hong Kong.

Karin Ling-Fung Chau is a MPhil/PhD student in the Department of Culture, Media and Creative Industries at King's College London.

How and what are we to examine if we wish to understand the commonalities across East Asia without falling into the powerful fictions or homogeneities that dress its many constituencies? By the same measure, can East Asian homogeneities make sense in any way outside the biases of East–West personation?

For anthropologists familiar with the societies of East Asia, there is a rich diversity of work that can potentially be applied to address these questions within a comparative tradition grounded in the region as opposed the singularizing outward encounter. This requires us to broaden our scope of investigation to include all aspects of intra-regional life, trade, ideology, culture, and governance, while at the same time dedicating ourselves to a complete and holistic understanding of the exchange of identities that describe each community under investigation. An original and wide ranging analysis will be the result, one that draws on the methods and theory of anthropology as it deepens our understanding of the interconnections, dependencies, and discordances within and among East Asia.

The book series includes three broad strands within and between which to critically examine the various insides and outsides of the region. The first is about the globalization of Japanese popular culture in East Asia, especially in greater China. The second strand presents comparative studies of major social institutions in Japan and China, such as family, community, and other major concepts in Japanese and Chinese societies. The final strand puts forward cross-cultural studies of business in East Asia.

Tradition and Transformation in a Chinese Family Business
Heung Wah Wong and Karin Ling-Fung Chau

For more information about this series, please visit: www.routledge.com/
Routledge-Culture-Society-Business-in-East-Asia-Series/book-series/CSBEA

Tradition and Transformation in a Chinese Family Business

Heung Wah Wong
and Karin Ling-Fung Chau

LONDON AND NEW YORK

First published 2020
by Routledge
2 Park Square, Milton Park, Abingdon, Oxon OX14 4RN

and by Routledge
605 Third Avenue, New York, NY 10017

First issued in paperback 2021

Routledge is an imprint of the Taylor & Francis Group, an informa business

Publisher's Note
The publisher has gone to great lengths to ensure the quality of this reprint but points out that some imperfections in the original copies may be apparent.

British Library Cataloguing-in-Publication Data
A catalogue record for this book is available from the British Library

Library of Congress Cataloging-in-Publication Data
A catalog record for this book has been requested

ISBN 13: 978-1-03-208274-5 (pbk)
ISBN 13: 978-1-138-91484-1 (hbk)

Typeset in Times New Roman
by Apex CoVantage, LLC

Contents

Illustrations

Figure

Tables

Acknowledgements

This is a long overdue book. We would like to express our deepest gratitude to all our informants, whom we are not able to name here, regrettably, as we have to protect their identity. We would especially like to thank: the founder of the company, who is a respectable figure in the jewellery industry in Hong Kong and from whom we have learnt a lot; the son and daughter-in-law of the founder, who respect our academic independence and autonomy; and the then Deputy CEO of the company, who has become a good friend of ours and whose passion and sincerity we highly cherish.

We are extremely grateful to Dr. Pui-tak Lee and Dr. Reuben Mondejar, who reviewed our manuscript and provided tremendously helpful comments to us. We would also like to express our greatest gratitude to Professor Eyal Ben-Ari, who went through the whole manuscript and provided insightful suggestions to us and much encouragement, as always, and to Dr. Andrew MacNaughton, who helped proofread the manuscript. Special thanks go to Professor Wayne Cristaudo, our comrade and intellectual soulmate, who went through the final draft of the manuscript and pointed out major areas in need of strengthening. Of course, all omissions and mistakes remain ours.

Karin Ling-Fung Chau would, in particular, like to thank all her former colleagues, especially her supervisor, in the Corporate and Communications department of the company for their care and tolerance. Loving thanks go to WW, who has always been the best friend and companion.

Wong would like to express his gratitude to the National Museum of Ethnology, Osaka, Japan which provided him with a comfortable academic environment when he was on sabbatical leave from January 2016 to January 2017 and wrote parts of this book there. Special thanks go to Professor Kenichi Sudo, at that time Director General of the Museum, who never fails to provide personal and professional support to Wong.

Lastly, we thank everyone at Routledge, whose professionalism has made this book possible. Special thanks to Peter Sowden, editor-in-chief of this series, for his invaluable support.

Notes

1   Both authors, Heung Wah Wong and Karin Ling-Fung Chau, have contributed equally to the manuscript.

2   *Currency*. Unless specified, the currency used in the book is Hong Kong Dollars (HKD). The HKD was pegged to the USD at a fixed rate of HK$7.8 = US$1 in 1983 following the introduction of the linked exchange rate system.

3   *Pseudonyms*. In order to protect the identity of our informants, we have attempted to remove all the unnecessary personally identifiable information from the book. Fong Bou Lung, the main protagonist of the book, and FBL, the company that he founded are pseudonyms. All the names of the employees of the company are also pseudonyms. For the same purpose, we have not included sources containing personally identifiable information in the reference list. For other names, we specify whenever pseudonyms are used.

4   *Name*. In the Chinese language, the surname precedes the first name. In Hong Kong, the majority of Chinese observe the same rule. Throughout the book, we respect the way how our informants give their names:

    a)   For those who give their names in the Chinese way, the first appearance of their names is in the format of: surname, first name. Thereafter, we refer to them by their first name (Chinese name).

    b)   For those who give their names in the English way, the first appearance of their names is in the format of: first name (English name), surname. Thereafter, we refer to them by their first name (English name).

    c)   For the main protagonist of the book, Fong Bou Lung (pseudonym), we refer to him by his surname, Fong, only.

5   *Transliteration*. In this book, we follow the *Jyutping* system for the transliteration of Cantonese names and terms. For other Chinese terms, the *Hanyu Pinyin* system is adopted.

Part I

1   Introduction

Fong Bou Lung, aged 78 in 2014, wakes up at 6:45 a.m. every day. He then has breakfast with his wife, exercises in a park nearby, takes a shower and prepares for work. When we visited Fong for the first time, he had, as usual, arrived at the office by 10:30 a.m. He wore a grey jacket, a plain white shirt, and a pair of khaki trousers. Nothing was showy or dramatic. The 'small' man in front of us looked like an ordinary Chinese elderly man except that he had distinctively thick, black hair, and a lot of energy. Fong walked amazingly fast, like a storm. As he was heading for his office on the second floor, Carrie To, the Head of the Corporate Communications Department, ran into him in the corridor and greeted him. 'Good morning, Kum *neoi*[1] (literally: Kum the little girl)!' he responded in a loud voice with a big smile. Fong addresses the employees with their Chinese instead of English names; the latter are commonly used in the white-collar workplaces in Hong Kong. The fact that Fong addresses his staff by their Chinese name touches many of his staff. As one of the employees of the company, remarked, 'I feel very warm, only my family members call me by my Chinese name.'[2]

Located at the back of the office area, Fong's room is the biggest in the company, like a mini-headquarters overseeing the whole operation of the floor. The name tag on his office door reads: 'Founder, Fong Bou Lung'. Fong usually kicks off his workday by reading newspapers, letters, and some company documents. Sometimes, Fong checks out the office of the Corporate Communications Department next door to find someone to help translate the English letters and documents into Chinese and look for some information on the internet for him. Fong also meets visitors, friends, and business partners in his office. He is also active in catching up with the operations of the company. For instance, he attends the meetings of the senior management team, but he has a hard time following the conversation as they tend to use English presentations and terms during discussions. When he needs to get information about a certain aspect of the business, he goes directly to the office of the person-in-charge to ask for the statistics and reports. After all, he is being employed by the company as 'Founder' to provide 'general advisory and strategic advice'.

When Fong is not in the office, he is, for most of the time, 'inspecting' the retail branches of the company scattered throughout Kowloon, Hong Kong Island, and the New Territories. As an icon of the company, Fong also needs to attend different business and social events. Fong usually gets off work and goes home around 6:30 p.m. But where is home? To Fong, the office is his home. Fong is inseparable from the company not simply because he founded 'Fong Bou Lung Jewellery Company' (FBL). It is also because he has dedicated almost his whole life to building, developing, and maintaining the company. As Fong told us:

> I have never had a day-off. I have never owed the company. I have only been sacrificing myself for the company.

Fong Bou Lung (FBL) the company and Fong Bou Lung the person, at least before the son of Fong took over the chairmanship in 2000, had been a *Schicksalsgemeinschaft* (community of fate) as we can see that the company is named after him. As Fong said, 'FBL is me and I am FBL.'

Born in Hong Kong, Fong comes from a very poor family. At the age of 13, he was sent to a goldsmith to become an apprentice. Around 1960, Fong started his own jewellery workshop. In about 30 years, he developed this workshop into one of the most popular local jewellery brands. Between the end of the 1990s and the early 2000s, the Fong family and FBL, however, underwent a series of crises. Fong went bankrupt. Subsequently, the senior management of FBL including Fong and his son were arrested, prosecuted, and sentenced to prison. Within a decade, FBL had gone from a reputable brand into a failing company on the brink of collapse. In the 2010s, Fong's daughter-in-law, Emma, tried to recruit professional managers to rebuild and rebrand FBL. The reform, however, ended in failure with the resignation of those professional managers.

These episodes are suggestive of several major questions we ask in this book: Why and how is Fong qualified as an entrepreneur? How did his entrepreneurial process proceed? What did the management of his family firm look like? And how and why did his successors professionalize the company? Narrowly conceived, this book is an anthropological study of entrepreneurship, management of family firms, and their professionalization. But it sets its sights more ambitiously in one respect: it is also an attempt to engage in a dialogue, especially with scholars from mainstream-US-dominated management sciences. In Wong's forthcoming article, 'It is Not that All Cultures Have Business, But That All Business Has Culture', he argues that culture is the essential condition of human existence rather than an additive factor to something more fundamental for human behaviour (Wong, forthcoming). As Marshall Sahlins (2000a, p. 158) effectively argued, culture is 'the organization of human experience and action by symbolic means. The persons, relations, and materials of human existence are enacted according to their meaningful values – meanings that cannot be determined from their biological or physical properties.' It follows that anything human including 'commercial' must be cultural, because business activities are meaningfully constituted (Sahlins, 2000b, pp. 9–32).

The implication of Wong's position on culture is important in our context because it speaks to the fact that the objects of anthropology share the same ontological status with those of management sciences, which is also to say that anthropology and management sciences should share the same epistemological stance. Scholars of these two disciplines, however, seem to adopt very different methodological approaches to and discourses on business phenomena, not to mention the criteria for assessing their work. It is not our purpose to identify the reasons for such differences between the two disciplines. What we want to do instead is to have a dialogue with our colleagues within mainstream-US-dominated management sciences through providing a critical review of their work on entrepreneurship, the management of (Chinese) family business, and the professionalization of family firms published in the top US-based management journals, because we believe that the first step to open up such dialogue is to engage with each other's work.

We, however, do not claim that our review covers the entire literature in the field. In fact, it is difficult, if not impossible, to make our review exhaustive given the fact that the entire literature is voluminous, and their theoretical discourses heterogeneous. We are only able to focus on those works that have been very influential in the field and/or address a common problem that mainstream management scientists and we anthropologists engage with in a constructive sense. The point of our review is to identify the major problems in the literature of mainstream-US-dominated management sciences concerning entrepreneurship, the management of (Chinese) family business and the professionalization of family firms on which this book can shed some light. Our review therefore is unavoidably selective, always idiosyncratic, and perhaps contains errors. Another necessary apology is that our review may not be able to pay sufficient attention to alternative theoretical discourses situated within the field, let alone those outside of the mainstream circle.

It is also important to clarify at the beginning of this book what this study does *not* set out to achieve. Our book is intended neither as a study of the economic and social history of post-war Hong Kong through the case of Fong and his company nor as an exhaustive ethnography of a Chinese family firm in Hong Kong. We believe that there are many other publications by more competent colleagues that have already covered those topics. While the scope of our book is relatively modest, our intention is perhaps excessively ambitious.

The individual–opportunity nexus

The literature of entrepreneurship to be reviewed here is the so-called Individual–Opportunity Nexus (ION) proposed in the article titled 'The Promise of Entrepreneurship as a Field of Research' by Scott Shane and Sankaran Venkataraman (2000). The reason that we choose ION is threefold. First, the article received the 2010 Academy of Management Review (AMR) Decade Award, the receipt of which, as Shane (2012, p. 10) admitted, 'confirmed that it [the article] has significantly impacted the field of entrepreneurship'. In fact, the article 'has influenced scholars within the fields of entrepreneurship and management, as well as scholars from a variety of other disciplines' (Venkataraman et al., 2012, p. 21), which can be taken to mean that ION has an interdisciplinary appeal. It follows that

ION can serve as a good opportunity for interdisciplinary engagement. Second, the definition of entrepreneurship 'as the identification, evaluation, and exploitation of opportunities' given in ION is widely adopted in the field to the extent that some scholars even regard the definition as the *consensus* definition (Shane, 2012, p. 12). Our engagement with ION is thus methodologically strategic in starting a conversation with the majority of scholars of entrepreneurship within mainstream-US-dominated management sciences.

Finally, and most importantly, the ION shares a similar theoretical framework with the one we are going to put forward in this book. As Shane (2003) pointed out in his seminal book, *A General Theory of Entrepreneurship: The Individual-Opportunity Nexus*, there are two major theoretical approaches to the study of entrepreneurship. The first one is what Shane (2003) called an individual-centric approach which considers core human attributes as independent variables that explain entrepreneurship. This approach assumes that there are what Shane called 'entrepreneurial individual' in the society who possess core human attributes such as inclination to bear uncertainty and ambiguity which explain their entrepreneurship (Shane, 2003, p. 2). The major problem of the individual-centric approach, according to Shane (2003), lies in the fact that even entrepreneurial individuals would not engage entrepreneurial activities all the time and in all situations. If the depositions of individuals *alone* could account for entrepreneurship, these individuals should have participated in entrepreneurial activity all the time. Obviously, 'it is impossible to account for entrepreneurship solely by examining factors that should influence all human actions in the same way all of the time' (Shane, 2003, pp. 2–3). The second approach is what Shane (2003) called an environment-centric approach. Scholars adopting this approach propose that entrepreneurship can be explained by an environment where 'entrepreneurial activity, often measured by new firm formation, is more likely to occur' (Shane, 2003, p. 3). The crucial problem of the environment-centric approach, to Shane (2003), is its ignorance of human agency. The execution of entrepreneurial activity requires human agency. Environment itself cannot engage in entrepreneurial activity. It follows from this that '[n]o amount of investigation of the environment alone can provide a complete explanation for entrepreneurship' (Shane, 2003, p. 3).

What is needed is, Shane (2003, p. 3) continued to argue, a comprehensive framework that 'incorporate[s] the effects of individuals, as well as the effects of opportunities and the institutional and industry environment in which the pursuit of opportunity occurs'. Shane (2003, p. 4; italics ours) then defined entrepreneurship as 'an activity that involves the discovery, evaluation and exploitation of opportunities to introduce *new* goods and services, ways of organizing, markets, processes, and raw materials through organizing efforts that previously *had not existed*'. This definition implies an approach to entrepreneurship which 'think[s] not just about the people who identify, evaluate, and exploit opportunity but also about the opportunities those people identify, evaluate, and exploit' (Shane, 2012, p. 15).

Several observations can be made in light of this definition. First, entrepreneurship requires the existence of both individuals and opportunities. Second, entrepreneurship should be seen as a social process in which the individual identifies, assesses, and exploits the opportunity (Shane, 2012, p. 14). The crucial question for scholars of entrepreneurship is the nature and character of the opportunity exploitation including 'the strategies used to pursue opportunities; and the organizing efforts to exploit them' (Shane, 2003, p. 5). Third, the objects of the entrepreneurial activity are not confined to new products but also include many different things ranging from ways of organizing, markets, processes to raw materials. The formation of new firms for exploiting opportunities is not considered to be the necessary condition of entrepreneurship because exploitation of opportunities, as Shane (2003, p. 8) argued, can also be done by existing companies or markets through franchising. Fourth, these objects have to be new, and thus *different* from the existing ones. As Shane (2012, p. 17) explained, 'the exploitation of entrepreneurial opportunities demands the creation of new means-ends relationships (ways to combine resources) rather than optimization within existing means-ends frameworks'. The final observation is the objectivity of the entrepreneurial opportunity. According to Shane (2012, p. 16), opportunities refer to 'situations in which people have the potential to make a profit'. In his response to the scholars who go for the subjective definition of opportunities, Shane (2012) argued that the concept of opportunities must be objective because if the opportunities were subjective, the ION would have become redundant. For it is not necessary to talk about the *nexus* between the individual and the opportunity any more as everything can be reduced to the individual (Shane, 2012, p. 16).

We have to say immediately that we agree with many of the arguments of ION; we share with ION the processual nature of entrepreneurship; we echo ION's view that neither the person-centric approach that there are only individuals nor the environment-centric respect for the deterministic power of environment turns out to be a good explanation for entrepreneurship; and we have no doubt that entrepreneurship should be understood as the result of the relationship between the individual and the environment. What we are not satisfied with is the non-symbolic cultural theory of ION with its ontological roots in Cartesian dualism, 'which suggested that the subject and object were two distinct realms of the world that could be methodically separated' (Deetz, 1992, p. 117). As a result, the argument of ION runs either from the subject to the object or vice versa, which is to say that the dualism can only reproduce either the person-centric or the environment-centric approach.

The subject of ION is seen as a typical *homo economicus* 'whose single-minded pursuit of his own pleasure or gain by the rational choice of the alternatives presented by a supposedly self-regulating market' (Sahlins, 2013, p. 163). Shane's 'entrepreneurial individual' is an abstract being except that s/he possess the dispositions of some psychological and cognitive characteristics which make him/her a machine of exploiting entrepreneurial opportunities. Sahlins (1976a) has already offered an effective critique of the *homo economicus* elsewhere, so we are not going to repeat the argument here. What we want to emphasize is the social specification of human subjectivity. Human subjectivity cannot be seen as abstract and universal but culturally specific and socially relative. As we will demonstrate in Chapter 3, Fong developed a set of attitudes from his social position as a child of lower-class families in the socio-economic environment of Hong Kong where he grew up. This set of attitudes constitutes Fong's entrepreneurial ethos because it is closely related to his entrepreneurial pursuit. In other words, Fong's dispositions cannot be attributed to his biological makeup, which is also to say that there is no biological determination of entrepreneurship.

But Sahlins (2000b, pp. 284–285; italics ours) also reminded us that '[t]he individual is a social being, but we must never forget that he is an *individual* social being, with a biography not the same as that of anyone else'. Fong cannot be seen as the actualization of the socio-economic configuration of the post-war Hong Kong society because 'there is no specific correspondence or adequacy between the two' (Sahlins, 1976a, p. 131). Between Fong's entrepreneurial ethos and his social position in the socio-economic environment there is a gap created by the intervention of his family. As we will show in Chapter 3, the configuration of Fong's family gives him an individuality that cannot be reduced to his social position. In short, Fong cannot be reduced to his socio-economic position in the Hong Kong society. There is no simple socio-cultural determination of entrepreneurship, either.

We have to emphasize not only the social specification of human subjectivity but also of the 'environment'. We learn from Marx that the environment is socially relative and historically varied. As we will demonstrate in the following chapters, the environment where Fong pursued his entrepreneurial activities changed with the transformation of Hong Kong from manufacturing to service economy, in the course of which the environment is constituted and reconstituted. It follows from this that human perception of the 'environment' does not mirror the environment but depends on the way it is *constituted* in a given historical occasion by culture. The 'environment' therefore is a humanized – not an 'objective' – environment.

However, we are not arguing for the subjective nature of 'environment' and opportunities. Nor are we suggesting that the 'environment' is irrelevant. What we are asserting is that the determination of entrepreneurship by the 'objective' environment is itself indeterminate. To borrow Sahlins' (1976a, p. 168) argument:

> For the material conditions, if always indispensable, are potentially 'objective' and 'necessary' in many different ways – according to the cultural selection by which they become effective "force." Of course in one sense nature is forever supreme. No society can live on miracles, thinking to exist by playing her false. None can fail to provide for the biological continuity of the population in determining it culturally – can neglect to provide shelter in producing houses, or nourishment in distinguishing the edible from inedible. Yet men do not merely 'survive'. They survive in a definite way. They reproduce themselves as certain kinds of men and women, social classes and groups, not as biological organisms or aggregates of organisms ('population'). True that in so producing a cultural existence, society must remain within the limits of physical-natural necessity. But this has been considered axiomatic at least since Boas, and not even the most biological of cultural ecologies can claim any more: 'limits of viability' are the mode of the practical intervention of

nature in culture. Within this limit, any group has the possibility of great range of 'rational' economic intentions, not even to mention the option of production strategy that can be conceived from the diversity of existing techniques, the example of neighbouring societies, or the negation of either.

The indeterminacy of entrepreneurship by the 'objective' environment is the result of cultural intervention, which gives 'force' to the 'objective' environment in the way that is not the only one possible but varies with historical occasions. We will see in Chapter 4, 5, and 6 how the economic structures of Hong Kong in different historical periods rendered Fong's various entrepreneurial pursuits meaningful and significant; and how the transformation of the economic structure from manufacturing-oriented to service-oriented changes the parameter of what constitutes meaningful entrepreneurial pursuits. As Sahlins quoted Marx's famous argument:

> A Negro is a Negro. Only under certain conditions does he become a slave. A cotton-spinning machine is a machine for spinning cotton. Only under certain circumstances does it become *capital*. Torn away from these conditions it is as little capital as gold by itself is money, or as sugar is the price of sugar.
> (Marx 1993 [1849], p. 28, 1967, 3:814 f., cited in Sahlins, 1976a, p. 132)

Here we are arguing that the determination of entrepreneurial pursuits and the significance thereof is a general specification of the socio-historical order.

Shane's assertion of objective existence of environment and opportunities, however, has a fatal consequence to the ION framework. If the environment and opportunities have an objective existence *out-there* waiting for individual entrepreneurs to discover, evaluate, and exploit, the reasons for the differential competence of discovering the opportunity among individuals must be sought *in-here* such as the psychological dispositions or cognition of individuals. Perhaps that is why Shane's (2000) recent studies of entrepreneurship tend to focus on the relationship between the motivation of individuals and their opportunity discovery, arguing how their motivations help them to *correctly* identify entrepreneurial opportunities. More recently, Shane has pushed this focus to an extreme, exploring the relationship between individuals' genetic makeup and their entrepreneurship (Nicolaou et al., 2009; Nicolaou and Shane, 2014; Nofal et al., 2018; Quaye et al., 2012; Shane, 2010). In other words, despite his critique of the person-centric approach to entrepreneurship, Shane himself ends up repeating the same approach and thus its errors as he himself pointed out.

Since Sahlins (1976b) has offered a thorough critique of the biological determination of human behaviour elsewhere, we are not going to repeat his argument here. What we want to point out, however, is the *discontinuity* between the motivation and the significance of human behaviours. There is a general agreement among anthropologists, sociologists, political scientists, and the man in the street that human behaviours are meaningful and take place in terms of that meaning. The constitution of human behaviours is necessarily in three terms: the act, the meaningful system, and the mediation between the two. The act itself has its own reasons *sui generis* such as the intention of the individual at issue to maximize his or her monetary return; and the meaningful system is what anthropologists call culture, which is symbolic by nature and therefore 'stimulus free', by which we mean that culture cannot be reduced to what Sahlins (1976a) called practical reason, be it biological, economical, or ecological. The meaning of a human act is the result of the mediation between the act and culture, meaning here is in the double sense of importance and significance. The significance of a human act is given by the mediation between culture and the act, which is also to say that the significance of a human act cannot be reduced to the intention of the individual who initiates the act. The intention of a human act and its significance are categorically different. The latter is the result of cultural encompassment of the human act. The intention of a human act cannot determine its significance because between them there is a gap created by the intervention of cultural context in which the human act occurs. That is why Fong, as we will demonstrate in Chapter 4, 5, and 6, could not predict the results of his entrepreneurial pursuit.

In short, between the individual (subject) and the environment (object), there is a gap created by the intervention of culture. The individual is not subjectively defined, the environment does not objectively exist either; but both are culturally constituted. As Lévi-Strauss famously argued:

> Without questioning the undoubted primacy of infrastructures, I believe that there is always a mediator between *praxis* and practices, namely the conceptual scheme by the operation of which matter and form, neither with any independent existence, are realized as structures, that is as entities which are both empirical and intelligible.
>
> (cited in Sahlins, 1976a, p. 56)

In other words, between the subject and the object, there is culture as a meaningful system which constitutes both.

An anthropological idea of entrepreneurship

We believe that we have theoretically prepared the reader for a new understanding of entrepreneurship. We argue that entrepreneurship is the significance an individual pursuit acquires from its mediation with the socio-cultural contexts in which the pursuit takes place. Or we can speak of the intersection of individual pursuits and the socio-cultural contexts. Entrepreneurship results from the ways different orders of determination intersect in which neither of them can totally determine the final outcome of the intersection. Following Shane's idea that entrepreneurship involves a *new* means-and-ends relationship, which must be *different* from the original means-and-ends relationship, entrepreneurial pursuits, first of all, should be seen as difference-makings; but analytically there are two categories of difference-makings. One is the difference that can acquire significance and importance from the socio-cultural context; the other is one that cannot. Entrepreneurship obviously refers to the former. We argue that whether a certain difference-making can acquire significance and importance is dependent on the power derived from the social position of the person who initiates the difference-making or/and the configuration of the socio-cultural contexts. The first is what Sahlins called structural power (Smith, 2002). Fong, as the founder and controlling shareholder of his company, had the agentive power within the company because his difference-making can lead to the structural changes of the company. The second is conjunctural power (Smith, 2002). As we will demonstrate in Chapter 5, the success of Fong's showroom business is due to the fact that his branching out into showroom business took place at the right time *and* in the right place. Fong was in a conjunctural position that enabled his venture into showroom business and determined the significance thereof. But it was the conjunctural situation – the complex relationships among overseas travel agents, local tour operators, and retail shops – that put Fong in such a conjunctural position.

The socio-cultural context cannot dictate what an entrepreneur would do as s/he is motivated by his or her idiosyncratic orientation. We will see how Fong's efforts in ever expanding his jewellery manufacturing business were driven by his unique business logic of maximizing production developed from his biographical experiences.

All of this speaks to one important feature of entrepreneurship: the *discontinuity* between the properties and the determinants of the phenomena so articulated as entrepreneurship. Neither the individual pursuit nor the socio-cultural contexts where it occurs can determine the pursuit as entrepreneurship. The crucial question then is how does entrepreneurship result from the intersection of these incommensurable phenomena? To answer this question, we argue for the importance of contexts. First, the individual is a unique person who cannot be reduced to either his biological-cum-psychological makeup or his socio-economic position, although his or her behaviour is somehow constrained by them. His or her uniqueness is created by the intervention of the family. That is to say, the entrepreneurial ethos and pursuits must be located in the context of his socio-economic position and his family. Second, the environment or Shane's concept of 'objective' existence of opportunity is socially relative and historically specific. We therefore also have to contextualize the environment in a specific historical setting. Finally, the mediation between the individual and the environment must also be put in the specific context in which the mediation occurs. The chapters concerning Fong's entrepreneurial process that follow (Chapter 2, Chapter 3, Chapter 4, Chapter 5, and Chapter 6) will exemplify ethnographically the importance of contexts in the understanding of entrepreneurship.

Family business and the management of Chinese family business

One of our major observations about the study of the family business by the scholars in mainstream-US-dominated management sciences is their focus on the differences between family firms and non-family firms. The majority of their studies tend to investigate *whether* the family firm is different from the non-family firm (Chrisman, Chua and Sharma, 2005; Denison, Lief and Ward, 2004; Gallo, Tapies and Cappuyns, 2004; Gudmundson, Hartman and Tower, 1999; Littunen, 2003; Navarro and Anson, 2009). Considering the needs to justify the study of the family business as a distinctive academic field, the focus, to a great extent, is understandable because in order to legitimize the field of family business studies, scholars have to establish the distinctiveness of the family business. We however are convinced that the field of family business studies has been sufficiently legitimized as the general consensus among mainstream management scientists on the fact that family firms are different from non-family firms in some if not all dimensions has already been empirically established and confirmed (Achmad, Rusmin and Tower, 2009; Bird et al., 2002; Chrisman et al., 2010; Chua, Chrisman and Bergiel, 2009; Galambos, 2010; Oswald, Muse and Rutherford, 2009; Parada, Norqvist and Gimeno, 2010; Sharma, 2004; Zhang and Ma, 2009). We believe that it is the time now to move the field forward to examine *how* and *why* family firms are different from non-family firms.

The first step to move the field forward is to examine the relationship between the family and the firm, and in order to do that, we need to investigate the family, the firm, and their relationship in a particular cultural context. As Wong (forthcoming) argued in his previously mentioned forthcoming paper, we cannot assume that the family or the firm as a social institution is the same cross-culturally and thus treat them as a constant. We have to take seriously the anthropological discoveries that different cultures have different concepts of the family and the firm and that, as a result, family businesses in different cultures will exhibit very different forms of organizational behaviour (Steward, 2003). In short, it is not that all cultures have families or firms, but that all families or firms have culture. It follows that we have to pay attention to the cultural specificity of the family, the firm, and their relationship, which is also to say that we should put them in their cultural context.

In Chapter 7, we will examine the organizational logic of the Chinese family through three native concepts pertinent to the Chinese family and demonstrate how the Chinese attach the overriding importance to the genealogical aspect of the family and why the Chinese always prepare to sacrifice the economic aspect of the family for the sake of its genealogical continuity. When this organizational logic is applied to the business context, the Chinese are willing to sacrifice the family *business* for the interest of the business *family*, which also implies that the Chinese tend to treat their family firms as an instrument to enhance the interest of their family. Chinese family firms, therefore, have no intrinsic value in themselves; they can be discarded if they are no longer needed. That is why Fong did not hesitate to sacrifice the interests of his company for the interests of his family. This further helps explain why there is a Chinese saying that family wealth in Chinese societies never lasts beyond three generations. In short, the relationship between the family and the firm in the Chinese context is that the former provides the organizational format for the latter and the interest of the former is more important than that of the latter to the extent that the Chinese are willing to sacrifice their family business for the sake of their family because the family firm for the Chinese is an instrument to enhance the family interests.

The concept of Chinese family can also help us understand the management of Chinese family firms. As we will show in Chapter 7, we argue that Chinese entrepreneurs tend to run their businesses through the organizational format of family as an economic entity because running a family business is also an important function of such an entity. The organizational dynamics of Chinese family as an economic entity therefore provides an important context against which the management of Chinese business can be understood. In running the family business, the head of a Chinese family is inclined to apply the kinship logic to his personal relationship with his employees, which makes the management of Chinese family business centre on the specific social relations instead of the formal organizational structure, resulting in an organizational dynamic characterized by the general ignorance of the organizational chart, autonomy and agency of individual workers, and the emphasis on the holistic relations between employee and employer as well as among employees themselves. We of course are not going to argue that this organizational dynamic represents all the cases of Chinese family businesses, but it is not uncommon to observe the display of all of these features in the Chinese family business context, as we will show in Chapter 7 through Fong's management regime.

We argue that the idea of the Chinese family is culturally relative and should be understood in the Chinese cultural context. The cultural idea of the Chinese family can help us understand not only the organizational logic but also the management of Chinese family businesses. Through the examination of the cultural idea of the Chinese family, we can understand why and how family firms are different from non-family firms in Chinese society. The same approach can also be applied to the study of family businesses in Japan, Korea, and other regions of the world. Unfortunately, there is insufficient academic attention paid to the cultural specificity of family, firm, and their relationship in the mainstream management sciences literature of family business.

Of course, we cannot treat Chinese family business as a homogeneous category as there are many different types of Chinese family businesses. Indeed, mainstream management scientists have become increasingly aware of the intra-cultural differences of family businesses (Neubaum, Kammerlander and Brigham, 2019; Rau, Schneider-Siebke and Günther, 2019; Sanchez-Ruiz et al., 2019; Sharma, Chrisman and Chua, 1997; Stanley et al., 2019). We would like to push this line of research further by focusing on a single Chinese family firm, FBL, because the company is a unique entity and cannot be seen as simply an actualization of the monolithic category of the 'Chinese family firm'. FBL has its unique features and therefore cannot be treated as the same as other Chinese firms in Hong Kong. It follows that we cannot adopt the formal quantitative methods of physical sciences that are widely adopted in mainstream management sciences:

> The physicist compares a series of *similar* facts from which he isolates the general phenomenon which is common to all of them. Henceforth the single facts become less important to him, as he lays stress on the general laws alone.
>
> (Sahlins, 2000b, p. 20; italics ours)

We suggest that what our colleagues should do is the same thing that Sahlins has said anthropologists are required to do. As Sahlins (2000b, p. 21) explained:

> In anthropology, the one move and the other required the submission of the analyst, the knowing scientific subject, to the arrangement of the culture, to its own meaningful construction – as opposed to an analytic dismemberment into classes which loses the culture's specific characteristics.

We will return to this in the methodology section soon but at this juncture we would like to stress that in this book, we submit ourselves to the specific characteristics of Fong's family and his family firm. We will examine the ethnographic peculiarities of Fong, his family, and his family firm in a particular context in order to understand how and why Fong's company behaved in a certain pattern; and how and why the company has been managed in a specific way.

The professionalization of (Chinese) family firms

As mentioned earlier, there is a general consensus among scholars within mainstream management sciences that family firms are different from non-family firms. The reason for the difference is naturally attributed to the involvement of family in the management and ownership of family firms. The typical argument runs like this: since the members of business families tend to dominate the management and ownership of their companies and business families have their own values, purposes, and norms, they are inclined to manage their firms according to the family culture which prioritizes the interests of the family over those of the company. As a result, the management of family businesses by family managers *must* be different from that of professional managers (Chrisman et al., 2010; Gedajlovi, Lubatkin and Schulze, 2004; Ram and Holliday, 1993; Westhead, Cowling and Howorth, 2001). Implied in this argument are a series of oppositions including those between family business management and professional management, family managers and professional managers, and its correspondent dichotomy between family managers as insiders and professional managers as outsiders.

Family business management and professional management are not treated as two different and equal management systems but as a hierarchical dichotomy with the former being 'primitive' and the latter 'advanced'. Such a hierarchical dichotomy is further understood as two stages in the evolutionary path of corporate management. Family firms managed by the members inside the family are considered as the earlier if not primitive stage of the path, which will become inefficient if not problematic when the company grows larger and becomes more complex. In order to survive, family firms at a certain point will recruit professional managers from outside to replace family managers to run the company in a professional and advanced way, which is called professionalization of family business by our colleagues in mainstream management sciences. As Gibb Dyer (1989, pp. 222–223) argued:

One of the most common reasons is a lack of management talent within the family. Family members sometimes lack skills such as marketing, finance, or accounting, and the family must acquire such skills if the business is to survive. As a family grows – particularly in a complex environment – it is unlikely that the family will be able to staff all the key positions and have all the necessary skills. Therefore, the family will, out of necessity, look outside the family for help or attempt to broaden the skills of family members. . . . A second reason for professionalizing management is to change the norms and values of business operations. . . . A third reason acquiring or developing management expertise is to prepare for leadership succession.

More importantly, the professionalization of family business is always seen as being able to benefit the company. As Alex Stewart and Michael Hitt quoted Martínez et al.:

When family-controlled firms professionalize their management and governance bodies, and have to be accountable to minority shareholders, they can overcome most of their traditional weaknesses and take advantage of their strengths and succeed.

(Martínez et al., 2007, p. 93, cited in Steward and Hitt, 2012, p. 59)

In light of the previous discussion, several observations can be made. The first is the sharp if not exaggerated distinction between family business management and professional management. Family business management is seen as a management regime characterized by nepotism, familial conflicts, and an informal atmosphere, while professional management represents a *rational* option for family business management. As Dyer cited Schein:

. . .founders of family business tend to be driven by their particular vision of their product or service. They tend to be intuitive in their decision making, their power based on ownership, and they motivate their followers through their charismatic behaviour. Conversely, those trained as professional managers generally derive their power not from ownership but from positions of authority. They tend to make decisions based more on logic and rational analysis than on intuition. Furthermore, these managers tend to be rather impersonal in their interactions with others, in contrast to the more personal style of the founder . . . Professional managers often have world views and assumptions that differ from the leaders of family-owned firms. Moreover, the organizational systems and methods of operation that are preferred by professional managers are often antithetical to those of family leaders, who are accustomed to a more informal (and, at times, seat-of-the-pants) management style.

(Schein, 1983, cited in Dyer, 1989, p. 224)

Annika Hall and Mattias Nordqvist (2008, p. 53), echoing Dyer (1989), argue that the organization professional management is stereo-typified as 'modern, efficient, and rational ways of organizing economic activities'. The authority of professional management 'is based on objective rules, norms, and rational decision making, where managers' authority is grounded in technical qualifications and rational values rather than in individual characteristics and personal ownership rights' (Hall and Nordqvist, 2008, p. 53).

It follows that professional managers and family managers are mutually exclusive. The former is assumed to 'have formal business training, often an MBA'; they are supposed to be generalists who 'should not pay much attention to context' (Hall and Nordqvist, 2008, p. 53). As Hall and Nordqvist quoted Dyer:

> [H]e or she must base actions on a 'general set of principles . . . independent of a particular case under consideration' be 'experts in the field of management and know what is best for their client,' make sure that 'relationships with clients are considered helpful and objectives,' gain status 'by accomplishment as opposed to status based on ties to the family,' and 'belong to voluntary associations of fellow professionals'.
>
> (Dyer, 1989, p. 221, cited in Hall and Nordqvist, 2008, p. 54)

The latter, on the contrary, are imagined as non-professional managers, whose behaviours are opposite to those of professional managers. Finally, the professionalization of family business is seen simply as an event in which professional managers from outside have replaced existing family managers.

Although the previous arguments contribute a lot to the understanding of professionalization of family business, we argue that they are too simple, if not incorrect; we can see from Fong's case that the professionalization of family business is not just an *event* in which professional managers have replaced family managers but a social process in which major players have interacted with each other to produce the effect of professionalization of family firms. Who the major players are cannot be theoretically assumed and thus *a priori* known but have to be *ethnographically* determined. As we will see in this book, Fong's second son and his daughter-in-law, his long-serving employees, and the newly recruited professional managers are the major players in the professionalization of Fong's company. In other words, the professionalization of Fong's family firm involves not only professional and family managers but also long-serving employees, which challenges the dichotomy of professional and family managers assumed by the earlier argument.

More importantly, these players are not a homogenous group. Fong's second son and daughter-in-law do not always agree with each other, while the professional managers have different views on their relations with the long-serving employees. The long-serving employees have played an important role in the professionalization of FBL but have adopted different attitudes towards the professional managers. The situation is even more complex in so far as some of the long-serving employees chose to make alliances with the professional managers, while some others were determined to resist the management system introduced by the professional managers. Some of the professional managers tried to communicate with the long-serving employees and find a way to encourage the latter to accept the new management system, while some other professional managers were inclined to ignore the voices and feelings of the long-serving employees and directly imposed their views on the latter. Which way a certain professional manager or long-serving employee would take depended on his or her motives, interests, and strategies that were underscored by circumstances. We will show in Chapter 10 that the motives, interests, and strategies of each major player vary with circumstances, which further changes the form and character of the interaction among the major players.

Finally, professional managers or long-serving employees cannot be assumed to have a social identity as 'professional' or 'long-serving' staff and form a social group as 'professional managers' or 'long-serving employees' right from the beginning. The genesis of their social identities lies in a particular context in which the newly recruited professional managers dominated the management of Fong's company. They enjoyed higher social status, more corporate power, and better salaries than long-serving employees, resulting in a structural inequality between the professional managers and long-serving employees. The inequality, however, requires meaningful signification and cultural legitimation. We will show that the professional managers, as the superior group, protected their privileges by denying the worthiness of the long-serving employees' experience in the industry, while at the same time stressing the values of their professionalism in modern management. The superiority of the professional managers was also strengthened by their middle-class background and the positive images associated with it and justified on some putative cultural grounds.

The long-serving employees reacted with the reciprocal denial of the values of the professional managers by emphasizing their industry know-how and the experience that the professional managers lacked. Many of them even denied that the managerial skills of the professional managers are transferrable and applicable in the jewellery industry. We will argue that it is this marked opposition between the professional managers and the long-serving employees that helped create the communal self-definition, the collective social identities for the professional managers and the long-serving employees as social groups. In short, the formation of the professional managers and long-serving employees as social groups is a function of the structural inequality between them within the company. The emergence of group consciousness among the professional managers and the long-serving employees is the product of historical processes which structured relations of inequality between them. We therefore cannot assume that the professional managers and the long-serving employees had their social identity from the outset and interacted with each other as social groups. Indeed, we should investigate the process in which the professional managers and the long-serving employees have formed their social identities as 'professional managers' and 'long-serving employees'.

The social identities of the professional managers and the long-serving employees, once formed, have been objectified as a social 'principle' by which the interaction between the professional managers and the long-serving employees as social groups is regulated. In other words, the professional managers or long-serving employees have to develop their social identity as 'professional managers' or 'long-serving employees' *before* they can behave like a professional manager or long-serving employee.

Seen in this way, the professionalization of Fong's company involves two processes. The first is the complex interaction among the major players and in our case including the owners of the family business, the professional managers and the long-serving employees, the form and character of which are determined by the motives, interests, and strategies of each player as a function of circumstances. It is this complex interaction which specifies the result of the professionalization of Fong's family firm. Second, underlying this complex interaction is the identity formation process which gives rise to the group consciousness of 'the professional managers' and 'long-serving employees', which in turn serves as the social principle that governs the interaction between the professional managers and long-serving employees.

In short, the previously mentioned scholars of mainstream management sciences have not paid sufficient attention to all players' voices; they therefore have not done justice to the complexities and contractions on the side of each player involved in the professionalization process. We therefore challenge ourselves to write an ethnography of professionalization of family business that takes into consideration all the players in the process including the motives, goals, and interests that drove their actions and the limitations that constrained them.

This further requires us to take John Comaroff's (2010, p. 530) position that anthropology as *methodology* is based on 'a few closely interrelated epistemic operations that lay the foundation for its diverse forms of theory work, mandate its research techniques, and chart its empirical coordinates'. Seen in this way, anthropology as a discipline should be seen as a mode of knowledge production by which Comaroff meant:

> the principled practice by which theory and the concrete world are both constituted and brought into discursive relationship with one another. And they are epistemic in that they entail an orientation to the nature of knowledge itself, its philosophical underpinnings and its notions of truth, fact, value. None of them is new, none of them absent from anthropologies past. Together, they underscore the point that our topical horizons ought to be configured by our praxis, not the other way around.

One of these epistemic operations involves what Comaroff (2010, p. 530) called 'being-and-becoming' which 'is the mapping of those processes by which social realities are realized, objects are objectified, materialities materialized, essences essentialized, by which abstractions – biography, community, culture, economy, ethnicity, gender, generation, identity, nationality, race, society – congeal synoptically from the innumerable acts, events, and significations that constitute them'.

Following Comaroff, we as anthropologists would not take any abstraction such as 'professional manager' or 'long-serving employees' for granted. We instead try to trace the historical processes in which the categories of 'professional managers' or 'long-serving employees' 'are pragmatically produced, socially construed, and naturalized' (Comaroff, 2010, p. 530).

Methodology[3]

The previous review speaks to the importance of contexts in understanding entrepreneurship, family business, and its professionalization as human phenomena. The importance of contexts constitutes a challenge to any methodology that ignores contexts. What we are pointing to is the formal quantitative method widely considered as the normative method by most scholars in mainstream management sciences. We have to emphasize immediately that we are not opposing the formal quantitative method, but the typical explanation embedded in the method: 'the presence of some phenomenon (a cause) determines the appearance of another phenomenon (an effect)' (Sewell, 2005, p. 347). Behind the explanation is the famous ideology of general linear reality which is predicated on philosophical assumptions about the way the social world works (Abbott, 2001):

> . . .the social world consists of fixed entities (the units of analysis) that have attributes (the variables). These attributes interact, in causal or actual time, to create outcomes, themselves measurable as attributes of the fixed entities.
>
> (Abbott, 2001, p. 39)

We find this ideology problematic as it denies the contextual influence on any attribute of the entity at issue. As Andrew Abbott (2001, pp. 39–40) pointed out:

> An attribute's causal meaning cannot depend on the entity's location in the attribute space (its context), since the linear transformation is the same throughout that space. For similar reasons, the past path of an entity through the attribute space (its history) can have no influence on its future path, nor can the causal importance of an attribute change from one entity to the next. All must obey the same transformation.

We want to invoke the long anthropological tradition from Saussure, via Lévi-Strauss, to Sahlins which considers human phenomena as the result of the *interpretation* of a human action in terms of culture which is not the only one possible. It follows that a physical object can only become a *human* object through culture and more importantly the same physical act can have different meanings in different cultural contexts. Take family as an example. In Chinese societies, the daughter is not a member of her father's family, while the son is. But in the United States, no one will deny that the daughter is a member of her father's family. That is to say, the cultural category of 'daughter' has different meanings in different societies and therefore cannot be seen as belonging to one single analytical category. More generally, no human phenomenon is context-free.

It is the logic of the culture which gives meaning to a physical act. As we will show in Chapter 7, the son in Chinese society shares the same *qi* (literally means breath; but in Chinese culture, it means the essence of human life) with his own father who also shares the same *qi* with his brother (his father's brother). He also shares the same *qi* with his father's brother's son because he inherits the *qi* from his father. According to this logic, a son is symbolically equivalent to his father, his father's brother, and his father's brother's son in Chinese societies. The mother shares the same *qi* with her husband, her husband's brother, her husband's brother's son and her son. All of them belong to the same family. The daughter, however, cannot inherit her father's *qi* and therefore the daughter is categorically different from her male siblings, her father's brother, her father's brother's son, and even her mother in Chinese societies, which is also to say that the daughter does not belong to the same family with her own mother. This is the logic of Chinese agnatic relations.

We argue that in order to understand human phenomena, we have to situate them into their own cultural contexts rather than imposing our theoretical assumptions or moral judgements upon them, which is also to say that: we have to submit ourselves to the cultural context in which the human phenomena take place. The epistemological stance is closely related to the ontological nature of human beings: human beings of different cultures share the same symbolic competence. The understanding of the Other inescapably involves the self. As Sherry Ortner pointed out, 'it [ethnography] has always meant the attempt to understand another life world using the self – as much of it as possible – as the instrument of knowing' (Ortner, 1995, p. 173). Seen as such, human sciences are *categorically* different from natural sciences because the latter require the separation of the subject from the object. More importantly, the notion of understanding for human sciences is also different from that of natural sciences. As Sahlins says (2000b, p. 30):

> Indeed, the more we know about physical objects the less familiar they become, the more remote they stand from any human experience. The molecular structure of the table on which I write is far removed from my sense of it – let alone, to speak of what is humanly communicable, my use of it or my purchase of it. Nor I will ever appreciate tableness, rockiness, or the like in the way I might know cannibalism. On the contrary, by the time one gets to the deeper nature of material things as discovered by quantum physics, it can only be described in the form of mathematical equations, so much does this understanding depart from our ordinary ways of perceiving and thinking objects.

Now it has become clear why the previously mentioned explanation widely adopted by scholars in management sciences contributes less to the understanding of business activities as human phenomena because the explanation simply appears to readers as 'unreal'.

Ethnographic methods

It, however, would be unfair to say that all management scientists ignore the ethnographic methods adopted by anthropologists, as we have recently come to know that more and more management scientists realize the utility of ethnographic methods in studying business activities. The question is whether ethnographic methods are properly understood by our colleagues in management sciences. First, ethnographic methods cannot be seen as equivalent to one-or-two-hour interviews with informants in the field. Second, the meaning of participant-observation cannot be vulgarized as a brief visit to the workplace. Finally, ethnographic methods are not just fieldworks or qualitative methods; it is a deep commitment to what Clifford Geertz (1973, pp. 3–30) called 'thick description'. As Ortner suggests, ethnographic methods are 'to [produce] understanding through richness, texture, and detail, rather than parsimony, refinement, and (in the sense used by mathematicians) elegance' (Ortner, 1995, p. 174). Despite the fact that 'thickness' could mean different things in anthropology, its core meaning is contextualization. Ethnography tries to reproduce the logic of the other culture as it is and thus appears to be *real* to us as human subjects by locating human phenomena in the context of different domains and at multi-levels. For human phenomena are very complex because they acquire different meanings in different contexts. Moreover, the human actor can also reflect on his or her behaviours and in the course of doing so, he or she can create new meaning. In a discourse of human sciences, individuals have their own agency.

Unfortunately, the value of individual voices or individual cases is invariably denied in mainstream-US-dominated management sciences literature. Being 'scientific' in management sciences is to do what the natural scientists are doing, that is, to search a universal law of human behaviours. Individuals or individual cases are relevant *only if* they serve as an 'example' or a 'counter example' of a general trend. What the voice of an individual or the dynamics of an individual case are does not deserve any academic concern. Fong's family business, for instance, is relevant *only if* it constitutes an example of Chinese family firms. What Fong's company looks like does not matter! Neither does it deserve any academic attention.

More importantly, the use of cultural categories in everyday life can sometimes transform the meaning of that category (Sahlins, 1981). The challenging task is to investigate how culture gives meaning to a cultural category and how the practice of that category in everyday life transforms the meaning of that category, a task that cannot be tackled simply by any context-free method. A statistical relationship among various variables, for example, is insufficient, if not impossible, to capture this dynamic process.

Our ethnographic study in this book therefore focuses on Fong as a unique person, his family as a specific Chinese family in post-war Hong Kong, and his company as a particular Chinese family firm. One of the authors, Chau, conducted ethnographic fieldwork in Fong's company in the capacity of a new staff member in the company's Corporate Communications Department from 2013 to 2014. During that one year of work at the company, Chau not only participated in the everyday operation of the company but also observed the interactive relationship between the owners and the professional managers, between the owners and their employees in different ranks, particularly the long-serving employees, and between the professional managers and the long-serving employees. She also analyzed what she observed in different contexts and reproduced the meanings of these interactions. All of this provided a context through which the data collected by in-depth interviews of one to two hours each with more than 30 employees in different levels of the company over five years from 2013 to 2018 is understood. Some of them were interviewed more than one time. Most of the interviews were conducted inside the company but we also conducted interviews with some professional managers outside of the company to make sure that their replies to our questions were not constrained by the corporate setting.

We have to mention that we spent a lot of time talking to Fong about his life, family, and company. Some of the conversations took place in formal interviews with him inside the company; but most of the time we socialized with Fong outside of the company. We did this after discovering that answers had always been prepared in advance for Fong when we interviewed him formally. We therefore tried our best to establish a personal relationship with Fong so that we could know more about him and his background from the informal conversations with him outside of the company, which proved to be as useful as, if not more useful than those formal interviews.

Our ethnographic research is not confined to conducting fieldwork in the company. We also spent a lot of time searching local newspapers published between 1970 and 1990 in order to collect all the news clips about Fong and his company, including the advertisements of FBL. The advertisements of FBL are particularly useful because they help us to reconstruct the marketing strategies of FBL, the location strategy of FBL's retail shops, and their pricing policies. We also consulted the annual reports of FBL as the company went public in the second half of the 1980s to understand the financial situation and corporate strategies of the company. We also expanded our search to the news clips about several major jewellery companies to understand the industry. Finally, we conducted an extensive search in the government archive office to uncover historical information about the industry between 1968 and 1983. All of this was done to reconstruct the historical and industrial contexts in which Fong developed his company from a small workshop to a famous brand in the jewellery industry in Hong Kong.

Organization of the book

The book is divided into two parts to address three core issues: the idea of entrepreneurship, the management of (Chinese) family business, and the professionalization of (Chinese) family firms. The first part (Chapter 2 to Chapter 6) examines the entrepreneurial process of Fong in relation to the broader societal context of post-war Hong Kong and Fong's own biographical background. The second part (Chapter 7 to Chapter 10) focuses on discussing Fong's management style and the professionalization of his company initiated by his successors.

The first part of the book starts with a selective description of the politics, economy, and society of post-war Hong Kong that have informed Fong's entrepreneurial process and the development of his company (Chapter 2). It is then followed by a brief biographical history of Fong together with his entrepreneurial process from which we identify Fong's personal characteristics and briefly touch upon his management style. We do this in order to highlight the general theoretical framework of entrepreneurship proposed in the book and to demonstrate how Fong's entrepreneurship should be seen as the result of the *mediations* between Fong's personal characteristics and the socio-cultural and political-economic environment in which Fong's entrepreneurship takes place (Chapter 3).

In the three chapters that follow, we examine in detail the three stages of Fong's entrepreneurial process. In Chapter 4, we demonstrate that the specific path of development of Fong's manufacturing business must be understood in terms of three registers: the broader socio-economic context of Hong Kong, Fong's unique business strategy, and the *mediation* of the two. Fong's unique business strategy can be understood as what we call the maximization of production logic, which emphasizes expansion through maximizing production. Fong's logic of maximizing production appears to be very different from the general tendency of the manufacturers who tend to limit expansion and avoid risks. We shall explain the reasons behind Fong's logic and show how this logic *forced* him to keep expanding his workshop, eventually resulting in the dominance of his company in the local manufacturing sector.

In Chapter 5, we shall examine how and why Fong branched into showroom business in the 1970s. This chapter starts with an ethnography of Fong's showroom which highlights the characteristics of his showroom business. These characteristics, especially Fong's management of the showrooms, contribute to the success of Fong's showroom business. However, we will argue that neither Fong's entrepreneurial move into showroom business nor the political economy of the tourism industry in Hong Kong with its complex relationships among overseas travel agents, local tour operators, and retail shops can account for the success of FBL's showroom business; rather, the success of Fong's showroom business is the result of the mediation between the two.

Chapter 6 discusses how and why Fong began to venture into the local jewellery retail market. In this chapter, we will describe Fong's adventure in establishing and expanding FBL's retail business and identify the key features of the transformation of the FBL retail network. But retailing was not the core business activity of FBL at the initial stage. The retail outlets mainly served, together with the showroom, as a platform for Fong to sell the stock of his factories. The retail business was originally established to support the production of the factories. However, FBL's retail business had experienced remarkable growth from the mid-1980s and reached a zenith in the 1990s. From that time on, FBL was known as one of the major local jewellery brands in Hong Kong.

Chapter 7 marks the beginning of Part Two which focuses on Fong's management of FBL as a Chinese family business and its transformation. In this chapter, we move to examine Fong's company as a Chinese family business and Fong as the *jiazhang* (head of the household) of the business. The first part of this chapter offers an anthropological understanding of Chinese family, arguing that there are economic (*jia*) and genealogical aspects (*fang/jia-zu*) of Chinese family. Chinese consider the continuity of the latter more important than that of the former. In the second part of this chapter, we shall show how Fong applied the Chinese family logic to his relations with the employees in FBL, which further explains the characteristics of Fong's management: ignorance of the organizational chart, autonomy and agency, and holistic relations. We suggest that Fong's management can best be captured by what his employees call '*jan cing mei* management' (literally means the taste of human warmth) which, we argue, characterizes many Chinese family firms. In the conclusion, we will highlight some major shortcomings of Fong's *jan cing mei* management style, which, we argue in the next chapter, is responsible for the two related crises of Fong and his company in the 2000s.

In the three chapters that follow, we focus on examining the background against which the transformation of FBL is to be understood, the actual process of professionalization and its result. Chapter 8 examines the events leading to the crises and explains the reasons for the outbreak of the crises. We will demonstrate how the crises are related to Fong's obsession with real estate, the formation of the speculative culture in Hong Kong, the cultural meaning of landed property in Chinese societies, and more fundamentally, the problems resulting from Fong's running of FBL as *jia*.

Chapter 9 examines the nature and content of the transformation of the company initiated by Fong's daughter-in-law. We will show that the transformation itself amounts to the professionalization of FBL that introduces 'modern' management to the company. The 'modern' management constitutes a point-to-point opposite of Fong's *jan cing mei* management regime outlined in Chapter 7. The relationship between the modern management and Fong's *jan cing mei* regime is seen as a hierarchical one, with the former being good, modern, progressive, rational, scientific, democratic, and efficient and the latter bad, old-fashion, backward, irrational, intuitional, feudal, and inefficient. The transformation is therefore a political contention between the modern management and Fong's *jan cing mei* regime. In the conclusion of this chapter, we will further point out that underlying this political contention is a more complex micro-political dynamics among the owners, the professional managers, and the *lou san zi* (long-serving staff) that, as will be demonstrated in Chapter 10, had facilitated the transformation at the beginning, and made the transformation a failure in the end.

In Chapter 10, we will demonstrate that the result of transformation outlined in Chapter 9 is the consequence of the interaction among Fong's son and daughter-in-law, newly recruited professional managers and the long-serving staff of the company. We argue that the nature, form, and character of such an interaction were ever-changing because they all depended on the goals, strategies, and actions of each player involved, which varied with circumstances. The consequence of the interaction therefore would be contingent on the specific circumstances. In this chapter, we first specify the specific circumstance in which Fong's son and his wife were motivated to start the transformation and why the transformation could be successful at the beginning. The circumstance, however, changed later, which altered the goals, strategies, and actions of the major players including Fong's son and daughter-in-law, professional managers, and the long-serving staff of the company. The form and character of the interaction among these major players therefore changed accordingly, which led to the resignation of most professional managers and thus the failure of the reform. FBL then has returned to a typical Chinese family firm under the control of the new *jiazhang*: Fong's son.

In the concluding chapter, we will highlight the theoretical implications of this book to the study of Chinese entrepreneurship, Chinese family business, and the professionalization of Chinese family firms in particular and explain the significance of these implications to the dialogue between anthropologists and management and business scientists on human business phenomena in general.

Notes

1 The first name of Carrie, in Chinese, is Kum.
2 In contemporary Hong Kong, people in the workplace tend to call each other by his or her English name to maintain a suitable distance because calling colleagues by their Chinese given name in the workplace seems to be too close while their Chinese surname is too distant. English names in Hong Kong society tend to be associated with relationships that fall somewhere between close friends and strangers.
3 This section is a substantial revision of a section of Wong's forthcoming paper entitled 'It is Not that All Cultures Have Business, But That All Business Has Culture'.

2 Politics, economy, and society of post-war Hong Kong

In Chapter 1, we have argued that entrepreneurship is the significance and importance individual pursuit acquires from its mediation with the socio-cultural contexts in which the pursuit takes place. The study of entrepreneurship therefore involves three terms: individual pursuit, the socio-cultural contexts, and the mediation between the two. It follows from this that the study of Fong's entrepreneurial process has to examine Fong as an individual, the socio-cultural contexts in which his entrepreneurship takes place and the mediation between the two. This chapter therefore examines the socio-cultural contexts that are most relevant to Fong's entrepreneurial pursuit. We will outline several causal chains of phenomena of different registers or levels, such as certain aspects of the politics, economy, and society of post-war Hong Kong, the intersection of which, as we shall demonstrate in the chapters that follow, shapes Fong's entrepreneurial process, in particular, and the development of his company, FBL, in general.

Hong Kong was ceded to Britain in 1841 as a result of the defeat of China in the First Opium War. A Crown Colony was then established and what happened in the over 150 years of British colonial rule seems to be too familiar and normal to be reiterated here. In the official documented history, the development of Hong Kong began with the establishment of the Crown Colony. Under the British colonial rule, Hong Kong was reportedly transformed from 'a barren island with hardly a house upon it' (Hong Kong Government, 1963, p. 333) into one of the most prosperous societies in Asia after the Second World War. Parallel to the development of Hong Kong as one of the most vibrant economies in Asia, was the establishment of a distinctive entrepreneurial ethos among the people of Hong Kong, including the founder of FBL, Fong. Before we turn to discussing Fong and his company, we have to understand the post-war geopolitical context of Hong Kong and the politicking of the colonial government which informed the development of a *specific* entrepreneurial ethos in Hong Kong. We will demonstrate how the post-war geopolitical circumstances gave rise to the depoliticization policy of the colonial government in Hong Kong (hereafter Hong Kong government) and how the policies in turn imposed a 'particular way of seeing and being' among the Hong Kong people (Comaroff and Comaroff, 1989, p. 267) and transformed them into the 'Economic Man': He does not care whether He is Chinese or British, a national of Communist China or Nationalist China; He only knows that He is a profit-maximizing machine. We will also show how the same depoliticization policy not only shaped the developmental path of Hong Kong industries but also gave rise to the famous 'Hong Kong model' of industrial production which, as will be shown in Chapter 4, also characterized the development of the jewellery industry in Hong Kong.

In the final part of this chapter, we will first identify the characteristics of the entrepreneurial ethos of Hong Kong people, arguing that the ethos was in fact a manifestation of the coloniality of Hong Kong society, in the sense that the development of the ethos was stimulated by the particular form of colonial politicking, discursive practices, and institutional arrangements which had become dominant in the society. Finally, we will introduce two major social mobility strategies adopted by the Hong Kong people – education and entrepreneurship – through two concrete cases and argue that the Chinese entrepreneurial ethos was neither culturally prescribed nor in-born. Entrepreneurship was a tool that Hong Kong Chinese adopted to seek upward social mobility. All of this is to provide socio-cultural contexts that help shape Fong's entrepreneurial process and the development of FBL.

Geopolitics and politicking in post-war Hong Kong

The Second World War turned the page of history for many countries and territories, including Hong Kong. After enduring the afflicted, catastrophic hardship under Japanese Occupation, Britain regained control of Hong Kong and set up an interim military administration until 1 May 1946, the date when civil government was fully restored. The restoration of British rule was not smooth as Chiang Kai-shek, then leader of the Republic of China, demanded the return of Hong Kong to China in 1945. It was argued that full restoration of British governance could not have been completed without the support of the United States (Tsang, 2007, p. 136; Whitfield, 2001, pp. 133–135; Louis, 1997, p. 1063). The primary task of the Hong Kong government during the early post-war period was to reinstate the colonial rule that had been substantially undermined by the Japanese occupation of Hong Kong, which contributed to the falling prestige of the British empire (Tsang, 2007, p. 142; Snow, 2003, p. 303, cited in Smart, 2006, p. 42). More importantly, the rising Chinese nationalistic and patriotic sentiment among the Chinese population in Hong Kong also made it difficult for the Hong Kong government to restore law and order in society immediately after the reinstatement of colonial rule in Hong Kong (Smart, 2006, p. 41).

The situation was aggravated by the outbreak of the Cold War. Given its status as a British Crown Colony and its proximity to China, Hong Kong became what Chi-Kwan Mark (2004, p. 19) calls a 'Cold War city' which was inevitably drawn into the broader political contentions among the major powers such as Britain, the United States, the Soviet Union and China, mirrored and exacerbated in the increasing demarcation of the world between the capitalist and communist bloc. Hong Kong, as a British colony, was expected to serve as a 'natural' support base in the fight against communism. However, given its close ties to China, the situation of Hong Kong became very complicated, as illustrated in the outbreak of the Korean War in 1950. The impact of the Korean War on Hong Kong demonstrated how the colony was wedged between the contentions of the great powers, and its susceptibility to changes in the broader geopolitical circumstances. In December 1950, the United States decided to impose an embargo on the export of goods to China, Hong Kong, and Macao. The General Assembly of the United Nations also passed the resolution to impose an embargo on the shipment of strategic goods to China in 1951. As China was the principal trading partner of Hong Kong, the embargos became a serious blow to the economy of Hong Kong. The government stated bluntly that 'it is no exaggeration to say that the Korean [W]ar and the world events following it have put Hong Kong in an economically impossible position' (Hong Kong Government, 1952, p. 9).

In addition to the broader division between the communist and capitalist blocs, the Sino-British relationship was further complicated by the dual existence of the Chinese Communist Party's (CCP) regime in mainland China and the Kuomintang (KMT) regime in Taiwan. The confrontational dynamic between the two regimes was strongly manifested in Hong Kong. After the end of the Second World War, China was immediately torn apart by the unfinished and prolonged civil war fought between the CCP and the KMT. The finale of the war was marked by the establishment of the People's Republic of China (PRC) by the CCP in mainland China and the exile of the KMT regime to Taiwan. The rise of communist China was alarming to the capitalist bloc led by Western powers such as the United States and Britain. Despite the strong anti-communist outlook of Britain, Britain's China policy was driven by pragmatic calculation instead of ideological concerns. Britain desired to 'keep a foot in the door' (Mark, 2004, p. 134) to preserve their vested interest in China. British pragmatism was evident when Britain, as early as in January 1950, became the first major Western power to recognize the PRC.

The Hong Kong government was forced to face a difficult political dilemma with the desire of Britain to be a close ally of the US to contain communism on the one hand, and the necessity of keeping its relationship with the PRC on a neutral, if not friendly terms, on the other. What Britain decided to do was to avoid provoking China – a strategy reflecting the diminished power of Britain and the surging decolonization tide. It explained why Britain 'found Hong Kong a colony too valuable to abandon in peace, and yet too peripheral to be worth committing scarce resources to for its survival at war' (Mark, 2004, p. 1). In fact, David Faure (2003, p. 1) points out that Britain increasingly lost interest in maintaining its colonies after the Suez Crisis in 1956. The pressure from and the lack of commitment shown by the British home government, along with the shadow of constant communist threats and the vulnerability of Hong Kong in the face of tremendous power politics, prompted the Hong Kong government to envisage effective policies to consolidate its rule and defend its cause in the colony. Against this background, it was not surprising to see that the maintenance of public order and the suppression of political provocation were the top priorities of the Hong Kong government during the post-war period. The colonial government emphasized that its policy had been 'to keep Hong Kong free of external political fraction' (Hong Kong Government, 1950, p. 3). The strict social control imposed by the government was evident in the enactment of ordinances such as the *Public Order Ordinance* (1948),[1] the *Societies Ordinance* (1949)[2] and the *Illegal Strikes and Lock-outs Ordinance* (1949),[3] all of which were aimed at achieving the dual goals of social control and depoliticization.

The 'dangerous' Chinese politics and the year of 1967

The target of social control, or to be more exact, the source of fear for the Hong Kong government was the surging political sentiment of the Chinese population in the colony, the propaganda of the two Chinese regimes and other forms of infiltration by Chinese politics. The fear of the Hong Kong government was not totally ungrounded as Hong Kong had been susceptible to the political transformation in China due to their close geographical, cultural, and political ties which were not cut off by the establishment of the British colonial rule in Hong Kong. In fact, Chinese could enter and leave Hong Kong freely until the Hong Kong government imposed a quota system in 1950. When the Chinese Civil War broke out amidst the intensification of the Cold War, the Hong Kong government was extremely anxious about the extension of 'Chinese politics on Hong Kong soil' (Lee, 1998, p. 158).

The early imported Chinese politics was mainly a product of the influx of political and economic refugees as well as immigrants from China. The outbreak of the Chinese Civil War and the subsequent victory of the CCP brought about an unprecedented influx of immigrants into Hong Kong. It was estimated that the population of Hong Kong increased by two million during the period between 1945 and 1956; among them there were around one million immigrants from China (Hong Kong Government, 1957, p. 3). The influx of political refugees comprising the KMT personages and different kinds of economic refugees and immigrants alike from China alerted the Hong Kong government of the potential instability that it might cause. The government, in response, started to tighten its immigration policy. There was a series of legislative initiatives to regulate immigration. For instance, the *Immigrant Controls Regulations* (1949) required the arrivals to apply for and carry entry permits while the *Registration of Persons Ordinance* (1949) stipulated that the people in the colony registered and carried an identity card (Law and Lee, 2006, p. 219; Madokoro, 2012, p. 412).

The immigration policy in Hong Kong came to a turning point in 1950 when the Hong Kong government introduced, for the first time, a quota system to control the immigration of Chinese into Hong Kong (Ku, 2004, pp. 334–335). The colonial government continued to tighten its border control in the late 1950s and early 1960s, eventually militarizing its border with China in 1967. The border control between Hong Kong and China remained even after Hong Kong's return to China in 1997. The imposition of immigration control was one of the defining moments of the relationship between Hong Kong and China as it reified the difference between the two places.

Apart from the issue of immigration, the power conflict between the CCP and KMT did not cease after the establishment of the PRC in 1949. Both sides continued to fight for political legitimacy and authority over the 'overseas' Chinese communities. In particular, they strived to gain the support of 'overseas' Chinese immigrants and refugees in Hong Kong. Rival labour organizations, for instance, were established – the Trades Union Council was the core support base of the KMT, while the Federation of Trade Unions supported the communist government in China. The sympathizers of each camp also scrambled to build their own schools and publish their own newspapers. Even the humanitarian aid issue was highly politicized and exploited by both sides in order to extend their political clout (Madokoro, 2014). The riots in 1956[4] resulting from the conflicts between the two camps convinced the Hong Kong government that the infiltration of the Chinese politics into Hong Kong was one of the greatest potential threats to the order of the society.

Hence, the strategy of the Hong Kong government was to discourage any political activities in the society on the one hand, and to balance the influences of the opposing camps on the general population of Hong Kong on the other. The *Societies Ordinance*, for instance, as mentioned earlier, was enacted to ban 'all societies or organisations which had affiliations with political parties outside the Colony' (Hong Kong Government, 1950, p. 3). The *Expulsion of Undesirables Ordinance* (1949) was also enacted to empower the government to expel any undesirable 'alien' residing in Hong Kong (Sutton, 2017, p. 162). The *Education Ordinance*, on the other hand, was amended to grant the government more control over schools. Political propaganda, for example, was strictly prohibited in public schools.

Despite the effort of the Hong Kong government to impose social control, the political agitation and the prevalence of social problems such as housing, poverty, and corruption alongside the high-handed colonial rule eventually contributed to the outbreak of riots in 1966 and 1967 respectively (Lee, 1999, pp. 109–133). The 1967 riots, in particular, were regarded as a watershed of post-war Hong Kong history. The riots evoked by the Cultural Revolution were mainly led by communist sympathizers, if not supporters, and were sparked by the labour dispute of the Hong Kong Artificial Flower Works in the spring of 1967. It quickly accumulated into a large-scale opposition movement against imperialism and the suppressive colonial rule in Hong Kong (Cheung, 2009, pp. 23–42). Nevertheless, by the end of 1967, the people of Hong Kong were generally disillusioned by the violence of the riots and the government successfully re-established order in society.

The 1967 riots, however, substantially transformed the socio-political landscape of Hong Kong. The communist camp was fatally discredited after the riots and rapidly marginalized in the society. Moreover, the people in Hong Kong were made conscious of the difference between communist China and Hong Kong. Gradually, the mainland Chinese 'Other' rather than the colonial 'Other' was perceived to be *the* cultural 'Other' in Hong Kong (Mathews, Ma and Lui, 2008, p. 33). The emergence of this alienated sentiment facilitated the measures of the Hong Kong government to respond to what Ian Scott (1989) describes 'a crisis of legitimacy'. The turmoil of 1967 forced the government to refine if not redefine its politicking. The top priority of the Hong Kong government was to improve its public image and rebuild the trust of its people. It was not a coincidence that official rhetoric of 'community', 'citizenship' and 'belonging' was first deployed on a large scale after 1967 (Turner and Ngan, 1995, p. 15). The government attempted to be *seen* as responsive to the social needs as it attributed the outbreak of the riots to an apolitical reason: the lack of communication between the government and the public. By doing so, it attempted to conceal the more fundamental and political cause of the riots – the oppressive nature of British colonialism. Governor Murray MacLehose initiated a series of social programmes such as the introduction of the nine-year free education plan, the ten-year housing programme and the social assistance scheme during the 1970s to extend social welfare to the people. The government also attempted to enhance the mutual understanding between the public and the government by launching local projects such as the City District Office scheme[5] and fostering the organization of local communities and advisory groups.

Depoliticization, denationalization and the birth of the economic man

We argue that the measures of the Hong Kong government to improve the public–government relations were part of its broader depoliticization efforts. The depoliticization policy here refers to some general principles rather than a set of concrete measures that guide the politicking, discursive practices, and institutional arrangement of the Hong Kong government. These principles include: (1) the emphasis on the social order and material advancement over political participation in the policy-making process, (2) the necessity of keeping politics out of the public arena and (3) the invisibility of the colonial state. The primary objectives of these principles were to consolidate the colonial rule by diverting the attention of the people away from politics so that they would focus instead on business and economy and to insulate the influence of communist China on Hong Kong, which continued to haunt the Hong Kong government even after the 1967 riots.

The government also aimed at marginalizing the left-wing and right-wing camps in society by taking up their roles in providing better social welfare such as free education, affordable but high-quality health facilities, inexpensive public housing, and so on. By doing so, the Hong Kong government was able to counteract the communist propaganda through the creation of a better, top-down alternative to those provided by the left-and right-wing camps from below. The provision of better alternatives can not only be described as the colonial government's effort to buy out the colonized people's loyalties to the government, but also as an effective way to marginalize both political camps. In short, the Hong Kong government constructed and emphasized *material progress, law and order* as well as *freedom* as better alternatives to political mobilization, Chinese nationalism, and anti-colonialism. More importantly, the government utilized these alternatives as important social markers to indicate the *categorical* difference between Hong Kong and China.

Interestingly, the depoliticization policy of the Hong Kong government became an unintended denationalizing project that anchored the loyalty of the people in Hong Kong to the market instead of any nation: be it Chinese, Taiwanese, or even British. In other words, the depoliticization policy encouraged, though indirectly, the transformation of the so-called 'refugee mentality' of the Hong Kong people to the 'market mentality' characterized by the depoliticized, denationalized, and de-territorialized-cum-consumption oriented life-style around which the Hong Kong identity was formed (Mathews, Ma and Lui, 2008, p. 29).

As Allen Chun (1996, p. 58) perceptively points out, the 1967 riots could arguably be considered the catalyst that strengthened the government's determination to develop a consumption-oriented market society via economic development to divert local people from the two Chinese nationalisms. Through the policy focus on economic development and the prioritization of economic interest over others, the Hong Kong government effectively mobilized people around the economy instead of politics. Since the 1960s, the Hong Kong government began to put more effort into fostering the industrial development of Hong Kong. Such effort, however, took place in terms of providing a more favourable environment for foreign investments to boost the export-oriented industrialization rather than directly subsidizing individual industries (Fung, 1982, p. 26). For instance, the Hong Kong government contributed to the establishment of public organizations such as the Federation of Hong Kong Industries (FHKI) (1960), the Hong Kong Trade Development Council (HKTDC) (1966), and the Hong Kong Productivity Council (HKPC) (1967) to support the manufacturing and trading sectors of Hong Kong as well as promoting Hong Kong products in overseas markets. The reluctance of the Hong Kong government to directly subsidize individual industries was justified on the grounds of the notion of 'positive non-interventionism', the major thesis of which, to simplify enormously, is the minimum involvement of the government in economic development or in a simplified phrase: small government, big market.

We argue that deemphasizing the importance of the state and exaggerating the function of market had one important discursive function: to create an image of the Hong Kong government as a 'minimal government' that aimed only to maintain market order and provide a necessary infrastructure for the 'self-regulating' market. This was intended to pretend that the Hong Kong government was not a *colonial* government because it did nothing politically and economically to exploit its colony but served as a rule-keeper only. The exaggeration of the function of the 'self-regulating' market helped provide the Hong Kong government a convenient excuse for not doing anything especially at the time when the British government was not willing to invest its already limited financial resources on its overseas colonies. All of this helped create an image of the Hong Kong government as a minimal if not a non-existent government.

The discourse of 'free market economy' also functioned to banish politics to the status of 'exogenous factors' in order to pretend that 'politics' and 'economy' were two separate and independent realms of Hong Kong society, with the former being not quite relevant, if not completely irrelevant, to the latter. Such discourse imposed an ideology of the separation between politics and economy on the Hong Kong people, by which the Hong Kong government shifted the attention and energy of the colonized from political resistance to economic pursuit, and in the course of which the government further fostered an image of 'Economic Man' among the people in Hong Kong. Martin Hollis and Edward Neil (1975, pp. 53–54), cited in Sahlins (2013, p. 164), wrote:

> He [Economic Man] is introduced furtively and piece by piece. . . . He lurks in the assumptions, leading an enlightened existence between input and output, stimulus and response. He is neither tall nor short, fat nor thin, married nor single. There is no telling whether he loves his dog, beats his wife or prefers pushpin to poetry [pushpin or Pushkin?]. We do not know what he wants. But we do know that whatever it is, he will maximize ruthlessly to get it.

'The Hong Kong Economic Man' likewise is very abstract; He does not care whether He is Chinese or British, a national of communist China or nationalist China; He only knows that He is a profit-maximizing machine. In other words, the national consciousness of the Hong Kong people was replaced by the single-minded ethos of money-making.

It is possible to observe that the single-minded ethos of money-making and its associated strategy of upward mobility that Hong Kong people adopted was in fact encouraged, if not created, by the Hong Kong government. Through the depoliticization process, the people in Hong Kong were transformed into 'Economic Men' who were characterized by the market mentality to devote themselves to maximizing monetary gains under the ever-changing circumstances. As Gordon Mathews, Eric Kit-wai Ma and Tai-lok Lui (2008, p. 151) observe, 'money, in the broadest sense of the term, became Hong Kong's raison d'etre'. Money-making has therefore become the major motive for many peoples to start their entrepreneurial processes in the post-war Hong Kong society.

A brief history of the post-war Hong Kong economy

Following closely the version of the brief history of the post-war Hong Kong economy outlined in *City-State in the Global Economy: Industrial Restructuring in Hong Kong and Singapore* co-written by Stephen Wing-kai Chiu, Kong Chong Ho and Tai-lok Lui (1997), this section shows how the laissez-faire policy mentioned earlier not only helped develop a remarkable Hong Kong model of manufacturing but also specified the developmental path of the post-war Hong Kong economy.

Prior to the Second World War, the economy of Hong Kong was dominated by the entrepôt trade between the West and China. But Hong Kong's entrepôt trade, as mentioned earlier, suffered tremendously in the early 1950s because of the Korean War and the subsequent trade embargo imposed by the United Nation on China that prevented Hong Kong from trading with its largest business partner: China. Under the previously mentioned discourse of 'free market economy', the Hong Kong government did not try to get heavily involved in the economic transition when the entrepôt trade with China suffered under the United Nations embargo. What the government did, was to leave the problems to individual entrepreneurs who had no alternative but to follow the market trend. Local entrepreneurs capitalized on the opportunities created by what Gary Hamilton and Cheng-shu Kao (2018, p. 98) call 'the retail revolution in the United States' which forced American buyers to source cheap but high-quality consumer goods from East Asia. As they explain:

> Japanese trading companies arranged most of the early contracts between American buyers and Taiwanese and Hong Kong manufacturers, but as demand increased, both sets of manufacturers were able to work closely with the buyers, on one hand, and to organize effective production networks, on the other. For this purpose, cooperative production networks proved to be flexible in response to Western orders and to be able steadily to upgrade in terms of quality, speed of delivery, and costs – characteristics that in turn brought in more orders. From 1965 through most of the 1980s, the emergent Taiwanese and Hong Kong economies were the result of the capabilities of would-be businesspeople to organize in response to increasing and rapidly changing demand. The comparative advantage that their form of organization gave them was that it allowed them nearly to monopolize the production of certain types of goods that needed to be produced in limited batches and that had short product cycles, a category of merchandise called nondurable consumer goods.
>
> (Hamilton and Kao, 2018, p. 98)

This is how the famous export-oriented industrialization started in Hong Kong and more importantly, it explains why the industrialization of Hong Kong was export-oriented.

The success of the manufacturing sector was evident: manufacturing's share of the GDP increased from 24.7 per cent in 1961 to 28.2 per cent in 1971 and the sector's percentage of total employment rose from 43 per cent to 47 per cent (Chiu, Ho and Lui, 1997, p. 52). Hong Kong had successfully transformed itself from an entrepôt hub into an export-oriented industrial centre. We, however, will not be examining why Hong Kong's export-oriented industrialization turned out to be a tremendous success, but will rather describe the macro-economic context contributing to the so-called 'Hong Kong Model' of industrial production.

The Hong Kong model

As mentioned earlier, the industrialization of Hong Kong during the post-war period was mainly driven by the export market. James Riedel (1973, p. 3) succinctly summarizes the Hong Kong industrial model as follows:

> Hong Kong (1) specializes in the manufacture of standardized consumer goods (2) for export (3) to high income countries in the West, and at the same

time, the Colony (4) relies on Asian countries for the provision of raw materials and (5) on Western countries for capital goods.

Lui and Chiu (1993) further identify other key features in the industrial structure of Hong Kong. The manufacturing sector, they observe, was dominated by small establishments, the majority of which were family-owned businesses. Most of the workshops engaged in labour-intensive and low-technology production. They were also highly sensitive to market changes. Sensitivity here refers to the acute awareness of the change of demand, price, and taste of the world market. Since the manufacturing sector of Hong Kong was largely export-oriented, the production and business of workshops and factories were highly susceptible to the slightest changes in the world market. The capacity to deal with such changes was the key to the survival of the manufacturing business. The Hong Kong manufacturers, in general, exhibited high flexibility in adapting to the volatility of the world market.

Flexibility, as Kim-Ming Lee (1997, p. 189) points out, has very often been considered to be the key to the success in Hong Kong industry. The meaning of flexibility, however, is not always clear since flexibility can be defined in various ways (Lee, 1997, pp. 189–190). We contend that the flexibility in the Hong Kong industrial context refers to the capacity to manage contingencies, and specifically to the capacity to adjust the production volume, the labour force, and the product range within a short period of time and at a low cost. The flexibility of Hong Kong industry was basically a combined result of the prevalence of extensive subcontracting network, the availability of a cheap, large labour pool, and the merchant mentality of the manufacturers.

The informal labour market

According to the conventional narrative of the development of Hong Kong industry in the post-war period, there were three factors which were crucial to the growth of the manufacturing sector: the supply of an almost inexhaustible labour force due to the Chinese emigration, the supply of fresh capital from businessmen from China, especially those from Shanghai (Wong, 1988), and the transfer of the entrepreneurial and management skills of these immigrants. Yin Wah Chu (1992), while acknowledging the important role played by the Chinese capitalists, argues that their contribution to this industrial development should not be exaggerated. The proliferation of the informal labour market, she points out, is one of the keys to understanding the flexibility of the Hong Kong industrial model (Chu, 1992, p. 420). It was not simply the availability of the vast amount of cheap labour, but *the specific way* in which the labour was flexibly organized, as embedded in the extensive subcontracting networking, that enabled the manufacturers to respond to the market swiftly and inexpensively (Lui, 1994; Chu, 1992).

The manufacturing sector in Hong Kong was supported by a sophisticated subcontracting network organized around a steady supply of both formal and informal labour. The description of production networks in Taiwan offered by Hamilton and Kao (2018, p. 114) can also be applied to the situation in Hong Kong:

By parcelling out the manufacturing process among many firms, each firm doing a set of tasks that contributed to the final product, the cost to individual firms as well as the general cost of administrative overhead was kept to a minimum.

Lui's (1994) study of the garment industry in Hong Kong examines in detail the mechanism of the subcontracting system and identifies the major forms of informal labour organization. Subcontracting refers to the outsourcing of certain parts of production to other firms. Horizontally speaking, the highest position in the subcontracting system would be the multinational firms that outsourced the whole or part of the production procedure for their goods to Hong Kong. What followed were the very few large local manufacturing firms that had the capacity to take part in the whole production process by producing their products in-house or subcontracting parts of their production to smaller workshops. Due to their limited production capacity, small workshops, which were predominant in the manufacturing sector in Hong Kong, specialized in only one or certain parts of the production process. Very often, they had to work closely with other workshops in order to complete a specific order. The workshops might in turn further subcontract the assignments to informal workers who work from home, and this gave them the ability to form the backbone of the production force in workshops.

Many workshops relied on the informal labour force to maintain their 'flexibility', in the sense that they helped workshops to lower costs and reduce risks during production. In contrast to formal workers, the workshops neither had to provide any labour protection nor make any commitment to informal workers (Lui, 1994, p. 65). Workers were summoned or dismissed anytime the workshops needed to enhance or reduce production capacity in response to market change. The system, however, could only operate effectively when the skills of the informal workers were transferrable, that is, non-firm-specific and when the workshops had established strong social ties which enabled them to recruit and mobilize the workers. Similar production activities were practised by many workshops in the same industry, allowing the skills of the workers to be largely transferrable.

Merchant manufacturers

The flexibility of manufacturers was also a result of the mode of investment. Many manufacturers in Hong Kong had a 'quick buck' mentality in that they did not think that it was necessary to make any long-term investment commitment such as the upgrade of technology in workshops (Carney and Davies, 1999; Glasmeier, 1994). Instead, they adopted the 'hit and go' strategy to swarm into the profitable sector and to scramble for profit maximization. Once the profit was exhausted, they simply shut down their business and looked for other opportunities. These 'merchant manufacturers' were primarily interested in maximizing short-term profit through guerrilla business investments, instead of running and developing the manufacturing business. In other words, money-making rather than business sustainability was their primary concern. As a result, manufacturers tend to invest only in transferrable production assets, so that they could continue to employ the assets when they shifted their business from field to field. The manufacturers demonstrated a high level of flexibility towards the volatile market in part because they were more than ready to abandon their existing businesses and move to another sector, continuing to scramble for new profit generated by fresh market demands. This explains why so many workshops in the industry remained small in scale: the manufacturers simply lacked both the motivation and capital to expand their business.

We would like to emphasize that the flexibility of Hong Kong industry should be understood primarily as the result of the specific industrial pattern of Hong Kong, which was characterized by the under-investment and high-risk aversion of the manufacturers, as well as the heavy reliance on the flexible labour market. The success of the model largely depended on the abundance of cheap, efficient, and flexible labour force which enabled the manufacturers to produce not only at a lower cost, but also with higher efficiency, thus attracting the multinational companies to outsource their production to Hong Kong.

Demand-responsive integration

To better understand the pattern of the industrial sector in Hong Kong, we would like to point to the fact that small workshops in Hong Kong, not unlike their counterparts in Taiwan, faced 'an economy-wide of oligopsony' (Hamilton and Kao, 2018, p. 118). According to Hamilton and Kao (2018, p. 118; italics original), 'when the imbalance [in economic power] is due to *a few* buyers and many sellers, it is an oligopsony'. They further explain:

> The big buyers were the funnel through which the exports from Taiwan had to pass in order to reach the consumers in the United States and Europe. Without this intermediary passage, the small and medium-sized firms would have been unable to establish contact with Western consumers. Therefore, by the mid-1970s, a relatively small set of big buyers controlled the economic behaviour of a large portion of Taiwan's economy. The price structure established in the export sector spread over the entire economy. All the players in the economy had to become demand responsive, had to adjust to a world market for the goods they produced.
>
> (Hamilton and Kao, 2018, p. 118)

Small workshops in Hong Kong in the 1970s faced similar situations. In other words, owners of Hong Kong small workshops had to calculate their costs and profits according to the production price set *solely* by the foreign buyers, who worked out the pricing according to the price competition in their own countries. It would be very difficult for small workshops in Hong Kong to bargain the price with the foreign buyers in the supplier market. The only thing they could do was to come up with new ways to produce better quality goods at an even cheaper price. Hence, the extensive subcontracting network and the availability of a cheap, large labour pool were two major means on which the small workshops in Hong Kong relied.

In short, the manufacturers in Hong Kong, not unlike their counterparts in Tai-wan, had to be extremely cost-sensitive and demand responsive not only because their profits depended solely on how well they could reduce their costs but also because they were vulnerable to the demand fluctuation given the fact that their survival solely relied on foreign buyers and they were not able to negotiate a bet-ter price from their foreign buyers in 'an economy-wide oligopsony'.

The politics of industrialization in Hong Kong

The Hong Kong model, however, should not simply be regarded as a natural result of the market mechanism. Lui and Chiu (1994), in their study of the garment industry in Hong Kong during the 1970s and the 1980s, point out that the strate-gies adopted by the manufacturers, were, at least in part, a result of the policies made by the Hong Kong government. The manufacturers, as they explain, did not intentionally engage in labour-intensive production, nor were they born with sensitivity and flexible knowledge on how to survive in the market. Instead, they had to adopt such strategy due to the lack of government support in the industry (Lui and Chiu, 1994).

Chiu's (1994) study sheds light on the relationship between the laissez-faire policy of the Hong Kong government and the trajectory of development of the industry. In contrast to the statist model of Singapore in which the Singaporean government played an active role in orchestrating the development of the indus-try, the laissez-faire model of Hong Kong suggested that the government provided only minimal and indirect assistance to the manufacturing sector (Chiu, 1994, pp. 5–6). The manufacturers could only rely on themselves to raise capital, to upgrade their technology and to face fierce competition without subsidy or pro-tection. In other words, the survival in the market was not guaranteed by anyone. It was the lack of the government's support and the imposed 'self-reliance' that led to the risk aversion tendency and 'quick buck' mentality of manufacturers.

For example, when the steel industry requested the Hong Kong government to use the locally produced steel in official building projects to help the struggling industry in 1968, the government rejected the proposal claiming that it would be inappropriate for the government to favour, against the market mechanism, a particular sector (Chiu, 1994, p. 10). The Hong Kong government also resisted the call from industry to offer any land concession (Mizuoka, 2014, p. 29). Unlike the commerce sector, the industrial sector required a vast amount of land to build plants and expand their production. The government, however, refused to sell the land to industrialists at a concession rate as land sale was the primary source of income for the government and was key to the maintenance of the low tax rate, which benefited primarily the business sector, another area the government dared not interfere in (Mizuoka, 2014, pp. 28–29). The industrialists also had a much harder time raising funds through the banks than their counterparts in the business sector (Lui and Chiu, 1994, p. 53). One of the major reasons was that commercial banks were simply not used to issuing loans to industrialists as they did not establish strong ties with the industry in the same way as they did with the business sector (Lui and Chiu, 1994, p. 58). As a result, industrialists attempted to persuade the government to help establish an industrial bank. The proposal was rejected by a committee which was set up by the government; none of the committee members, however, was from an industrial background (Chiu, 1994, pp. 82–83).

We are not suggesting that the Hong Kong government intentionally suppressed the growth of industry because the government in fact did play a significant role in building a business-friendly environment, although it appealed to foreign investments rather than local industrialists. As an umpire of the market game, the Hong Kong government strived to construct and maintain the 'framework' essential to the operation of the market. The government, as mentioned earlier, established semi-official institutions such as the HKTDC in 1966 to link the local traders and manufacturers with the international market. The organization, for example, helped organize local fairs and delegations to participate in overseas trade shows. As will be mentioned in Chapter 3, the HKTDC played a significant role in helping Fong to establish his export trade market, as it created the opportunity for Fong to not only join overseas fairs, but also to get to know overseas clients.

While it may seem inappropriate to criticize the Hong Kong government for doing minimal work to assist industry, we would like to point out that the support of the Hong Kong government to industry was largely indirect and trade-oriented, that is, to facilitate the trading of the manufactured goods. The government, we contend, did not provide direct assistance to the production activities, which were the core of the industry, to help boost the productivity of the industry or to help them upgrade technologically.

The unwillingness of the manufacturers to invest and expand, as we have shown, was in fact a result of the lack of support and protection from the Hong Kong government. The manufacturers had to bear all the risks by themselves, had limited access to bank loans and did not receive active assistance from government. Under such circumstances, they could hardly develop any long-term business structures and had low motivation to take more risks to expand their businesses. In fact, the policy of the Hong Kong government also encouraged manufacturers to engage in labour-intensive production through its pro-employer labour policy. Despite the pressure from London, the Hong Kong government did not actively push for labour protection until the late 1960s. With weak if not non-existing labour laws, the employers were not obliged to provide benefits such as health care to the workers and could request them to work for very long hours without compensation. This effectively drove down labour cost. More importantly, the Hong Kong government was highly suspicious of labour unions as they were often linked to the Communist party or the Kuomintang. As a result, the rate of labour unionism was very low and the workers in general had minimal bargaining power vis-à-vis the employers (Lui and Chiu, 1994, p. 58). The lack of direct support from the government and the maintenance of the low labour wage further encouraged manufacturers to engage in labour-intensive production.

The relocation strategy of Hong Kong manufacturers in the 1980s

Such industrial politics continued to shape the trajectory of the economic development when the export of Hong Kong manufacturers was threatened by the competition from other newly industrializing countries and the protectionism in their exporting markets in the second half of the 1970s. During that period, there were voices in the community that called for expansion of the industrial base of local manufacturing industries, and more importantly the upgrade of production technology (Chiu, Ho and Lui, 1997, pp. 53–54). However, all of this could be very costly and thus risky. Most local manufacturers could not afford to upgrade their production technology because they were small-to-medium sized companies with limited capital. It would be necessary for the Hong Kong government to intervene with practical, financial subsidies or establish policies that could support the manufacturers' effort in upgrading their production technology. Legitimized by the discourse of 'free market economy', the Hong Kong government again refused to intervene because doing so would imply the provision of financial support by the government and thus the possible creation of a 'big government' image that the Hong Kong government strived to avoid. Fortunately, China decided to open herself to the outside world in 1978 and this revived Hong Kong's entrepôt trade. At the same time, the influx of immigrants from China helped ease the shortage of labour in Hong Kong. The fresh supply of cheap labour enabled Hong Kong manufacturers to maintain the labour-intensive, low-wage, low-profit-margin production in the 1980s rather than moving to technological upgrades and capital-intensive production, since such a move was no longer necessary (Chiu, Ho and Lui, 1997, pp. 53–55).

However, the labour-intensive, low-wage, low-profit-margin production of Hong Kong manufacturers was very vulnerable to rising production costs, especially labour costs. In the 1980s, the fresh supply of labour was no longer available since the 'touch base' policy[6] was cancelled by the Hong Kong government. In other words, the manufacturers could no longer hire recent immigrants as low-wage labour (Chiu, Ho and Lui, 1997, pp. 55–56). The Hong Kong government again left the problems to local manufacturers who had no alternative but to relocate their production bases to South China to exploit the rich supply of cheaper labour there.

The implications of this relocation strategy to Hong Kong's industrial structure were various, one of which was the change in the employment structure: while the absolute number of employees in the manufacturing sector reduced, there was an increase in the percentage of professional, technical, administrative, and managerial personnel within the same sector. Such a change also revealed that the manufacturing sector, not unlike what had been happening in the general economic structure from the 1970s onward, had been commercialized in the sense that the sector itself has shifted from being production- to commercial-oriented (Chiu, Ho and Lui, 1997, pp. 71–77). In other words, the economy of Hong Kong was undergoing what Chiu, Ho and Lui (1997, pp. 75–76) call a 'double-restructuring process'; as they explain:

First, there is the general trend of a sectorial shift towards finance, trading, and services in the economic structure. . . . Second, as noted above, within the manufacturing sector itself, the direction of change is towards a more commercially oriented center than a production base.

This double-restructuring process and the subsequent occupational shift from production to commerce in turn changed the class structure of Hong Kong society.

Social mobility in Hong Kong

The change of class structure was supported by the result of a study presented at the beginning of the 1990s. The study was a joint-research project conducted by two local sociologists (Wong and Lui, 1992). They interviewed 1,000 male household heads, aged 20 to 64 randomly chosen from district- and block-stratified sample blocks provided by the Census and Statistics Department of the Hong Kong government in January 1989 (Wong and Lui, 1992, p. 24). The study discovered that more than 60 per cent of the service classes had no service class origin (Wong and Lui, 1992, p. 50), testifying to the expansion of the service classes, because otherwise there could not have been so many newcomers joining the classes (Wong and Lui, 1992, p. 47). As Lui and Wong (1994, p. 13) point out in another paper, '[i]n other words, structural changes of the economy have created vacancies for a significant portion of the people of Hong Kong to move to class positions different from their fathers', which is also to say that in post-war Hong Kong, 'class origins do not form unsuppressable hurdles for social mobility'. Our intent of adopting the version of the brief history of Hong Kong economy by Chiu, Ho, and Lui (1997) was to point out that the double de-industrialization process described in the previous section led to the expansion of the service classes, which made the social mobility in the last two decades of the twentieth century possible.

The 'survival trio'

Despite the structural changes of the economy that facilitated social mobility for the people of Hong Kong, not everyone could be successful in this mobility game. We are tempted to ask what characterized those who were successful in their social mobility. According to the previously mentioned survey, 65 per cent of the service class owned their property, 'while for the working classes, the majority (ranging from 67% for the unskilled workers to 76% for the skilled workers) rented their premises' (Wong and Lui, 1992, p. 33). As mentioned earlier, 60 per cent of the service class had no service class origin, which is also to say that they should be considered as successful mobility seekers. Since 65 per cent of the service class owned their property, most of the successful mobility seekers should also be property owners. It is therefore safe to assume that the property owners and the successful mobility seekers shared similar features. We therefore suggest that an analysis of the characteristics of property owners is methodologically strategic in identifying the features of the successful mobility seekers.

In his analysis of the motivation for housing ownership among the people of Hong Kong, James Lee (1999) argues that it could be attributed to the early living conditions, investment return on housing ownership, and identity construction. Most people in Hong Kong, according to Lee (1999), experienced congested living conditions in their childhood. This can be attributed to the large-scale influx of immigrants from China soon after the establishment of Communist China in 1949, which made the living conditions crowded and deprived (Lee, 1999, pp. 112–113). Immigrants from China who had no place to stay, had no alternative but to illegally build themselves a house anywhere in town, which resulted in a quarter of a million people in the squatter population between 1956 and 1958 (Lee, 1999, p. 116). Squatter living conditions were of course very congested. However, it was these congested conditions that cultivated a worldview, of which the concept of *ngei* (extreme endurance) became an important characteristic. *Ngei* 'essentially means more than just endurance or tolerance' (Lee, 1999, p. 114). As Lee (1999, p. 114) further explains:

It [the concept of *ngei*] refers to the unquestioned willingness of the individual to sacrifice personal comfort and old values in order to survive in the new environment. One accepts enduring of the most unfavourable conditions of life without repentance. It also means the readiness to live anywhere as long as there is shelter and to take up any work that comes along, even if followed by personal degradation.

The people of Hong Kong could not just be *ngei* when the Hong Kong government determined to go for a mass construction of seven-storey H-shaped resettlement blocks with communal facilities after the famous fire in Shek Kip Mei on Christmas in 1953.[7] Although the inhabitants of the settlement blocks no longer needed to worry about environmental safety, the fact that there was no toilet, washing or cooking facilities inside individual households gave rise to interpersonal conflicts, and more importantly 'extremely competitiveness to survive in the living environment' (Lee, 1999, p. 123). Lee (1999, p. 123) quotes one of his informants, Mr. Wan, saying:

When I was about 10, I was assigned by my mother as a 'sentry' for the washing tap and the toilet. I developed a system of warning and communication with my family so that they knew exactly when to come forward to the communal place (we called it the 'pit') for washing. I mustn't let the fat lady next door get it first because if she did, we wouldn't be able to have the shower room before 10. I was extremely good at that, and nobody in my family would beat me.

This harsh social environment helped cultivate a survival strategy that could be summarized by the concept of *shingmuk*, as Lee (1999, p. 124) explains:

Shingmuk, like ngei, is a Cantonese slang, meaning a combination of smartness, vigilance, swiftness, worldliness, assertiveness, agility and independence.

When somebody is described as being shingmuk and also capable of ngei, that somebody is almost certainly destined for success. This mundane set of cultural concepts carries a wide impact across all social sectors.

In the 1970s, the rising living standards in Hong Kong also cultivated the *pok* (proactive and risk-taking) attitude among many working-class families. The 1970s was a very important decade in Hong Kong's modern history as it was a decade when Hong Kong society underwent a rapid and radical change. The rapid growth of the garment-making and electronic industries in the 1970s inevitably caused labour shortages and thus salary increases (Chiu, Ho and Lui, 1997, p. 55). The incomes and living conditions of Hong Kong workers improved tremendously in the 1970s. Working-class families could now afford to send their children to universities. At the same time, the shift of Hong Kong's economic structure from manufacturing to finance, trading, and services in the 1970s created opportunities for well-educated young people to leave the working class and join the service class (Wong and Lui, 1992, pp. 47–50). More importantly, the expansion of the service sector helped nurture the children of working-class families to seek for social mobility, which in turn made the second generation of working-class families adopt a *pok* orientation, which 'stands for the combined meaning of proactivity, fierce competition and risk-taking' (Lee, 1999, p. 133).

It has become clear now that the congested living conditions in post-war Hong Kong gave rise to three core values instrumental and essential to survival, namely, *ngei, shingmuk*, and *pok* which Lee (1999, p. 133) calls 'survival trio'. The 'survival trio' speaks for the combination of the determination to survive, the flexibility to adapt, and the will power to act. We argue that the 'survival trio' of the property owners whom Lee (1999) studied were also the major characteristics of the successful mobility seekers.

Managers and entrepreneurs[8]

The 'survival trio', we argue, motivated many people in Hong Kong to seek social mobility. Lui and Wong (1994) further argue that there were two general strategies of social mobility adopted by the second generation of working-class families in Hong Kong. One was education and the other was entrepreneurship. Some worked hard in school, hoping to climb up the social ladder through pursuing their bureaucratic careers in government offices or multinational companies in Hong Kong. In fact, the majority of those who performed well on the school examinations in the 1970s became first-generation college graduates. Many then joined multinational companies or government offices upon graduation and moved up the corporate ladder or civil servant hierarchy within the government; some achieved top management positions in their companies or in the Hong Kong government. In this regard, the story of Ricky Szeto Wing Fu, the managing director of a very successful herbal tea chain in Hong Kong, Hung Fook Tong Holdings, is very illustrative.

Ricky was born to a poor family in the 1960s. He spent his childhood with his grandfather because his mother passed away very early, and his father had to work in a distant area to support the family. Ricky, however, had a very happy child-hood with his grandfather, who influenced him deeply; as he recalled:

> My grandfather was a persistent, hard-working, and selfless person. At that time, we, like other poor new immigrants from Guangdong Province after the Second World War, lived in an old tenement block. My grandfather always cleaned the public area of the building for all the people there, although he was not that young at that time. I think I am heavily influenced by him and we have similar personalities.

Ricky's childhood, however, was not without problems, one of which was that he had a speech problem. Since he did not have enough money to consult medical specialists, he had to solve the problem by himself. However, it was this problem that cultivated his patience, as he explained:

> During my postgraduate study abroad, I realized that my mind functioned so quickly that my body could not catch up. I therefore decided to train myself so that I could think quickly but I consciously control my body to make sure that my actions were always accurate, and I would not make mistakes. The people of Hong Kong are famous for their efficiency, but their re-do rate, according to an international survey, is 12 per cent, while the rate for people in Singapore and Japan is only 7 per cent. The people of Hong Kong may be more efficient than their counterparts in Singapore and Japan, but at the same time they make more mistakes. More impor-tantly, perhaps correcting the mistakes we made will take more time. . . . Everybody knows the story of the match between the tortoise and the hare. The tortoise may walk slowly and must do so cautiously because if, for example, it makes a mistake in directing itself, it will take much time to correct the mistake. The hare can run quickly but always wants to be lazy. The final winner is always the tortoise! I always tell my staff to be the tor-toise rather than the hare. We should always remain calm and pragmatic. If we face a problem, don't rush to solve it. Stay calm until we can come up with the best solution.

Like other young men from poor families during that time, Ricky wanted to move up the social ladder through university education. However, he was not lucky enough to attend either the University of Hong Kong or the Chinese University of Hong Kong, the only two publicly funded universities in Hong Kong at that time. Ricky ended up enrolling in a private university: Shue Yan University. Upon graduation, Ricky went abroad to obtain his Ph.D. When he returned to Hong Kong, he decided to teach at Shue Yan's business school while managing Hung Fook Tong Holdings at the same time.

Ricky's example has showed how people in Hong Kong sought social mobility through education and moving up the corporate ladder; some, not unlike Ricky, even achieved top management positions in their companies.

Of course, not everyone has the educational talent. Less academically minded people sought social mobility by starting off their own companies as family businesses. The case of a well-known Hong Kong restaurant, Yue Kee Restaurant Ltd ('Yue Kee' hereafter), serves as a supporting example. In 1958, the restaurant's founder, Ng Ceon Yim, started Yue Kee with his wife in Sham Tseng, New Territories, Hong Kong. The Yue Kee of that time could hardly be called a restaurant: they did not own a physical shop and instead sold food to customers in bamboo baskets slung from the ends of a shoulder pole. In 1966, Ceon Yim saved enough capital to buy a wooden hut for Yue Kee. At the same time, Yue Kee expanded its menu to include roast duck, marinated duck, chicken, and so on. The Ng couple together with their newly joined brother-in-law Ceon Yim continued to run Yue Kee. Two years later, the government removed Ceon Yim's wooden hut but gave him a stone house in return. Ceon Yim continued to operate Yue Kee from the stone house and simultaneously rented some wooden huts to raise his ducks. The first half of the 1970s saw Yue Kee's first business boom when even factory workers could afford spending a sunny day at a beach near Sham Tseng with a dinner at a restaurant such as Ceon Yim's restaurant nearby. Another boom occurred from 1980 to 1981 when the government built the Tuen Mun Highway to connect the new town of Tuen Mun with Tsuen Wan. Many construction workers patronized Yue Kee during this time.

Despite its booming business, Yue Kee did not employ any staff and was still run by members of the Ng family. By this time, in addition to Ceon Yim, his wife, and his brother-in-law, Ceon's six children also joined their father's business. The workload was heavy, especially for Ceon Yim himself. Hence in 1982, he decided to close Yue Kee and move on to property investment.

Ceon Yim's property investment, however, did not go well, and he decided to return to the restaurant business. In 1984, together with his brother-in-law and children, Ceon Yim reopened Yue Kee at its original location. This move proved fortuitous, because that decade became the golden period of Hong Kong's economy. Living conditions improved substantially, and many low-income families could afford to go out for dinner. Yue Kee also started to employ other staff members, at the same time expanding its business scale by renting additional stone buildings nearby. In 1992, Yue Kee however encountered its first major crisis: the sudden death of Ceon Yim and his wife in a fire. This was a heavy blow to the Ng family and to Yue Kee. With the help of their uncle, however, Ceon Yim's children reopened Yue Kee six months after the fire and at the same time updated its facilities and turned Yue Kee into a modern restaurant.

Yue Kee now has a new leader: May Ng, Ceon Yim's third child. Before Ceon Yim and his wife passed away, Yue Kee had been entrusted to her. After their death, May took up the management of the restaurant and has proved herself a competent successor, making Yue Kee more successful under her leadership. Nowadays, Yue Kee is one of the most famous roasted goose restaurants in Hong Kong.

We have demonstrated through the cases of Ricky Szeto Wing Fu and Ng Ceon Yim two major strategies whereby lower-class families in post-war Hong Kong sought upward mobility. The strategy one adopted and the way the entrepreneurial process proceeded, however, were the results of the mediation between entrepreneurial characteristics of individuals that are given by their biographical background including class and education level, and the socio-cultural contexts. As we shall see in the next chapter, Fong pursued a similar entrepreneurial path as Ng Ceon Yim, the founder of Yue Kee.

Conclusion

In this chapter, we have outlined several causal chains of phenomena in different registers or levels. First, we have demonstrated how the specific post-war geopolitical dynamics and politicking gave rise to the depoliticization policy of the Hong Kong government. One of the major consequences of the depoliticization policy was that the people of Hong Kong were interpellated as 'Economic Man'. In other words, the self-identity of the people of Hong Kong as 'Economic Man' is the consequence of the colonial policy of the Hong Kong government.

Second, the depoliticization orientation, especially its positive non-intervention policy, also contributed to the formation of the famous 'Hong Kong Model' of the manufacturing sector which is characterized by the domination of small family-owned firms. These small family businesses tend to adopt the labour-intensive and low-technology production mode and exhibited high flexibility in adapting to the volatility of the world market. We also argued that the flexibility of Hong Kong manufacturers was a combined result of the prevalence of an extensive subcontracting network, the availability of a cheap, large labour pool, and the merchant mentality of the manufacturers. All of this enabled the local manufacturers to be extremely cost-sensitive and demand responsive in 'an economy-wide oligopsony'.

The Hong Kong model, however, should not simply be regarded as a natural result of the market mechanism but, at least in part, as a result of the positive non-intervention policy made by the Hong Kong government. The local manufacturers did not intentionally engage in labour-intensive production, nor were they born with sensitivity and flexible knowledge on how to survive in the market. They were forced to do so as the result of the lack of government support in the industry.

Third, the same positive non-intervention policy also helped shape the developmental path of Hong Kong manufacturing industries which further facilitated the social mobility of a sizeable portion of the people of Hong Kong. This segment of the Hong Kong population was characterized by the 'survival trio' – *ngei*, *shingmuk*, and *pok* – which constituted the typical ethos of the entrepreneurs in Hong Kong.

Finally, it is this survival trio that motivated the second generation of working-class families in Hong Kong to adopt two major strategies for their social mobility: education and entrepreneurship. Chinese entrepreneurship in the context of Hong Kong could be argued as a strategy for upward social mobility. As Lui and Wong conclude (1994, p. 26):

The entrepreneurial spirit works as a "tool-kit" and is called upon for selecting the line of economic actions, rather than defining ends and objectives. In this way, we see entrepreneurship as an economic strategy through which individuals, under given conditions and constraints, work out their ways for climbing up the social ladder.

That is also to say, Hong Kong Chinese entrepreneurs are not culturally determined to become entrepreneurs, not to mention that they are not born to be entrepreneurs.

Any of these causal chains of phenomena, when considered in isolation, is neither novel nor our own discovery. Their significance lies in the *specific* way they intersect with each other. In the chapters that follow, we will show how the determination of Fong as an entrepreneur and his entrepreneurial process result from the intersection between these causal chains of phenomena on the macro level described in this chapter and Fong's unique personal characteristics. Next chapter therefore will be devoted to the identification of Fong's personal characteristics through examining his biographical history together with his entrepreneurial process.

Notes

1 The ordinance, for instance, restricted the right of association with political organizations in public, as it stated: 'Any person who in any public place or at any public meeting wears uniform signifying his association with any political organization or with the promotion of any political object shall be guilty of an offence.'
2 All unregistered local societies, according to the ordinance, were deemed unlawful. The Registrar would refuse to register a society if it was regarded as 'a branch of or is affiliated or connected with any organization or group of a political nature established outside the Colony'.
3 The ordinance restricted the right to strike of employees.
4 The riots were largely staged by the pro-KMT immigrants in Hong Kong. On 10 October 1956, pro-KMT groups were celebrating the National Day of the Republic of China in the resettlement area in Kowloon when officials tore down the national flags on the wall of the buildings. The conflict soon escalated into large-scale riots. During the riots, leftist unions and factories were attacked.
5 It was initiated by the government as an effort to establish the local administrative system in the colony. The offices helped disseminate governmental information to the public, foster social campaigns, and facilitate communication between the government and the public.
6 Illegal immigrants from mainland China who could successfully reach the urban area of Hong Kong, in a 'touch base' sense, would be granted the right of abode by the Hong Kong government.
7 The fire destroyed the homes of 50,000 families and thus forced the Hong Kong government to make up its mind to build resettlement blocks on a massive scale to resettle not just those 50,000 families but also other illegal squatters (Lee, 1999, pp. 121–122).
8 Some passages included in this section are drawn, in amended and abridged form, from Wong's (2013) previous article.

3   A life history of Fong

This chapter focuses on Fong and his personal characteristics. We will examine, though briefly, the biographical history of Fong together with his entrepreneurial process, beginning with Fong's childhood and apprenticeship. It is then followed by an exploration of how Fong started and developed his first workshop, diversified the scope of his company into the export, showroom, and retail realms and successfully developed FBL into one of the most popular jewellery brands in Hong Kong. From Fong's entrepreneurial process, we will identify Fong's personal characteristics and briefly touch upon his management style for a more ambitious goal: to outline the general theoretical framework of this book which is that Fong's entrepreneurship and the development of his company are seen as the results of the mediation between Fong's personal characteristics and the socio-cultural and political-economic environments in which Fong's entrepreneurship took place.

The formative years

Fong was born in Hong Kong in 1936. It was a year before the Marco Polo Bridge incident which sparked off the Second Sino-Japanese War and five years before the Japanese occupation of Hong Kong. Fong's childhood memories are occupied by wartime images and the daily scenes of poverty. He grew up in Yau Ma Tei on the southern tip of the Kowloon Peninsula. Yau Ma Tei was one of the major local Chinese settlements in Hong Kong. Fong's father was a hawker who sold snake meat and soup in a local market. His mother was a housewife. He has a brother who is two years older and a sister who is three years younger. Fong told us very little about his siblings for reasons unknown to us. The Fong family lived at a shabby tenement building in Yau Ma Tei. At that time, the housing facilities in Yau Ma Tei were predominantly old tenement blocks of three to four floors without any lavatory facilities inside, as described by Pryor, quoted by James Lee:

> In terraced houses, only the front rooms had windows so that the inner compartments were dark and airless. At the rear of each floor was a cookhouse, normally about 2 metres deep, which also frequently served as a latrine, storage room and even sleeping quarters. Chimneys were the exception and

smoke escaped by means of holes, usually about 1.2 square metres, cut in the upper floors and roof. Such smoke holes were not very effective with the consequence that fumes permeated the living space. . . . Tenement houses were constructed so that each floor was one undivided room. On the ground floor a space was boarded off in front of the kitchen for a bedroom or store and above this a platform was often erected as a workplace or for sleeping. While the regulations required the provisions of latrines, these were rarely to be found. Women and Children normally used a pot kept either under a bed or in one corner of the cookhouse. The menfolk had to resort to the use of public latrines which, although supervised by the government, were run as a business enterprise with the products being shipped to China and sold at considerable profit to farmers.

(Pryor, 1973, pp. 10–11, cited in Lee, 1999, p. 112)

Fong and his family lived on the second floor of the building and shared the 600-square-foot flat with six other households. Fong's mother was a sub-landlord. She rented the flat from the landlord, divided it into compartments and sublet them to the other households. The 'compartments' could not strictly be called private. There was no real privacy to be spoken of. Some tenants could only afford a bed space. It was very common in Hong Kong for several households to share a single flat before and even after the Second World War. The ordinary people were simply too poor to afford individual housing.

The five members of the Fong family had to squeeze themselves into a 100-square-foot room on the veranda. Apart from the lack of privacy, overcrowding is another dominant characteristic of the everyday life in the compartment within a flat. One of Lee's (1999, p. 113) informants who spent his childhood in an old tenement block recalled:

As a child I can remember my mum didn't allow us out for fear of bad elements on the streets. During weekends and holidays, we usually played together inside the room where we lived. There were other families in other rooms. When my mom cooked in the kitchen, my brother would drag out a wooden panel from the bunker and use it as a slide at a corner of the room. That's all we had in the childhood as 'playground'. We had no toys because they were expensive. We played with stones and tiny bags filled with sand. In the evening when bathing time came, all three of us, including my sister, bathed in the same tub of water. Not exactly a tub in the modern sense, mind you, it's just a big wooden basin. Because there wasn't a bath room and we were too small to go to the public bath, we bathed either in the kitchen or in the corridor where everyone passed by. We did that all the way until I was about ten and my sister about eight, when we began to feel a bit shameful of exposing our bodies like that. At night, my brother slept on the top of the double bunker with me. It was a small bed: 3' x 5'. I always woke up in the middle of the night and discovered my brother charging his toes right into my mouth.

The poor life of Fong and his family grew even more miserable after the Japanese army invaded Hong Kong. At that time, Fong was around five years old. The scenes of hunger and death remained vivid in his mind, as he told us:

> We starved all the time. I always felt very hungry, damn hungry. I remember my little sister kept crying all the time because she was so hungry. My uncle (Fong's father's elder brother) starved to death. I am not kidding. He was really a poor guy. He was sick and did not have anything to eat. When we found out, he had already been dead. His body was bloody cold. I helped my father to bring the corpse downstairs and leave it in the alley. That's it. What else could we do?

Fong's father could not resume his trade in the market during wartime. To make ends meet, Fong's mother went to work in a teahouse. She would try to bring back the leftovers to feed her children. Later she was laid off too. She then went to Huizhou in southeast Guangdong Province to take up a job there. She could not leave all the children with Fong's father in Hong Kong, so she decided to take the eldest son with her to Huizhou. Fong and his younger sister stayed with their father in Hong Kong. Fong's mother had to take up construction work for the Japanese army. It was a very physically demanding job and Fong's mother, after working there for a year or two, found it difficult if not impossible to stand the harsh work any longer. She finally decided to quit the job and returned to Hong Kong. Foreseeing that she could not feed her three children anymore, Fong's mother decided to sell the eldest son to a household of boat people[1] in Huizhou. 'They didn't have any choice. Not enough food. He [Fong's brother] could have a better chance to survive,' Fong said. The absence of his elder brother naturally forced Fong to assume the role of the eldest son in his family and share the economic burden with his father.

While Fong's mother was working in Huizhou, Fong's father became a rag-and-bone man in Hong Kong. Fong became his father's assistant. Carrying a large, heavy gunny sack, the little boy had to walk from block to block every day to collect second-hand items. 'I had to keep shouting, "Collect metal scrap and worn-out clothes!" Otherwise people didn't realize what you were doing,' Fong said. In the evening, they would just find a spot on the street, spread out the items collected, hoping to resell them. Since both Fong and Fong's father had to work outside the whole day, they had to leave Fong's younger sister who at that time was just four years old at home by herself.

One day, when Fong and his father were doing their business as usual, they heard the sound of bombings. As Fong recalled:

> I was really scared and immediately hid under a stair. I didn't even know where my father was. I waited and waited. We learnt later that many people were killed during the bombing.[2] Phew. That's war.

Following the Japanese surrender on 15 August 1945, Hong Kong was liberated. Immediately after the war, Fong enjoyed a very brief period of sheer happiness.

He got the chance, finally, to go to school. He was enrolled in a school in Yau Ma Tei and was assigned to start with the primary one curriculum. At that time, he was ten years old. Just two years later, however, he was forced to drop out. The Fong family was haunted by poverty again. Fong's father fell ill so he could no longer get to work. Not only did Fong have to cease his studies since his parents could not afford it, he himself *alone* also had to support the family. At the age of 13, Fong was sent to a goldsmith to become an apprentice. All of this just happened so suddenly that Fong simply had to accept the arrangements. As he recalled:

> My mother told me they didn't have any money. My father was ill. They couldn't support me, so I couldn't go to school anymore. Then one day, my mother told me that I would take up an apprenticeship in a goldsmith. I have to leave home and stay there for five years. A relative had helped to arrange this.[3] She helped me pack some clothes and daily necessities. That's it. I then became an apprentice in goldsmithing.

Fong was sent to a goldsmith on Shanghai Street in Yau Ma Tei. Shanghai Street was one of the busiest roads in the area. It was also the major cluster of goldsmiths on the Kowloon side. Fong's apprenticeship was to last for five years. During the period, the boss provided Fong with meals and accommodation. The accommodation was not really a benefit as Fong was required to live in the workshop to help guard the store. A folding bed supported by several wooden sticks was all he got. Fong was not entitled to any salary or holidays either. He could at best get a dollar each month from the cashier to get a haircut.[4] Altogether there were ten employees working for the goldsmith. Fong was the only apprentice there, meaning that he was at the bottom of the hierarchical ladder. Fong's major duties were to satisfy every need of his seniors, and do the cleaning, grocery, and cooking for everyone. At the beginning, Fong lived in enormous fear and shame. He explained the situation to us:

> I was so afraid of the 'masters' (the senior goldsmiths).[5] I did not dare get off work if the masters were still working. I was the youngest there. I had to be obedient otherwise I would have a very hard time. But I really hated sweeping the floor at the entrance of the store! It was embarrassing and humiliating as people on the street all stared at you!

What Fong found most disappointing was that no one taught him anything on goldsmithing. It was not until the very last stage of the apprenticeship that he was able to get a desk to do the real work. He basically acquired the craft through self-learning. He would observe the work of the masters and practice the techniques during his own free time. 'It was completely a waste of time! I spent several years doing all the cleaning and cooking, what's the point?' Fong was still very upset by the experience when we interviewed him in the 2010s. 'It's utterly unproductive. So, I changed the system once I established my own workshop.'

Despite the hardship, the apprenticeship did guarantee Fong's own survival. Although he did not have any salary, he still managed to save some money and give it to his parents because he had to support his family as his father could no longer work. Fong was still very proud of this as he told us:

There is one thing that I am really proud of myself. Ever since I left home when I was 13, I have never asked for a single penny from my parents. Instead, I have been sending money back to my family all the time.

We could not help asking immediately, 'But how could you send money to your family when you were an apprentice? You said you didn't have any salary?' Fong further explained:

No, I didn't. But I did some tricks. I was responsible for doing grocery and cooking for the staff. I would receive several dollars for that. I would buy food which cost less than the amount and secretly save what remained. I could save around ten to twenty cents a day. Days after days, it's not a small sum! At that time, you could get a bowl of congee at five cents.

Five years later, Fong completed his apprenticeship and *could* become a goldsmith master, but he chose to leave the industry and work in a cotton mill as an intern. We were quite amazed by the twist when Fong told us about his brief working experience in the textile industry since we had not read anything about this in media coverage on him. Fong explained to us:

Not many people are aware that I had worked in a cotton mill. When I completed my apprenticeship, I just didn't want to become a goldsmith. A master could only earn around $30 to $40 a month. There's not much prospect. I could earn a lot more in the cotton mill. I could get $6.5 per day. If I was willing to work overtime on Sunday, I could earn as much as $10 a day. In other words, I could earn around $300 a month. That's a huge difference. I needed money; I mean not for myself, but for my family.

We learned from Fong later that when he was still undertaking his apprenticeship at the goldsmith, the Fong family was forced to leave their home. The tenement building where the Fong family lived was designated by the government as a 'dangerous building'. They could no longer live there and were forced to move to the squatter village in *Loufu ngaam* (Tiger Cave)[6] in Kowloon. As mentioned in Chapter 2, many immigrants from mainland China came to Hong Kong to flee the communist rule after the Second World War. The influx of immigrants resulted in an explosion of squatters in the territory. The living conditions in the squatter village were very poor. These squatters were living in simple huts supported by wood or iron plates that would be easily destroyed by typhoon and fire. The residents had to live in fear and discomfort, as Lee's (1999, p. 122) informant recalled:

I can remember the 1960 Typhoon Wendy, you know, which killed many people and made 10,000 homeless. At that time our family lived in a squatter hut in Tai Hang Tung. It was one August evening, I don't remember exactly when Signal No. 10 was hoisted. During dinner time my father and I were trying to stabilize the hut by some more external wiring . . . and you know what, by ten, the whole roof was blown off, just like that! We all clutched together under a plastic sheet for 2 hours before the rain turned light and then we ran for cover in a nearby school.

Obviously, Fong decided not to be a goldsmith but to work in a cotton mill because he wanted to earn more money so that he could change the fate of his family.

Fong started his first job in a cotton mill in Tsuen Wan in the New Territories, an area that was gradually developed into a light industrial centre during the post-war period. The textile industry was one of the major pillars of the rapid industrialization that took place in Hong Kong in the 1950s. Fong thus followed others' steps to join the booming industry hoping to earn more money. The money did not come easily though. The cotton mill adopted a rotating shift system. Fong would take up the night shift for two weeks followed by a week of day shifts. For each shift, Fong had to work for 12 hours either from 7:00 a.m. to 7:00 p.m. or vice versa. Fong told us that the work experience in the cotton mill was one of the toughest times in his life:

It's really miserable! I basically worked nonstop. We only had a half-hour lunch break each day. We had to stay on guard all the time as the cotton was very vulnerable, they would be easily broken in the machine. Of course, there was no air-conditioning in the factory. The air was very bad. All the machines were operating. It's like you were thrown into a big steamer. I know that many workers got lung-related illness. You see I am very thin right? That's because of the overwork in the mill. The harm was so great. In order to earn more money, I would also work on Sunday too. Can you imagine? Work seven days a week under such pressure and condition! The company provided us a dormitory. I remember that I could not sleep at all. I always felt like I was being pressed by ghosts on the bed (sleep paralysis)! Nothing is more miserable than those crazy days. I had a feeling that if I could endure this, then I could endure anything. Money was the reason why I endured all of this.

Fong had been working in the cotton mill for a year until it was closed one day with no prior notice. Fong was at a complete loss when he suddenly became unemployed. 'I was very anxious,' Fong recalled. 'I needed to feed myself and my family. I needed a job desperately.'

Through the recommendation of his masters at the goldsmith shop where he took up the apprenticeship, Fong took up another apprenticeship in a workshop attached to a jewellery store to learn the craft of gemstone setting. During the early post-war period, goldsmith and jewellery stores were two different kinds of business operations in Hong Kong. Traditional goldsmiths (*gam pou*) mainly sold pure 24K gold (pure gold) products (*zuk gam*, literally, full gold) to local and ordinary Chinese customers. Jewellery stores (*zyubou hong*), on the other hand, mainly sold karat gold accessories set with gemstones, such as diamonds, to tourists and rich Chinese customers. Insiders in the industry would differentiate *zuk gam* from karat gold jewellery (*sai gam*, literally, Western gold). *Sai gam* masters earned much more than *zuk gam* masters. That's why Fong was willing to take up another apprenticeship.

The workshop was attached to Coeng Faat Hong at Humphreys Avenue in Tsim Sha Tsui in southern Kowloon. Tsim Sha Tsui was and still is a major tourist centre in Hong Kong. It was also the hub of jewellery stores on the Kowloon side. Fong's second apprenticeship lasted for two years. This time, he received $30 a month as 'salary'. After completing the apprenticeship, Fong continued to work in the workshop for a while, but his master never mentioned a salary increase. Fong then left the workshop and found a job in Maan Sing Hong, a large jewellery company in Tsim Sha Tsui, as he told us:

> It's [Maan Sing Hong] a big one. They specialized in taking orders from the seamen. Usually I could earn around $500 to $600 a month. I was paid by piece rate, so I had to work extremely hard. Once I stop working, I would not have money. It was very tough, but I was quite happy with the money.

The entrepreneurial adventure

Day after day, Fong's life was occupied entirely by work. He did not have the leisure to think about the future. Around 1960,[7] the visit of a lady changed his whole life. Mrs. Wong, the boss of Coeng Faat Hong, visited Fong one day. Recall that Fong previously took up an apprenticeship in gemstone setting at the workshop attached to Coeng Faat Hong. Mrs. Wong told him that his former master had already gone, and she would need someone to replace him. Obviously, Mrs. Wong came to ask if Fong would want to run his own workshop.

> I had never thought about setting up my own business. I mean, I simply didn't have the time to dream about this. When I was an apprentice in Coeng Faat Hong, I had made a good impression on Mrs. Wong. She thought that I was an honest and reliable guy. I just said yes when she asked me if I wanted to replace my former master. I didn't think much. I just thought that being a boss could earn a lot more than being a worker. I only have two hands. But if I employ people, I can multiply what I earn.

Mrs. Wong was willing to lend $3,000 initial capital to him if he was interested. Fong did not hesitate and said yes, and this was the beginning of Fong's entrepreneurial adventure. Fong got $3,000 from Mrs. Wong, as promised. He used $1,500 to buy raw materials and the remaining money to purchase tools and equipment. The gold price at that time, as Fong recalled, was around $300 per Chinese tael (*loeng*).[8] The workshop was an annex to Mrs. Wong's store. Fong could only manage to put five desks – or what the insiders called '*kung fu* desk'[9] – inside the 100-square-foot room. From the start, it was a one-man workshop. Fong subsequently recruited four apprentices until all the desks had been occupied. Fong's very first apprentice, after 50 years, is still working in the company today.

At the early stage of operations, Coeng Faat Hong was the only client of Fong's workshop. His workshop was basically responsible for manufacturing jewellery products for Coeng Faat Hong upon request. Since Coeng Faat Hong was just a small retail business, it could not provide enough orders to support Fong's workshop. Fortunately, Mrs. Wong was willing to 'free' Fong from his obligation. She not only allowed Fong to take orders from other clients but also recommended him to other jewellery stores such as Maan Sing Hong, the large company in which Fong worked before.

Over the next several years, Fong put all his energy into expanding his workshop in Tsim Sha Tsui. He first rented another 600-square-foot flat in an old building on Carnarvon Road and shared it with his friend. Later, he relocated his workshop to a nearby building. He rented two units and linked them together, using one side of the 1200-square-foot space as a workshop and leaving the other side as his own residence.

The first breakthrough: expansion after the 1967 riots

While Fong was busy expanding his business, Hong Kong society was experiencing tremendous changes. In 1967, for the first time, the British colonial rule in Hong Kong came under serious threat. As mentioned in Chapter 2, the Cultural Revolution in China invoked a series of protests and boycotts by workers supported by left-wing groups. The protests soon turned into a large-scale opposition movement against imperialism and colonialism in Hong Kong. The confrontation between the communist sympathizers, if not supporters, and the Hong Kong government escalated quickly. The opposition movement became more and more violent. Bombs were set up randomly on the streets causing widespread anxiety and panic among the people. It was a time of chaos. Many people lost confidence in the future of the city and attempted to emigrate. Many factories stopped operating or were simply closed.

Fong, however, was unaffected by the turmoil. His workshop continued to operate as usual as if nothing had happened. Since some of his competitors suspended or even abandoned their business, Fong grasped the chance to absorb their orders as well as workers. The development of Fong's workshop experienced a giant leap after the riots. We were impressed by his boldness. 'Why did you make this decision? Weren't you worried about the situation?' we asked. 'You had such strong confidence in Hong Kong!' Fong explained:

> I just didn't think much. I mean I just didn't know how and what to fear about. I was just concerned about my own business, that is, whether my workshop could get enough orders, whether my workers and I could earn more money.

'So you never thought about closing down your business during the riots?' we asked as we were eager to find out the answer. Fong said in a firm voice:

> No! Absolutely not! I have never for a second thought about closing my business! It's all I had, how could I close it down? How could I, my family and my workers survive without the workshop? I really didn't think much: the danger, the chaos, the uncertainty or anything else. The only thing I had in my mind was how to keep my business.

After the riots, the number of Fong's workers doubled. His workshop expanded from occupying two to 13 units in the building. Fong had already established his name in the local jewellery manufacturing sector. His clients included all the major local jewellery retailers in Hong Kong. In 1971, Fong relocated his workshop to a building at Minden Row, still in Tsim Sha Tsui. He bought 18 units in a single purchase. In the same year, he incorporated his company, which became a milestone in his entrepreneurial adventure.

Fong told us that he decided to incorporate his company only after listening to the advice of his friends. He personally did not have much knowledge about the meaning and implication of incorporation. He recalled the details:

> I incorporated my company because my friends told me to do so. They said I should do so to further expand my business. Ha! I didn't really know much about these kinds of things. They said the procedure was easy, I didn't have to care about the details, the accounting firm would take care of everything. The firm told me that I had earned $0.97 million in a decade! They helped me to round up the figure to one million. I was very surprised! It was a great sum of money! I had never really sat down to calculate how much I got.

The second breakthrough: the beginning of export trade

The development of Fong's workshop business was not smooth all the way. His emphasis on expanding the labour force to maximize production resulted in overstock and put him under constant pressure to find a way to sell the products. Fong understood that he had to explore more channels to get more orders and to sell off the stock. He first started to engage in the wholesale trade, asking some of the masters to become middlemen to help sell the products. It still was not enough. Fong needed to obtain more big orders. A golden chance came in 1971.

In that year Fong was invited by the Hong Kong Trade Development Council (HKTDC) to participate in an international trade fair held in the United States. As mentioned in Chapter 2, the HKTDC was established by the Hong Kong government in 1966 to help promote local products to, and link the local traders and manufacturers with, the international market. Export trade in fact became the major driving engine of the Hong Kong economy in the 1970s. Fong gladly accepted the HKTDC's invitation without hesitation. It was in fact a very bold decision, given that Fong spoke no English and had no prior experience in export. But Fong believed that going overseas would be a good chance for him to promote his products and more importantly get new and large orders as the volume of transactions in the export business was much bigger than the Original Equipment Manufacturer (OEM) orders, which could help Fong to solve the overproduction problem.

The normal practice was that Fong and his team would first join a jewellery fair or show in the United States. Fong would not travel alone; he needed someone who could speak English and drive. New York usually would be their first stop. After the show, Fong and his team would stay behind and travel from city to city to peddle the products. This explained why Fong and his team would have to stay in the United States at least one month with each trip. All these journeys could be very risky and sometimes even dangerous, but Fong was still determined to develop his export business. He actively recruited staff with high educational backgrounds and experience in export businesses to help him.

The third breakthrough: the establishment of showrooms

Before turning to Fong's adventure in the 1980s, we would like to go backwards a little bit to the early 1970s first. When Fong started to embark on his export business, he faced a very big problem at home. He kept receiving warnings from the Labour Department and Fire Services Department. In fact, when Fong's workshop was still located on Carnarvon Road, he had already received similar warnings causing him to move his base to Minden Row. It was illegal to undertake any industrial activities in a residential building. But back in the 1960s, many small workshops, commonly known locally as 'cottage workshops' (*saan zai cong*), like Fong's, just sprang up to meet the surging market demand. Most of these workshops were in residential buildings in urban areas. By convention, these workshops were generally tolerated. However, Fong's workshop had grown too big and thus attracted the attention of the relevant government departments. After ignoring the warnings several times, Fong received an official 'notice to quit' from the government ordering him to remove his workshop from the residential building.

Given the ever-expanding scale of his workshop, Fong understood that it would be very difficult to find another suitable place in Tsim Sha Tsui. He thus decided to relocate the workshop to Hung Hom, an industrial area adjacent to Tsim Sha Tsui. He found a new site in an industrial zone so that he would no longer have to worry about the intervention of the government. Eventually, he got several units on the eighth floor of an industrial building. With a 10,000-square-foot space, the workshop was much bigger than before. The immediate problem was solved.

After moving to Hung Hom, some friends of Fong working at travel agencies visited his new site. They looked around the vast space and told Fong, 'you are wasting such a big space here; you should establish a showroom!' Fong told us that his friends could bring some tourists to the showroom to buy the jewellery.

Fong thought it was a promising idea. He then recruited people to help start and run a showroom to sell jewellery directly to tourists.

From its opening, the showroom began attracting quite a lot of customers, all of whom were tourists brought in by travel agents or tourist guides. Following the rapid development of tourism in Hong Kong, the showroom business seemed to have promising prospects. The number of tourists visiting Hong Kong was over one hundred thousand in 1958 (Hong Kong Tourist Association, 1959, p. 15); the figure reached almost one million in 1970 (Hong Kong Tourist Association, 1971, p. 3). Fong decided to expand the showroom business and bought several factory units in a nearby building in 1977, which has since become the headquarter office of the company.

Fong's involvement in the showroom business was a great breakthrough as his company started to move forward in the supply chain to deal with consumers directly. When Fong moved the company into the new building in 1977, he also opened his first retail branch, signifying the full transformation of his company from a manufacturer into a retailer.

The fourth breakthrough: the founding of the retail empire

The chance came when the Ocean Centre opened in Tsim Sha Tsui in 1977. It was one of the most high-end shopping malls in Hong Kong. One of Fong's clients encouraged him to try his luck and open his own retail branch in the new mall. Fong told us the story:

> I got to know the third-generation owner of a century-old jewellery store. He was one of my former clients and was very kind to me. He helped me to buy a lot of products and was willing to lend me money whenever I was in need. He really helped me a lot. He always told his staff, 'Look at Fong, see how smart he is! You should all learn from him!' [Fong laughed] He had a store in the Ocean Centre. He told me that I should also try my luck there. He encouraged me to set up my own retail store and gave me a lot of confidence. I was grateful to him. The profit margin of running a jewellery manufacturing workshop was very low, only around one-tenth of that of a retailer. I had no capital before. When I got enough money, of course I would like to have my own store. I could earn much more!

In 1977, Fong opened his first jewellery retail store in the Ocean Centre. To enhance the grandeur of the store, Fong hired two security guards to stand guard and borrowed a rare pink diamond to display it in the store. The business, however, did not turn out to be as good as Fong had expected. Fong was very frustrated until he came across an idea, as he told us:

> I just got very few customers. I kept thinking what I could do to attract the people. Then I suddenly got an idea. At that time, it was popular for people in Hong Kong to buy gold Krugerrand coins. I remember the bank sold a coin

at the price of $328. I bought some from the bank and sold them at $320 each in the branch. People rushed to my store to buy the coins because they were cheaper! You may think that I did attract people but at the expense of profit, right? It's not true. Some of them preferred to wear the coins, so they bought a necklace in my store. At the end, I was able to attract customers and earn money at the same time.

The success prompted Fong to come up with another unusual strategy in the industry at that time: to use mega sales to attract people. Fong regarded himself as the major driver of the massification of jewellery products in Hong Kong, as he said:

In the past, very few local people would dare to go into a jewellery store. Jewellery stores were for rich and foreign people. They were too grand for ordinary people to go in. This was something I wished to change. I wanted to sell affordable jewellery. I was the one who initiated the massification of jewellery in Hong Kong. I emphasized quick returns with small profits. My strategy was to organize sales and promotion events from time to time. I would put a whole-page advertisement in the newspapers stating clearly the prices of the items. The strategy worked because people thought that it was really a good bargain.

Fong's tactics proved to be very successful. The sales and promotion events did attract a lot of customers to Fong's store. An employee of FBL, who joined the company in the mid-1970s, told us that whenever there was a mega sales event, customers would swarm into the store:

I was working in the billing department. I mean I was not really a frontline staff. But whenever there was a mega sales event, we would all be summoned to help in the store. There were really a lot of people. They basically scrambled for the products! We had to bring mah-jong boxes to collect money. We just stuffed money into the boxes. The queue was very long.

The success of Fong's campaigns, however, led to the closure of his store in Ocean Centre. Fong was still a bit displeased when he talked about what happened:

The Ocean Centre refused to renew the lease. They didn't tell me the reason directly, but I knew that's because I held those sales events and attracted a bunch of people. They thought that my store was too 'low', damaging their high-end image. When the lease expired, they immediately kicked me out. Even until today, we still don't have any stores there.

In addition to the store in Ocean Centre, Fong had also set up branches in Central, Causeway Bay and North Point on Hong Kong Island. In 1986, after Ocean Centre refused to release his lease, Fong returned to the goldsmith industry. He established a goldsmith and jewellery store in Yau Ma Tei, an area in which he grew up and first learnt the trade of goldsmithing. Fong told us his motivation behind this:

> My first retail store was a jewellery store. But in fact, I had been thinking of running a goldsmith because I was a goldsmith and I understood the properties of gold. I didn't want to waste my knowledge of both *zuk gam* and *sai gam*. So, I started to establish goldsmith and jewellery stores selling both pure 24k gold products and jewellery. That's my biggest strength. During the opening ceremony of the Yau Ma Tei store, I wrote a couplet saying that, 'Though the Ocean is Big, One Still Can't Be Accommodated' [Fong looked proud] You understand what that means right? The Ocean Centre kicked me out, but I showed that I wasn't defeated. During the opening period of the store, I made some mini gold qilins[10] to celebrate the event. They were extremely popular among the customers.

A year after, in 1987, Fong listed his company on the Hong Kong Exchange. He became the chairman and one of the two executive directors of the listed company. According to the prospectus, the turnover of his company was estimated to be $448 million. Fong told us that he did not really understand the procedure of going public:

> We were the first listed jewellery company in Hong Kong.[11] My friends told me that if my company was listed on the stock market, it's easier to raise funds and to expand. One dollar could be easily turned into ten dollars. So, I set it [going public] as my target and I finally achieved the goal. I didn't know much about the procedure. I just found some people to help me with this.

By that time, Fong had already extended the retail network to cover the New Territories, Kowloon, and Hong Kong Island. In 1989, according to the annual report of the company, it became 'the largest chain of jewellery stores in Hong Kong in terms of number of retail outlets employing over one thousand employees'. An ordinary goldsmith had become a chairman of a listed company. Fong of course could not have foreseen this and would never have dreamed about it.

Fong also aggressively extended his retail network beyond Hong Kong to places such as Taiwan, Singapore, and Malaysia. Fong's jewellery empire reached its zenith in the mid-1990s. During the fiscal year of 1996/1997, his company had altogether 19 retail outlets and five showrooms in Hong Kong, 27 franchised or joint-venture retail outlets in China, 13 franchised retail outlets and four counters in Taiwan, four retail outlets in Malaysia, and one showroom in Singapore.

The development path of Fong's jewellery business is a textbook case of forward integration. From building a manufacturing workshop, through engaging directly in wholesale and export trade, to establishing showrooms and retail outlets, Fong led his company to go beyond manufacturing. But we would like to emphasize that Fong's forward integration of production and circulation, however, was not the norm in the jewellery industry in Hong Kong. Most of the jewellery workshops, including large workshops, tended to remain in the manufacturing sector, although it was common for jewellery retailers to extend their business backwards to manufacturing as they had accumulated sufficient capital to claim control over the suppliers. In other words, Fong had made a difference that had a significant difference on the local jewellery business. The developmental path of Fong's jewellery business can be considered to be an *entrepreneurial process* because it has made an extraordinary difference to the local industry.

Fong's family

In the early 1990s, when Fong's business reached the peak, his children had also finished their studies overseas. Fong had three children altogether with his wife whom he married in 1964. Joseph Fong, the eldest child, was born in 1965; Daisy Fong was born in 1967 and Jackson Fong, the youngest son, was born in 1968. All of Fong's three children were educated in the United States. Joseph got a doctoral degree while Daisy and Jackson had master's degrees. This also explains why Fong referred to them by their English instead of Chinese names. The children prefer to be called by their English names. According to Fong, Joseph and Daisy were smart in their studies while the performance of Jackson in school was just so-so. It is very typical for Chinese entrepreneurs to send their children to study abroad. The children are expected to return to help with the family business after finishing their studies.

The peculiarity of Fong's case is that Joseph, Fong's eldest son, has never participated in the family business. On the other hand, Daisy, Fong's daughter, once played a major role in the company. Daisy and Jackson were appointed as the executive director of the company in 1993 and 1994 respectively. Daisy was responsible for the jewellery business in China and Jackson took care of the marketing and retail business in Hong Kong. Fong was not willing to talk much about Daisy's experience in the company,[12] he just briefly mentioned that she was a housewife now. He talked more openly about his eldest son:

W&C: We are so interested in Joseph. It's very strange that, in the Chinese context, the eldest son does not join the family business.
F: Joseph had already expressed that he was not interested in the family business since a very long time ago. He's very good at studying. Sometimes I just think that he is really a nerd! He had worked in the university for a long time before becoming a freelance programmer.
W&C: And you are alright with this? We mean that with Joseph's not inheriting your business.
F: What can I do? He said that he just wants to live a very simple life. His whole family now lives in Canada. He just doesn't want to be involved in the business. But Joseph is a very good guy. He has never asked for a penny from me ever since he graduated from university.

Fong's youngest son, Jackson, told us that, in contrast to his brother, he has always wanted to take part in the family business:

I don't know why but I started to develop an interest in the family business since I was very young. I guess it's because of the influence of my father. He always brought us to the workshop. He also taught me a lot about the interior design of a store. My brother has never been interested in the business, however. I remember that he wasn't interested in visiting the store in the Ocean Centre at all. He would just bring a book to read there.

Since his elder brother was not interested in inheriting the family business, Jackson was regarded by Fong and the employees as the apparent heir to the jewellery empire which Fong had built. However, Fong had not really thought about the succession question since he had never thought about getting retired. It was only due to a series of unexpected incidents taking place after 1998 that Jackson, the crown prince, unexpectedly and smoothly succeeded his father to become the leader of the company in 2000. We will get back to this in Chapter 8.

Who is Fong?

What does this life history and entrepreneurial process tell us about who Fong is and especially who Fong, *the entrepreneur*, is? As we have described earlier, Fong's formative years were all about endurance. In order to survive, Fong had to bear the unbearable. He believed that he could only change the fate of his family and himself through earning more and more money. Fong exhibited what we described in Chapter 2 as the 'survival trio', which have a lot to do with the socio-economic environment in which he was brought up. Fong, not unlike other Chinese sons in Hong Kong, grew up in a very poor family. He suffered a lot during the Japanese occupation of Hong Kong such that he had to help his father collect metal scraps and old clothes on the street and resell them under the threat of Japanese bombings. It is therefore not surprising that Fong developed the attitude of *ngei*. Fong also developed an attitude of *shingmuk* when he was sent to work as an apprentice in a goldsmith. It was here that his characteristics of being smart, vigilant, swift, worldly, assertive, agile, and independent were nurtured since Fong, as the most junior worker, had to learn how to read the minds of his boss and all his masters. Finally, Fong developed a *pok* attitude in his business as the Hong Kong economy developed rapidly from the 1960s to 1980s which presented him with many business chances. In other words, Fong's personal traits mentioned earlier, not unlike the 'survival trio', cannot be attributed to his biological makeup. There is no biological determination for entrepreneurship!

Fong, however, cannot be seen as the personification of the socio-economic configuration of Hong Kong. He is not purely a passive instrument of the socio-economic configuration of Hong Kong because he is a *real* individual: he *lived* the hardship, uncertainties, and insecurities throughout his whole life and suffered from them. Neither can he be considered as an abstract 'Economic Man'. Fong is a concrete individual: he was born into a very poor family and was forced to take up the heavy economic burden of his family, which together nurtured him as unique person. As Sahlins explained in an interview with the anthropologist Adam T. Smith, '[a]ctual individual subjects are products of very complex mediations of family life, positions in family life, and a multitude of particular lived institutions experiences' (Smith, 2002, p. 289). In other words, there is no direct relay of the socio-economic configuration of Hong Kong to Fong and vice versa, because there is always a gap between the two created by the intervention of all sorts of institutions such as the family as we can see from Fong's case. If the socio-economic configuration cannot totally interpolate Fong, Fong should have an individuality. We can transpose to Fong what Sartre (1963, pp. 55–56) also said of Valery: there is no doubt that Fong Bou Lung is a lower-class person, but not every lower-class person is Fong Bou Lung.

In short, between Fong and the socio-economic configuration of Hong Kong, there is a gap that makes the direct reduction of the former to the latter and vice versa impossible. The relation between Fong and the Hong Kong society is mediated by Fong's biographical experiences in familial and other institutions. Fong therefore is an individual who 'express[es] the cultural universals in an individual form' (Sahlins, 2004, p. 151). There is no simple cultural determinism either.

Faat cin hon *(craze for money)*

The individual form of Fong's expressing the cultural universals is characterized by his two unique qualities: the pragmatism driven by his craze for money (*faat cin hon*) and his guts in making highly risky decisions (*gau geong*). When Fong narrated his story to us, he was very honest about his thirst for money. He never failed to emphasize that *faat cin hon* was the reason that kept him going forward as he emphasized:

> I did not receive much education. I could only use time to exchange for more and more money. I think that I am *faat cin hon* [jokingly]. Honestly, I really think that *faat cin hon* is the primary motivation of my work. For me, everything is a matter of survival. My biggest fear has always been losing a job and becoming penniless. Money is the most important thing to me.

Fong's *faat cin hon* driven pragmatism is reflected in his business approach as well as management style. Fong neither attempted nor was able to come up with a unique business idea or to design, produce, and market an original product. What he did was to feed the market with what it needed as accurately and efficiently as possible. He did not really care what he made and how to sell them all as long as the products brought him profits. Fong had never pretended that he was a great entrepreneur, an artisan or a dreamer who was eager to show the world his wonderful ideas or skills. When we asked him, for instance, to pick ten masterpieces that best represented his craftsmanship, he just seemed very reluctant to do so and explained:

> Frankly speaking, I don't know what 'craftsmanship' or 'artisanship' means. I am just a goldsmith. For us, there's nothing artistic about the jewellery products. We simply don't think in that way. Goldsmithing and gemstone setting are just some practical skills for us to earn a living. I don't know what an

artwork or a masterpiece is. But of course, there are differences in the skills required. Some works are difficult and take a lot of time while others are easy jobs. For me, as long as the products can generate profit, I will try my best to make them. For every product I made, it was intended for sale, not for art.

Fong's *faat cin hon* tendency explains how he was able to shift swiftly to different business scopes and made breakthroughs one after another. Fong could run a workshop to serve retailers, establish an export network to cater to overseas clients, set up a showroom to receive tourists, and open his own retail branches to reach the consumers directly as long as he believed that all of this was profitable. Fong's decision to convert some of his retail outlets into optical stores in 1987 is an especially illustrative case. Fong's retail business suffered heavily from the financial crisis in 1987 because at that time many banks in Hong Kong not only became very cautious in their loan business, but also started to request the clients to repay their loans immediately. As a result, Fong had problems in raising capital to finance the supply of the merchandise for his retail outlets, not to mention that he had to find financial resources to pay for the rent of the outlets as he could not simply terminate the rental contracts whenever he wished. In short, Fong needed to keep his retail outlets operating and he came up with the idea to convert some of his retail shops into optical stores and continue the business. 'But, why optical stores?' we asked. Fong explained:

> The setting of optical stores was very similar to that of jewellery shops. I didn't have to spend much to change the layout of the stores. There was no particular reason why I sold glasses except profit-taking. When our jewellery did not sell well, I could compensate that part by selling glasses. That's just an expedient arrangement. I stopped doing that later. But I didn't really think that it's odd. As long as I could make a profit, I could basically sell everything.

Following the same logic, Fong did not care, if not failing to comprehend, much about the images and values associated with the brand of the company. Branding was something that he considered abstract and thus incomprehensible, impractical, and therefore useless. 'I am the brand; I am the best symbol! haha!' Fong added.

FBL's retail strategy was particularly illustrative of Fong's pragmatism. Instead of marketing the products as grand and luxurious, as other jewellers usually did, Fong turned to mega sales promotional campaigns to emphasize that his products were good value for money. To Fong, the most important thing was to get the attention of the people and to convince them that they could get the best bargains at his stores. In other words, Fong did not attempt to sell his products through his own brand, nor through the image and value, or the fantasy and style associated with it. These were all 'impractical' things that Fong would not consider. What Fong concerned was the down-to-earth stuff: the manufacturing of the product, the pricing strategies and the profit generated.

Fong's pragmatic attitude was also reflected in his management style. He was not interested in ideas such as team-building or corporate culture, he only believed in money. Money, as he perceived it, was the best motivation and reward to the workers. As long as workers had enough monetary incentive, they, Fong believed, would work as hard as possible. Following the same logic, Fong also adopted a relatively lax attitude towards the employees. He was not concerned about setting up rules, regulations, or codes of procedures. He just cared about the result: whether the employees helped him earn money, as he explained:

> I just want my employees to get things done. I don't really care about the process. I give them a lot of freedom. Say, I don't set any regulations concerning the business hours of the retail stores. As long as the salespersons have enough economic incentives, they will be motivated, automatically, to work hard and strive to get more sales orders for you even if that might mean extending the business hours of the retail stores voluntarily. You understand what I mean? You don't have to use the stick because the carrot is good enough. And you don't have to control their every step. The salesmen are experts, they are better than me.

Fong's *faat cin hon* driven pragmatism also enabled him to entrust different people to help run his business. As we have seen, most business opportunities were brought to Fong by his friends or institutions such as the HKTDC, but Fong very often did not know how to exploit these opportunities. He had to recruit some capable staff members to help him. For instance, he had to rely on others to help him with the export and showroom business, as he did not speak any foreign languages. Fong did not care much about the details of the operation as long as the employees could help him achieve the goal. He did not hesitate to give them discretion. Reuben Cheung, Director of Group Product Planning & Trading, who joined the company in the early 1970s, explained:

> Mr. Fong was willing to trust and use different people throughout the process of developing the company. He didn't care *how* you get things done, he just cared *if* you really can get things done. He signed a lot of documents that he didn't really understand or maybe he even didn't remember that he signed those things! Because he trusted that the employees would handle the operation. He thought the employees were highly educated, so they should know better than he did. He's really a boss. I mean he expects that after he throws out an idea, you will help him to realize it. He complains sometimes that the subordinates simply can't follow his mind [Reuben laughed].

Fong's trust in the employees, however, is to a large extent driven by necessity. As we have seen, Fong came from an extremely poor family; he received little education, let alone mastering the English language; and he did not have the necessary expertise to exploit business opportunities. Fong was well aware that he needed the help of others to exploit business opportunities and that he alone could not handle the complicated details. To get things done, he could only choose to give the employees a free hand. Even though some employees betrayed him, Fong was not angry at them, as he said:

> I understand that one simply has to survive. Sometimes, the employees stole my clients or stole money from the deals, I knew that, but I also understood that they just wanted to survive. I was not worried about getting into business fields with which I was not familiar, because I could hire somebody else to help manage and operate. You can't do all the work by yourself, you have to trust people and know how to motivate them to help you. You have to trust the person in position otherwise you can't move on.

Gau geong (boldness)

Fong's *gau geong* (boldness) mentality also enabled him to solve many problems during his entrepreneurial process and to lead his company to make one break-through after another. *Geong* literally means ginger. In Cantonese slang, a man is said to have taken enough *geong* if he has the guts to take on whatever risks and challenges that may lie ahead and which many people, otherwise, would hesitate to go through. Many critical events in Fong's entrepreneurial journey – such as his decision to stay in business during the 1967 riots, to establish a showroom without any prior experience in tourism in the early 1970s and to expand into the retail market as early as the late 1970s – reflected his boldness and eagerness to keep moving, instead of standing still, amidst extreme uncertainty.

We have to add hastily that Fong's *gau geong* mentality cannot be simplified as equivalent to 'risk-taking'. The term 'risk-taking' implies that the person involved knows what the risks will be and makes decisions after careful calculation. Fong's *gau geong* mentality, however, implies not only risk-taking but also the ignorance of potential risks involved. As we shall explain in a moment, Fong could not always realize that what he did was in fact very risky either because he could not fully comprehend the situation or because he was so overwhelmed by the single motive of profit-taking that he either did not have time or simply was not able to think carefully about the potential risk involved in his entrepreneurial move.

Fong, his family, and Hong Kong society

We argue that Fong's *faat cin hon* driven pragmatism has to be understood against his specific family background, class, and early experiences. Recall that Fong's elder brother was sold to another family when Fong was a child, which is also to say that Fong was brought up *as if* he were the eldest son of the family. That also explains why when his father lost the ability to work after the war, Fong believed that it was he – rather than anyone else in the family including his elder brother or younger sister – who had to bear the economic burden of the whole family. We found out later – after completing our research work – that in fact, four years after the war, Fong's mother found Fong's elder brother and took him back to Hong

Kong. After returning to Hong Kong, Fong's elder brother helped his father to sell snake meat and soup in the local market. When Fong's father was forced to stop his business because of his sickness, Fong's elder brother accepted Fong's suggestion and worked in Fong's jewellery workshop as an apprentice. Obviously, Fong's elder brother was not as successful in his career as Fong was. When Fong's brother decided to emigrate to Canada later, Fong provided financial support for him so that the latter could start a jewellery shop there. Fong's younger sister also worked in his workshop until she married. Fong had been taking care of his parents until they passed away. All of this seems to suggest that although Fong is not the eldest son of his family, he has been financially supporting his family including his elder brother. Perhaps that is also why Fong never mentioned his brother and sister because they, to Fong, simply did not have a role to play in the family's struggle for survival. We therefore argue that Fong's personal fate is the same as that of his family: he lived the life of the whole family and he had the sole responsibility for the survival of his family. The ultimate reason for Fong's *faat cin hon*, we argue, lies in his strong motivation to enable his family to survive and make it prosperous, which is also to say that Fong was motivated more by the family interest than by his own self-interest.

The fact that Fong was forced to take over all the financial burdens from his father made him believe that he had to make as much money as possible to support his family. What Fong chose to do later was thus mostly out of the consideration of profit maximization. He decided to become an intern in a cotton mill instead of being a goldsmith, to learn the trade of gem-setting and to leave Coeng Faat Hong and work as a master in Maan Sing Hong all because of his desire to get more money. He had not thought about opening his own workshop until Mrs. Wong invited him to take over his old master's workshop. From Fong's own perception, he did not really choose to become an entrepreneur. He just thought *at that particular moment* that he could earn more money by recruiting people to produce more products.

In addition, the life of Fong and his family was full of uncertainties that added insecurity to his and his family's situation. Recall that Fong was suddenly forced to quit school when his father became sick; and he lost his job in the cotton mill when it was shut down unexpectedly. All of this speaks to a life of uncertainties and insecurities. Fong learned to respond to uncertainties and insecurities by maximizing monetary gain, which in turn gave him security. In the event, profit-maximization became his only goal in life. Fong did not have any dreams.

We, however, cannot take Fong's *faat cin hon* superficially as his longing for money because money was just a concrete and material symbol that represents the importance of Fong's money-making activities to himself, as David Graeber (2007, p. 97) argues:

> Different kinds of labor will tend to get reflected back in the form of a concrete, material medium which, like money, is both a representation of the importance of our own actions to ourselves, and simultaneously seen as a valuable in itself, and which thus ends up becoming the actual end for which

action takes place. Tokens of honor inspire honorable behavior. Really, their value is just that of the actions they represent, but the actors see them as valuable in themselves.

Likewise, Fong's value of *faat cin hon* represents the importance of money-making actions to himself and thus explains his endless pursuit of money, in the course of which Fong came to see money as valuable. It follows that it is not the concrete, material money that inspired his continuous money-seeking activities. Rather it was the importance attached to the action – the endless pursuit of money – that makes Fong never give up making money.

But why is such importance attached to the action of the endless pursuit of money in Hong Kong society? We argue that the importance of the endless pursuit of money is related to the colonial policy of the Hong Kong government mentioned in Chapter 2. Recall that the geopolitics in post-war Hong Kong presented a series of difficulties to the Hong Kong government, which forced the government to adopt a depoliticization policy that aimed to shift the attention and energy of the people of Hong Kong from politics to business and economy. In the event, the Hong Kong government successfully fostered a singular focus on material and monetary rewards among the people in Hong Kong. Money therefore was the ultimate motivation and the only life-long goal of many Hong Kong entrepreneurs, especially for those such as Fong who came from the lowest strata of the society and whose existence was always ignored by society. Fong had a burning desire to prove himself so that his personal importance could be recognized by society.

Fong's *gau geong* mentality was also developed through his biographical experience. Fong told us that very often he did not really feel scared at all. The 'risky' decisions he made, as perceived by others, were really nothing to him. He just thought that he had to do something to survive. We believe what Fong said and we contend that the reason for his seeming fearlessness is that he just did not have the capacity to fully comprehend the situation. He just took the risks without really realizing that what he did was in fact very risky. For instance, he did not really understand what joining a foreign fair and export business really means, what a showroom business is, and what listing his company on the Hong Kong Stock Exchange really means.

The impact of the specific biographical experience of Fong on his decision-making during the entrepreneurial process was also reflected in his spontaneity. For most of the time, Fong just responded to the contingencies. Let us recall the four major breakthroughs in Fong's entrepreneurial adventure. Fong had not really planned them in advance or made the decisions based on any business analysis. Fong's workshop experienced an explosive growth after the 1967 riots not because Fong had known in advance that the situation would turn better shortly but because he had to keep the workshop to support himself and the family; he engaged in the export business because he had to settle the problem of overstock at the workshop and to generate enough orders to feed the employees; he engaged in the showroom business because his workshop was relocated to an inconvenient location; and he established his retail stores because he still needed to create more orders. Fong's decisions were more an outcome of his constant reacting to contingencies instead of any strategic planning.

Finally, Fong's humble class background again should not be ignored when we attempt to understand Fong's *gau geong* mentality. Recall that Fong neither received much education nor had any training in managing a company, let alone the knowledge of marketing skills as he simply could not afford them. In addition, Fong hardly spoke any foreign languages or had any expertise in dealing with foreign customers. All of this contributes to the fact that Fong simply could not comprehend the risks involved in his decision-making.

In short, Fong's subjectivity cannot be seen as being prescribed by the socio-economic configuration of Hong Kong, for it is very complex, multi-faceted, creative, and always contradictory. Recall that although Fong, as mentioned earlier, is a very practical person, he still felt embarrassed and humiliated when he was ordered to sweep the floor at the entrance of the goldsmith store where he served his first apprenticeship in the industry. It is this complex subjectivity which, as we will demonstrate in the following three chapters, shaped the ways Fong made his decisions when he dealt with contingencies in his entrepreneurial process.

Conclusion

We have examined the biographical history of Fong Bou Lung together with his company's history. Specifically, we have delineated in detail the childhood and apprenticeship of Fong, how Fong started and developed his first workshop, diversified the scope of his company into the export, showroom and retail realms, and successfully developed FBL into one of the most popular jewellery brands in Hong Kong. What we attempted to achieve in this chapter was to identify from Fong's background his unique personal characteristics and management style: *faat cin hon* driven pragmatism and *gau geong* mentality. We, however, do not suggest that the individual-centric approach adopted by some of our colleagues in mainstream-US-dominated management sciences produces a good explanation for entrepreneurship. We instead have to emphasize here and will repeat throughout the book that the personal characteristics of Fong and the corporate features of FBL *alone* cannot account for Fong's entrepreneurship and over more than 50 years' history of the company as we can find many Hong Kong people who share similar characteristics with Fong and many similar Chinese family firms like FBL in Hong Kong. We shall show in the following chapters that the socio-cultural and political economic developments of post-war Hong Kong were clearly necessary conditions for the development of FBL.

Nor are we going to argue that the environment-centric approach adopted by some other colleagues in mainstream-US-dominated management sciences can explain Fong's entrepreneurship and the development of his company because not every entrepreneur in the same environment was, or, became Fong, and not every Chinese family business was FBL. As we shall show in the chapters that follow, Fong's own unique qualities – *faat cin hon* driven pragmatism and *gau geong* mentality – are also important variables in shaping the course of the company.

What we intend to do in this book is to propose a general argument – one that will be reiterated in the chapters – concerning the determination of Fong as an entrepreneur and his entrepreneurial process: that Fong's entrepreneurial process is a result of the *mediations* between his own specific qualities and the socio-economic-political context. This is an argument which is to be necessarily understood in three terms: Fong's personal characteristics, the socio-economic-political context of post-war Hong Kong, *and* their mediations.

This general argument is not our own discovery nor is it something novel; we are just, to quote Sartre (1963, pp. 47–48; italics original):

> restat[ing] what everybody has always known: the consequences of our acts end up by escaping us, since every concerted enterprise, as soon as it is realized, enters into relation with the entire universe, and since this infinite multiplicity of relations goes beyond our intention. If we look at things from this angle, human action is reduced to that of a physical force whose effect evidently depends upon the system in which it is exercised. But for *this very reason* one can no longer speak of *doing*. It is men who do, not avalanches.

In Chapter 2, we have already outlined several causal chains of phenomena of different registers or levels that inform Fong's entrepreneurial process. In this chapter, we, in turn, have identified Fong's unique personal characteristics that are also relevant to Fong's entrepreneurial pursuit. In the chapters that follow, our analytical focus will be on the mediation between Fong's personal characteristics and the socio-economic-political context of post-war Hong Kong, each of which is relatively independent from the other – as the former refers to the register at individual level and the latter that at societal level. We will show what characterizes the mediation is the discontinuities in Fong's individual characteristics and the determinants of the effect of Fong's economic pursuit as entrepreneurial, and we will show that in the forthcoming chapters. Hence the question now is: How did Fong's individual characteristics and the environment relate to each other to produce Fong's unique entrepreneurial process?

Notes

1 The boat people or the Tanka people live along the southeast Chinese coast. They are designated as one of the four indigenous communities of Hong Kong.
2 Fong probably referred to one of the air raids of the Allies. Quite a number of civilians were reported to be accidentally killed during the bombings.
3 According to Harry Mak, a long-serving employee of FBL who joined the jewellery industry in the 1970s, due to the nature of the business, traditional Chinese goldsmiths normally do not recruit strangers. The bosses want to hire someone whom they can trust. Recruitment is usually done through recommendation from the staff or friends and relatives of the boss.
4 In 1950s' Hong Kong, a dish of fish ball noodles cost around 20 cents.
5 In Hong Kong, people usually call craftsmen 'masters' (*sifu*). In the context of the local jewellery industry, masters refer to those who have completed their apprenticeships. We will explain the difference between masters and apprentices in the next chapter.

6 The area was later renamed as Lok Fu.
7 Fong could not remember the exact year.
8 In Hong Kong, 1 *loeng* is equivalent to around 37.7 grams.
9 The goldsmiths were regarded as 'masters'; their work desks were thus referred to as a kind of martial art desk for them to demonstrate their skills.
10 Qilin is a mythical creature in the ancient Chinese mythology symbolizing good luck.
11 The information provided by Fong is wrong. According to the local newspapers, Fong's company was the second listed jewellery company in Hong Kong, and the first one should be Chow Sang Sang, which went public in 1971. On the official website of Chow Sang Sang, the company also states that it became, in 1973, the first jewellery company to be publicly listed in Hong Kong.
12 Daisy stepped down from the Board of the company in 2000.

4 To produce or to die

The development of Fong's manufacturing business

As we have shown in Chapter 3, Fong vigorously expanded his workshop in the 1960s and 1970s by engaging in production as an original equipment manufacturer (OEM) and developing the wholesale business and export trade subsequently. In this chapter, we shall demonstrate that the specific path of development taken by Fong's manufacturing business must be understood in three terms: the broader socio-economic context of Hong Kong, Fong's unique business strategy characterized by the logic of maximizing production, and the mediation of the two. Fong's logic, as we shall demonstrate, was very different from the general tendency of local manufacturers to limit expansion and avoid risks. We shall explain the motivation behind Fong's logic and how this logic *forced* Fong to keep expanding his workshop. Fong's maximization of production logic, however, cannot explain its own effect, not to mention determining the developmental path of Fong's company. The broader growth of the jewellery industry driven by the increasing overseas demand for jewellery products manufactured in Hong Kong and the political economy of the city, as we will show in a moment, in fact enabled Fong's idiosyncratic business logic and amplified the effect thereof. In the conclusion, we will spell out two important implications of this chapter.

Jewellery manufacturing in Hong Kong

In Chapter 2, we have shown that the 'Hong Kong model' of the local manufacturing sector was characterized by the dominance of small-scale workshops which mainly engaged in labour-intensive production and exhibited a high-level sensitivity and flexibility to market changes. We also pointed out that the flexibility of Hong Kong industry was a result of the emergence of an extensive subcontracting system supported by a large pool of informal workers and the risk aversion tendency of the manufacturers. The flexibility was a product of the colonial policy of the Hong Kong government. Due to the lack of active and direct support from the government, the manufacturers did not have the motivation and capacity to upgrade the technology and expand their businesses. The jewellery manufacturing industry, not unlike the general manufacturing sector, was characterized by the dominance of small workshops and the reliance on labour-intensive production at least until the 1980s. The competitive edge of the local jewellery manufacturing industry in the global market lay in the ability of the local jewellery workshops to manufacture jewellery products at a relatively low cost and within a relatively short period of time. In order to understand the operation of the jewellery workshops, we should first understand the manufacturing process of jewellery pieces.

Production

Before the introduction and spread of the casting technique in the late 1970s, jewellery products were largely hand-made, and so the production process required intensive labour involvement. According to our ethnographic study of Fong's factory in mainland China, there are four major steps in producing jewellery pieces by hand: sculpturing, gem-setting, electroplating, and polishing. The most difficult and crucial part is sculpturing, in which the jeweller bends, hammers, and rolls a single piece of metal into the desired shape of a jewellery piece. In the case of complicated jewellery pieces, the jeweller must have a very clear conceptual image in his mind so that he knows how to fabricate different parts into a finished product. Once the jewellery shape is finished, it will be sent for initial polishing before gem-setting. Gem-setting is the art of securely setting or attaching a gemstone to a piece of jewellery. It is a specialized field since there are many different types of gem-setting depending on a wide range of factors such as the material, the size, and the design of the jewellery piece and the cost involved. After that, the piece of jewellery will be polished thoroughly. Before the item is sent off, it will go through the process of electroplating through which the colour of the surface of the piece can be enriched according to the design using rhodium. For instance, electroplating can make an 18K jewellery piece look 'whiter'.

Sculpturing is the fundamental step in jewellery making. No matter whether it is a pure gold or karat gold product, the craftsman must sculpture a prototype first. To learn the art of *zuk gam* – or gold hammering (*daa gam*) – is to learn how to turn a metal into a prototype by hitting, blending and assembling and to do the necessary polishing and finishing. The crucial difference between manufacturing pure gold and karat gold products is that the latter usually must be set with a gemstone. In the world of jewellery making, gem-setting is an independent field. To learn the art of *sai gam* basically refers to the mastery of the art of setting gemstones into a jewellery piece.

The complicated handmade process of jewellery pieces explains why skilful masters were highly sought after. The handmade jewellery pieces are certainly unique products of craftsmanship. However, there are two major problems associated with the handmade production. First, it takes a long time to finish a product. Second, as the jewellery pieces are individually made by hand, it is difficult to standardize their shapes and sizes.

The technology of casting enables jewellers to overcome these disadvantages. Making jewellery by casting involves several steps. First, a silver master copy must be made, from which a rubber mould will be created. Next, wax will be injected into the mould. The wax mould will then be duplicated to make a 'wax tree'. Third, plaster will be casted around the wax tree, a candle-like plaster mould will then be put into a furnace to be heated. The wax will melt out resulting in a cavity inside the plaster mould. Gold will then be molten and poured into the cavity. Then each individual mould must be cut off from the 'gold tree'. Before being sent off for gem-setting and electroplating, the mould must go through disc finishing and polishing.

The major advantage of casting is that it enables mass production. A mould can be recreated through the silver master, and the moulds on the 'tree' are similar to each other. By using the technology of casting, manufacturers can produce a large volume of standardized products in a relatively short time. This is particularly important for workshops engaging in export trade, which typically requires the delivery of a large volume of standardized products within a short period of time. It explains why, since its introduction in the late 1970s, casting has gradually become the dominant production method in the jewellery manufacturing industry in Hong Kong.

Casting, however, cannot replace handmade jewellery completely. The major disadvantage of casting is that the quality of the metals will be damaged through the process. It is also difficult to include lots of details in the jewellery pieces made by casting. While casting is widely used in mass-production, premium jewellery pieces still must be made individually by hand. Although machines boost productivity, skilled labour remains the key to the jewellery production process.

The jewellery manufacturing establishments in Hong Kong, as mentioned earlier, were slow to introduce new technology and machines to enhance productivity. As long as they were able to recruit and keep skilled workers, the owners had very low motivation to upgrade the workshops. In a survey conducted by a local newspaper, less than half of the jewellery workshops surveyed had adopted the casting technique in production by 1980 (SCMP, 1980). Not many manufacturers, especially those whose workshops were relatively small, were keen on modernizing their production (SCMP, 1980). As a result, most of the local workshops specialized in producing low- to mid-priced products, which did not have a high requirement of sophisticated machinery.

The business model of local jewellery workshops

Most of the workshops in the industry provided OEM services to the local jewellery retailers and trading houses which then engaged in the export trade of jewellery. Some workshops, such as Fong's, might also take orders directly from the foreign importers. The total cost of an OEM order normally comprised the expenses of raw materials (usually gold), labour fee, and the design fee, if applicable. Depending on the deals, sometimes, a workshop had to pay for the raw materials first, and the clients would pay the lump sum after receiving the products. In other cases, clients would provide the raw materials and the design in advance, and the workshop would simply ask for the labour fee after delivering the products.

The labour fee was all the owner of a workshop could earn, out of which the manufacturers paid their employees, that is, the masters, a certain percentage of the labour fee. For instance, if a manufacturer received a $10 labour fee for making a ring, he might only earn $2 as he needed to pay $8 to skilled masters. The actual percentage of labour fee payable to the masters depended on the latter's experiences and skills. A junior master, for instance, might only get $5 from making the same piece. Other costs of running the workshop included the fuel, electricity, and the rent.

The profit margin of running a jewellery workshop was therefore very low. According to Fong, the production cost of making a jewellery product could be as low as 10 per cent of the retail price, which is also to say that the profit margin of the workshop was even lower. Since the manufacturers could only earn very little per order, in order to survive, they had to win by quantity, that is, to acquire as many orders as possible. Labour here played a key role. As the jewellery manufacturing process relied heavily on skilled labour, the manufacturers had to retain as large a pool of skilled masters as possible in order to complete as many orders as possible.

The relationship between the manufacturer and the master, however, was not always stable. Some masters might work for several workshops at the same time. The workshop, to them, was like an outlet or platform through which they could get 'orders'. The masters would pay a 'desk fee' to the owner of the workshop as if they rented a workspace from the manufacturer. The manufacturer, in turn, was like an agent who helped the masters to get orders; they earned commissions from each of the 'transactions'. This illustrated why a manufacturer just kept 20 per cent of the labour fee earned. Of course, this model did not apply to all masters and workshops. Some masters just got a monthly salary from the manufacturers. We would like to emphasize that labour was key to the jewellery manufacturing sector and that a flexible labour arrangement, like other manufacturing sectors in Hong Kong, was also common.

Made in Hong Kong

We, however, have to point out that the jewellery manufacturers in Hong Kong did not just focus on the domestic market, which was too small to sustain their workshops. Hong Kong's manufactured jewellery products began to gain popularity in the world market in the 1970s. The total export value of jewellery in Hong Kong was $687 million in 1976; in 1986, the figure reached $3.611 billion (HKTDC, 1987, p. 1). The destination for manufactured jewellery products was concentrated in rich, developed economies. The United States was, for a long time, Hong Kong's major jewellery export market. This explained why Fong mostly travelled to the United States to peddle his products. The export sector experienced exceptional growth in the early 1970s because of the so-called 'China fever'. Following the oil crisis and the economic recession, the US market started to shrink. At the same time, Japan gradually emerged as an important export market to Hong Kong. In 1983, the United States remained the largest market for Hong Kong's jewellery exports followed by Japan, Singapore, and Europe (HKS, 1983). For manufacturers who were also exporters, such as Fong, they also had to procure raw materials directly from suppliers in various countries. According to Fong, for diamonds, the supplies mainly came from India, Belgium, and Israel. For other precious stones, he had to visit countries in Southeast Asia such as Cambodia, Vietnam, and Indonesia. For pure gold, he could find what he needed in the local Hong Kong market.

The primary factor contributing to the growth of the export of jewellery products manufactured in Hong Kong was that the Hong Kong manufacturers could produce the same products at a lower cost with higher efficiency than their competitors. Montilla (1970) explains that the workshops in Hong Kong, for instance, were far more efficient than their Japanese counterparts. Moreover, Hong Kong's free port status also facilitated the export trade. Although Hong Kong had to import raw materials from elsewhere, there was no tax on the imports or sales of precious stones in Hong Kong.

The efficiency of the Hong Kong jewellery manufacturers could be explained by the flexible labour arrangement and the extensive subcontracting network supported by many small workshops specializing in certain parts of the production process. As we have pointed out, most of the jewellery workshops were small establishments. These small establishments tended to specialize in only certain parts of the production, such as diamond-setting. The workshops would collaborate with each other. For example, Workshop A might specialize in sculpturing the prototype and find it more cost-effective to subcontract the gem-setting process to Workshop B. In another scenario, Workshop A might get an urgent order of delivering 100 rings within a week, which it did not have the capacity to complete on time. Workshop A might then seek the help of workshop B to split the work. Large workshops usually could perform the whole production process, but even they might subcontract the orders to other workshops to meet the demand of clients. The main point here is that Hong Kong jewellery manufacturers were able to be successful in the overseas market because they produced not only cheaply but also efficiently through the flexible labour arrangement and the extensive subcontracting network.

The increasing popularity of the Hong Kong manufactured jewellery products in overseas markets was also partly due to the promotion work of the Hong Kong Trade Development Council (HKTDC) and the trade unions. The HKTDC, together with trade unions such as the Hong Kong Jewellery & Jade Manufacturers Association (HKJJA), actively organized local fairs and delegations to overseas exhibition. For instance, local jewellery manufacturers, under the leadership of the HKJJA, first joined an International Jewellery Trade Fair in New York in 1971 (HKS, 1971). These overseas exposures were highly important and relevant to the local manufacturers. Without the assistance of the HKTDC and the trade unions, it would be extremely difficult for the manufacturers to get in touch with foreign clients due to the language barrier and the lack of information and connections. Fong, for instance, still felt very grateful to the HKTDC for helping him to develop the export business as he told us:

> I really need to thank the HKTDC for their help. They introduced many foreign clients to me. You know it'd be extremely hard for me to find these

contacts because I don't speak English. My first overseas exhibition was only made possible by the HKTDC.

In this section, we have shown that the industrial ecology of the jewellery manufacturing sector in Hong Kong basically echoed the Hong Kong model discussed in Chapter 2. The sector was characterized by the dominance of small workshops which engaged in labour-intensive production for local and export markets. Most of the workshops lacked the motivation or capacity to upgrade the technology and to expand the business. Through examining the jewellery manufacturing process and the business model of jewellery workshops in Hong Kong, we have also demonstrated how the availability of skilled labour and the way the skilled labour was flexibly organized were critical to the survival and development of the workshops. Now, let us turn to Fong's entrepreneurial path to examine how he managed to develop his jewellery manufacturing workshop into one of the largest jewellery production centres in East Asia against this specific industrial context.

To produce or to die: Fong's core business logic

In Chapter 3, we have illustrated how Fong, since the establishment of his workshop in 1960, kept expanding his manufacturing business vigorously. A decade later, he even became directly involved in the wholesale and export trade. The never-ending expansion of Fong's manufacturing business, we argue, was primarily driven by his distinctive business logic: the maximization of production at all costs. Only by maximizing production, in Fong's mindset, could he maximize the output, and thus the profit.

As mentioned earlier, in order for a jewellery manufacturer to maximize profit, he had to increase output, which further required the manufacturer to recruit more skilled workers *as well as* secure sufficient orders. Once enough skilled workers are recruited, the manufacturer must have enough orders, otherwise these workers would just move to other workshops that could provide them enough work. More importantly, if the workshop could not get enough orders after securing its labour force, the workshop would lose money because it still needed to pay its labour force. As a result, most of the local jewellery manufacturers were particularly cautious when they were contemplating making additional capital investments in equipment and labour. Local jewellery workshops, not unlike the producers of different industries in the manufacturing sector of Hong Kong, faced the similar economy-wide oligopsony with their counterparts in Taiwan. They could not negotiate the prices in the supply market with the foreign buyers. What they could do was to be cautious with their investments in equipment and labour. As Gary Hamilton and Cheng-shu Kao (2018, p. 119; italics ours) pointed out:

> Production networks in Taiwan had to respond to falling prices and precarious orders. Increasingly, manufacturers facing uncertainty about the terms of the next contract had an incentive to figure out how to produce better quality goods ever more cheaply. In practical terms, this incentive encouraged the

formation of more extensive networks. *Everyone was cautious about making additional capital investments in equipment and labor.* When there were large orders, core manufacturers in a production network would outsource a significant part of their production; when the orders shrank, the core manufacturers did most or all parts of the manufacturing process themselves. Networks expanded, contracted, overlapped, and intensified.

The Hong Kong jewellery workshop owners likewise tended not to overproduce their products or expand their labour force vigorously.

Fong's logic, however, was completely supply-driven. He learned from his experience as an owner of a small workshop that he could only maximize the profit by maximizing the output of his workshop. He was not really concerned about the demand side or the risks associated with overproduction and overexpansion. Fong simply did not take these factors into consideration. But Fong's logic could only work as long as sufficient orders could be secured, otherwise overproduction and overexpansion would cost his business. We asked Fong if he ever thought about the potential risks, and he repeated that he did not really think about anything much.

The formation of Fong's logic should be understood in the context of his previous work experience. Recall that Fong first served as an apprentice in goldsmithing for five years, then he learned the trade of gem-setting, and later he became a master in Maan Sing Hong, a jewellery store. All the experiences Fong gained, before establishing his own workshop, were related to jewellery manufacturing which mainly provided OEM services to the local jewellery retailers and trading houses. Fong got to learn that in order to maximize his monetary return, he had to maximize his output. When Fong established his workshop, the maximization of production thus naturally became his possible business logic. This logic was clearly reflected in his decision to establish his own workshop upon Mrs. Wong's invitation. Recall that Mrs. Wong, the owner of Coeng Faat Hong, asked Fong if he would like to take over the workshop of his former master. Fong told us that he made up his mind very quickly:

> I didn't think much. My logic's very simple. I just thought that, one worker, say, could help you earn $100 for an order, if you got 100 workers then you got $10,000. If you got 1,000 workers, wow, the sum would be very large! It's just a very simple calculation.

We shall demonstrate how this logic informed the path of development of Fong's manufacturing business.

The initial stage

Recall that when Fong established his workshop, he did not really think much about whether or not he could get enough orders. Mrs. Wong had loaned him $3,000 as the initial capital but he would have to help her complete the orders in order to repay the loan. Fong was only concerned about how to recruit more people to enhance the production capacity of his workshop. The question was that since he did not have much money, how could he attract skilled workers to work for him?

Fong first made use of his own social connections to recruit the son of his former neighbour to become his first apprentice. Chan Keung was only a Primary 4 student when he was sent by his mother to work for Fong. Based on his own experience, Fong was determined to make the apprenticeship more productive for both the master and the apprentice. Fong did not ask Keung to do irrelevant work as he was once required; from day one, Fong actively taught Keung the craft and urged him to master the skills as soon as he could. Fong believed that the apprentices should do what they were supposed to do, that is, to produce:

> They [the apprentices] shouldn't waste time doing irrelevant things like what I did before. I just employed someone else to do the cleaning and the cooking. I told them that they were here for a single purpose. They had to get down to the real work. I needed them to produce and earn money, not to fool around. The old practice was just a waste of resources.

Fong adopted this new form of apprenticeship which was targeted at turning the apprentices into a productive labour force as soon as possible. To Fong, transforming the apprentices into a productive force as soon as possible meant their labour could then be further converted into profit. Since the profit of a jewellery workshop depended on the number of items it produced, Fong strived to boost the productivity of the workshop by giving proper training to the apprentices. Through this new system, Fong hoped to achieve a win-win situation. On the one hand, the apprentices could focus on mastering the craft without wasting time on irrelevant work, which was crucial to their future money-making capacity; on the other hand, Fong could boost the productivity of the workshop at a very low cost.

One cannot deny the fact that the apprenticeship system was, in part, exploitative by nature. The apprentices would not receive the labour fee to which they were entitled even though they participated in the production. The crucial difference between being an apprentice, a junior master, and a senior master was the proportion of labour fee for which one could bargain. A senior master could get as much as 80 per cent of the labour fee the manufacturer received from the client while a junior master could only get 50 per cent of it. Fong gradually recruited more apprentices until all the workspace of the workshop was occupied. In this way, he could increase the production capacity while keeping the labour cost at the minimum during a period when the workshop was too small to yield any significant profit.

The production capacity of Fong's workshop kept increasing up to the point that Mrs. Wong could no longer provide enough orders to sustain the growth of his workshop. This put Fong in an embarrassing position. Fong's workshop, at this stage, should be understood as a 'residential workshop' in the sense that it basically attached to Mrs. Wong's store. In theory, Fong's workshop should just serve Mrs. Wong's store, taking care of her orders exclusively. As mentioned in Chapter 3, Mrs. Wong gave Fong another essential helping hand. She not only allowed Fong to take orders from other clients, but also actively referred Fong to other jewellery stores with which she had a connection including Maan Sing Hong where Fong previously worked as a master. Fong could now freely expand his workshop.

Expansion

After gaining independence from Mrs. Wong's store, Fong kept expanding his workshop by increasing the labour force. To attract and maintain the labour force, Fong implemented a dual salary system. He would pay the workers a monthly salary for their day-time work and pay them at piece-rate for night-time work. The time-rate salary was considerably lower than the piece-rate. 'I invented this system to attract the workers. During the daytime, I would distribute difficult tasks to them. But during the night time, I would just give out easy and regular jobs,' Fong said. Noticing our puzzled faces, he further explained:

> You don't understand? Well, imagine you were the worker. You didn't have to rush to finish the difficult tasks during day time since you were paid by time-rate. You wouldn't think that you were exploited, right? But during the night time, you had a feeling that you could earn a lot because you were paid by piece-rate and you could finish the easy tasks very quickly. It's all psyche. The workers would have the feeling that they could earn more in my workshop.

In addition to adopting the dual salary system to allure the workers, Fong also actively recruited new blood to strengthen his team. He would pay attention to the display areas of jewellery retail stores. Whenever he spotted some finely crafted products, he would try to find out exactly which workshop and which worker had produced it. Fong said, 'I love to recruit workers from the competitors. I don't need to be an exceptional master myself. I just need to scout and catch the best master.' He also needed the masters to serve as a 'human billboard' as he told us:

> When I started my business, I was nobody. You needed to build up your own reputation. You needed to convince the clients that your workshop had the capacity to complete the orders. It means that you can meet the deadline and can make sure that quality of the products meets the expectation. It's thus important to get the reputable masters. They reflected the standing of my workshop.

At the initial stage when Fong did not have the muscle to recruit great masters, he chose another route. He focused on recruiting junior masters who had just completed their apprenticeships at the renowned workshops.

Fong's strategy in maximizing production through an expansion of the labour force soon put him under intense pressure to secure and create more orders for his workers. As a new player in the market, Fong faced two critical problems: to get to know more clients so that he could get more orders and to attract more workers to work for him. These two problems were interrelated. The size of the labour force of a workshop was a major factor affecting the decision of a client whether to place an order there or not. The larger the size of the labour force in a workshop, the client believed, the higher the possibility that the order could be completed satisfactorily and on time. On the other hand, the more orders a workshop could secure, the higher the possibility it could attract the workers. Since skilled workers were in great demand, they tended to commit only to those workshops which could provide enough orders for them. To retain the labour to keep up and enhance the production level, Fong had to create demand for his products.

One of the strategies he used was to get in touch with as many potential clients as possible. Fong befriended the salesmen (*hang gaai*, literally, walking on the street) who helped the wholesalers to sell the jewellery pieces and diamonds to the retailers. Fong explained to us:

> I asked them if I could follow them to meet the retailers. I would then grasp the chance to show some samples to the person in charge there. If they were interested, they would then contact me to place orders. So, I would always carry some samples with me.

When we asked Fong why those *hang gaai* were willing to cooperate with him, Fong grinned and said:

> We were friends! We were willing to help each other. That really didn't do them any harm either. You know, it's just like they gave more choices to the retailers. Of course, I would return the favour. It's always like an exchange, you know, a win-win situation.

Fong also paid attention to maintaining the relationship with the clients. He told us the story of Mrs. Chow, the owner of a big jewellery retailer, who treated Fong not only as a business partner but also as a 'son'. She referred many clients to Fong and lent him money when he was in need. As Fong recalled:

> Like how I met many of the other clients, I just got into Mrs. Chow's store randomly and showed her the samples. She did not show great enthusiasm but was willing to give me a chance. Her store was located under the staircase of Miramar Tower [in Tsim Sha Tsui], not a very conspicuous one, but the business was good. Tourists and seamen were her main clients. One day, Mrs. Chow told me that I would need to finish an urgent order by 6:00 a.m. the next day. She asked if I could do that. I just said yes without any hesitation. Then I rushed back to my workshop and worked overnight. At 5:00 a.m., I carried the products and virtually ran to her place. She was very satisfied; thereafter she kept referring many orders to me. I later learned from her that

the order was not really that urgent. She just wanted to test if I was a trust-worthy person, and I had proved myself.

It took time for Fong to gain the trust of the clients and build his own reputation. For a very long period of time, Fong struggled to make ends meet, as he told us:

> Very often, after paying all the bills and the salaries to the workers, I barely had enough money to take the bus! I am not exaggerating, that's really the truth! It was very tough in fact. I had to borrow money from time to time as the workshop didn't have enough cash flow. Of course, I never delayed any payment. Other-wise, no one would ever be willing to help me again. I took it very seriously.

The rough situation did not deter Fong from expanding his workshop. On the contrary, he remained aggressive in enlarging his pool of labour and enhancing production. Even during the low season, Fong still kept up the production in the workshop. Fong explained his rationale to us:

> There were two reasons behind it. First, to keep my men busy. I had to make sure that even during the low season they still got something to do and could earn money. The second reason was to create order opportunities. I discussed with my employees all the time to develop new designs and products. I would then show the samples to the clients hoping that some of them would attract them to make an order. Since I had already kept up the production, once the clients placed an order, I could then deliver it swiftly.

This clearly illustrates that Fong's strategy in running his manufacturing busi-ness was underpinned by the logic of prioritizing production. Fong did not cease to expand his labour force and production when he was under pressure to create demand for the products nor did he hesitate to keep up the production when he was not even sure if he could find buyers for the products. He just kept expand-ing the labour force and production without calculating or considering the conse-quences. If problems arose, he would try to solve them, but under no circumstance would he compromise at the expense of the production.

This explained why Fong would just keep up the production of the workshop dur-ing the 1967 riots. According to his maximization of production logic, Fong would simply scramble for the chance to absorb the workers and orders of other workshops to further boost the scale of his workshop. The uncertainty ahead was simply out of his mind. Fong stressed, 'I was just concerned about my own business, that is, whether my workshop could get enough orders and whether my workers and I could earn more money.' Fong's insistence on maintaining production resulted, uninten-tionally, in the rapid expansion of his workshop after the 1967 riots.

Wholesale and export

By 1970, Fong's workshop had already become, by the local standard, a large-scale workshop employing over a hundred workers. The entire production process could be completed at this one workshop. It seemed that Fong could relax and enjoy the fruits of the development, but he faced tremendous pressure as a result of the rapid growth of the workforce. Fong struggled to obtain enough orders for his workers. On the other hand, his maximization of production logic also led to the problem of overstock. He had to create new channels to get more and bigger deals and to sell the manufactured products. Fong subsequently entered into the wholesale and export business in the 1970s. Getting involved in the wholesale business forced Fong to bear an even higher risk as he was not sure whether he would eventually find a buyer for the products he produced. To take part in export trade directly was even more risky as sometimes it would be difficult for the producer to get money back from foreign buyers. Again, Fong did not really perceive the risks at all when he decided to explore the new business channels. He just thought that he had to do so to feed his employees.

Instead of waiting for clients to place a small order requesting a limited number of products, he sent his workers to be *hang gaai* to sell the finished products to retailers and other clients directly on a wholesale basis. Recall that Fong had already established connections with many *hang gaai* in the early stage when he had to reach out to the local retailers. 'There were a lot of *hang gaai* in the 1970s and 1980s,' Harry Mak, an FBL employee who joined the jewellery industry in the 1970s, told us. 'They tied the gold bars on to their own bodies and walked around. This sounds crazy, but this was the only way for them to peddle the products from door to door." Reuben Cheung, who worked as a *hang gaai* from 1977 to 1986, added:

> The business area was vast covering Tsim Sha Tsui, Central, Causeway Bay and North Point. Wherever there was a jewellery store, we had to go peddle. And, we did not just visit retail stores; shopping malls and hotels were our targets as well, as we might encounter some buyers there. We had to walk a lot every day, so much walk that I even got bone spurs in the feet!

The middlemen worked and walked so hard because their major source of income was commission. As Reuben continued to explain:

> My basic salary at that time was only around $1,000 a month. I received around 2 per cent commission on the sale of each order. But don't forget that we are talking about a wholesale order. A big order could amount to two million dollars. We could make good money. The lead time of a wholesale order was typically two months. We were very nervous when the credit period was due, because we had to make sure that the customers did actually pay before we could get the commission.

Although the wholesale business helped Fong to clear some of the stock of his workshop, Fong still struggled to generate new orders to provide enough work for his workers. Then the chance came when he was able to connect with the world market through the help of the HKTDC. As Fong recalled:

> One day, the guy [from HKTDC] asked me if I was interested in joining a delegation to exhibit my products in a show in New York. I was really thrilled.

So, I joined the show and it was the start of my export business. After that, I had been travelling back and forth to the United States and other countries for a decade.

Despite his lack of knowledge of English, inexperience in export business and low capital, Fong simply said yes. Fong justified his decision as follows:

Many people were surprised by my decision. I didn't know any English. And what's New York? I had completely no idea either. To attend a foreign trade show, to us at that time, was a very big deal. To prepare for the trip, we had to do a lot of preparation. I had borrowed around a million dollars to purchase goods and raw materials! Many people thought that the whole thing was too risky. But at that moment, I really didn't think much. When the HKTDC guy asked me if I was interested, I just thought, "What a great chance! I can't miss this opportunity!" I am grateful to the HKTDC. They referred many foreign buyers to us. I didn't really have time to think about the consequence. I was so anxious to make sure that we got everything ready. In addition to jewellery, I also bought a lot of Chinese souvenirs including Chinese masks for the show. I just tried to grab things that I thought could sell well in the fair.

On the day before his departure, Fong and his workers were still busy finishing and packing the products. Fong got on the plane to New York without having a clue of what to be expected. He, along with the representatives of six other local jewellery companies, joined a Hong Kong delegation to participate in the JA (Jeweller of America) New York International Jewellery Show (JA Show). Fong could never forget the trip. He could still recount the details to us:

I remember every detail about the trip. It was my first time to go overseas. The whole experience is simply unforgettable. On the first day of the exhibition, I didn't get any orders. I hadn't expected this, so I was very nervous, I couldn't sleep at all! On the second day, we finally got a long-awaited order. A very beautiful middle-aged woman came to our booth. She kept pointing at this and that. We didn't understand her intention. She told us that she wanted to buy all those items. It's nearly half of what I brought to the show. I simply didn't understand what was going on because she didn't ask about the price. I thought it might be a scam. I was so worried that I could not sleep again. Luckily, on the next day, the customer did turn up. She closed the deal with us and took away the products. I later learned that she owned several jewellery companies in New York. I was so relieved that I could finally fall asleep that night.

Eventually Fong had succeeded in selling most of the items before returning to Hong Kong. The fair turned out to be an enormous success to Fong. After he arrived at the airport in Hong Kong, his employees came to drive him home.

When Fong was about to go inside his flat, he burst into tears in front of them. As he told us:

> I was really stressed out, I had to admit. At that time, a million dollars meant so much to me. I basically bet everything on it. If I had failed to get the money back, I would have had to close my business. I didn't think much before and during the show. I was just so focused on the show itself. But after everything was over, I realized how overwhelming the pressure was. When I looked at my employees, I just thought that I couldn't imagine what would have happened if they hadn't been with me. I cried really hard. I have never had such a profound, complex feeling in my life. It was a mix of anxiety, relief, gratefulness and joy.

After the show, Fong started to engage in the export business. He had to travel with his staff frequently to the United States to meet with clients and to explore new buyers. Fong and his team would first join a jewellery fair or show in the country. After the show, Fong and his team would stay behind and travel from city to city to peddle the products. As he told us:

> Whenever we arrived in a city, we would immediately look for the jewellery stores there. We would simply go into a store and show the owner our products. We didn't really care how many pieces they would buy on the spot. One piece was fine; five pieces would be fantastic. Some would take a look at our products. Some customers were really nice. They would invite us to visit their home and ask their friends and neighbours to come over and check out our products. Some owners would just kick us out. In that case, we would drive to another place to try our luck.

Fong would ask his employees to communicate with the clients directly on his behalf. He would only jump in when they started to talk about the price. 'I used my fingers to indicate the figures,' Fong said. For each trip, Fong and his team would have to stay there for at least a month. The journeys, Fong said, were quite dangerous sometimes:

> I bought insurance for the products whenever I took a business trip overseas. Many Colombians committed robberies in the United States at that time. There was nothing we could do, we still had to go there. One of my employees once drove to the China Town to get some food. He parked the car, which was loaded with goods, outside the restaurant. He did lock it of course. When he finished the meal and came out, he found that all the goods had already been taken. I negotiated with the insurance company for a long time and it only agreed to compensate for a half of the products.

After that, Fong had been travelling back and forth around the world. He not only travelled to America and Europe to sell his products, but also had to visit India and

Southeast Asia to purchase the raw materials. Fong found it extremely exhausting to keep on travelling like that. As he told us:

> I found it quite difficult to adjust. I don't know why but I just couldn't get used to it. First, I always had jet lag, I couldn't sleep well when I was outside [in the foreign countries]. And I didn't speak any foreign languages. That was a very big problem. I could not understand what others were talking about and therefore could not follow what was going on. The whole thing was very exhausting. I travelled like an astronaut for ten years and then I decided to focus on the local market instead.

On the other hand, Fong was eager to adopt the casting technique to produce a large volume of standardized products efficiently by acquiring workshops which owned the technique. He also installed machines manufactured in Germany and Japan, for instance, in the workshop. Fong told us:

> None of us knew how to operate the machines. We couldn't understand the manuals which were written in foreign languages. So, I either sent my men abroad to learn how to use the machines or invited the technicians to come over.

All these examples demonstrated how Fong made every effort to develop his export business to keep up the expansion of the workshop. Fong's involvement in the export market helped bring the development of his workshop to another stage as the workshop no longer had to rely solely on the rather small local market but could seek orders directly in the wide global market.

The money-oriented incentive system

Fong's maximization of production logic could work only if he was able to attract and retain workers for his workshop. The incentive system of Fong's workshop, we argue, was characterized by Fong's *faat cin hon* driven pragmatism, which we identified in Chapter 3. Money, in Fong's view, was always the biggest if not the only motivation behind work. As long as the workers could help Fong to increase profits, he was flexible on the salary payments. As Fong told us:

> I told my workers that I didn't really care how much salary they asked from me, as long as they could help me to earn money. I am always happy to share my profits with my employees. They work hard to help you earn money, of course you have to reward them. It's fair enough.

We have to emphasize that Fong did not aim at maximizing the profit per production unit, he was more concerned about whether he could generate more profits by getting and finishing more orders. As a result, he was willing to reward employees who could help him to get and complete more orders instead of squeezing their salaries to maximize the gain.

As Fong shared a similarly humble background with his workers, he understood that only monetary reward could give a sense of security to the people. He never hesitated to satisfy his employees monetarily as he understood that it was the best way to keep them. As he told us:

> I really think that I have the responsibility to help my employees to earn money. If the employees of another company can afford a Mercedes-Benz, I have to make sure that my employees at least earn enough to buy a Toyota. Otherwise I will feel ashamed. I will think that I am a very useless boss. Imagine my employees can only afford a bicycle! What a shame!

In fact, Fong always emphasized his sense of responsibility as he repeatedly stressed:

> I am always concerned about the livelihood of those who work for me. I think, as a boss, I need to take care of them. To help them earn more money so that they can have a better life. I think that's the responsibility of a boss, to help your men to benefit from your own business. This is the source of my pressure. I mean, I am not afraid of failures for I had nothing at the beginning anyway. But if my business fails, what should my men do? They will be very miserable. I have to make sure that my followers won't starve.

Fong was eager to emphasize that he was not a selfish person. Although he was hungry for money, he was not just concerned about himself. Fong perceived and presented himself as a 'big brother' who had to take care of his fellow workers because they were like his family members. We contend that Fong's effort to demonstrate that he was a responsible, caring boss was not just a presentation of self. Based on our own fieldwork observation and interviews conducted with other employees, Fong indeed was very concerned about the welfare of the employees.[1]

Notwithstanding Fong's own sense of responsibility, his emphasis on helping the employees to earn money also had a very practical aspect. If Fong failed to secure orders to feed the employees, they would simply go and work for another workshop. As the labour force was the lifeblood of a workshop, it was extremely important for Fong to increase and maintain the pool of labour if he would like to further expand his business.

Fong's *faat cin hon* driven pragmatism also led him to adopt a decentralized approach to the management of his workshop. Decentralization here does not mean that Fong did not closely monitor the work of the employees. Fong in fact was very strict about punctuality and would station himself at the workshop whenever he could to monitor the workers. Decentralization here refers to the lack of organizational restraints and the flexible work arrangement. Fong was a very practical person in that he simply wanted his employees to help solve the problems and get things done. He did not care about the details or would not bother to intervene in the process. Fong gave enough autonomy and even power to the employees to act on his behalf to complete the tasks. Recall that Fong allowed his employees to take charge of the export business. The trust, however, was partly a result of Fong's inability to control and manage everything, which is to say that Fong's trust in the employees is driven by necessity. He understood very clearly that he needed the expertise of others to expand his business and that he alone could not handle the complicated details. To get things done, he could only choose to give the employees a free hand. Even though some employees had betrayed him, Fong was not angry at them. We shall further examine Fong's management style in Chapter 7.

Instead of highlighting the power relationship between the employer and the employee to enjoy a sense of superiority, Fong was more interested in motivating the workers to work and therefore to gain profits. Many employees commented that Fong was an easy-going, approachable boss. One of the 'masters', who joined the workshop in the early 1970s, told us:

> Mr. Fong never scolded me. I was very young when I joined the workshop. I remembered that he just said, 'Where did this chap come from?' He did not care about your background; he was just concerned if you worked hard and did well. I proved my skills and very soon he asked me to help manage the teams for him. He never used his power as boss to coerce you or bully you.

We, of course, are not suggesting that Fong perceived the employees as an equal to him. He was in fact very conscious, proud, and defensive of his role as a boss. Our main point is that Fong's primary concern was to motivate the workers to help him earn money. His management strategy was thus dictated by this concern. In order to achieve the goal, Fong was more than willing to reward the workers monetarily, provide them autonomy at work and adopt a less authoritative, if not authoritarian, attitude towards the workers. All these measures reflected Fong' single-minded pursuit of a practical goal: money.

Conclusion

We have shown in this chapter that Fong – guided by his logic of maximizing production – kept expanding the labour force and enhancing the output of the workshop because he believed that he could continue to make a profit by maximizing production. In contrast to many local manufacturers, Fong therefore did not take risk into consideration when he developed his workshop. He had not calculated in advance if the existing demand could absorb the supply of his workshop to achieve equilibrium. Other manufacturers might make use of the flexible labour market to adjust the labour force accordingly so as to save costs during the low season and to meet the market demand during the peak season. Fong, on the contrary, simply did not adjust the labour force. His strategy was to keep expanding the labour force to increase the production capacity, while at the same time he explored all possible ways to secure more orders. In other words, Fong never compromised on production. It follows that he was always under pressure to create new demand to meet with the ever-growing supply of his workshop and to secure new orders to feed his workers. It was this constant pressure which motivated him to expand the business scope to engage in wholesale and even export business in addition to taking OEM orders.

Of course, Fong was able to implement his determination of expanding the business scope to generate more and more profits by virtue of his position as the sole owner of his company. In the legal order of the corporate system of Hong Kong, the owner is empowered to transmit his will in the company. In other words, what Fong did was always agentive; he had the institutional position of difference-making.

But the consequence of Fong's agentive power is not always his intention. As Fong himself confessed, he could not imagine that he could expand his manufacturing regime so quickly, not to mention the fact that he subsequently branched into wholesale and export businesses. Recall that Fong started as a petty manufacturer working for retailers and bigger workshops and he developed his small workshop into a large wholesaler over a brief period. But if there was no retail revolution in the United States leading to a substantial increase of demand for the locally manufactured goods or the ever-increasing similar demands from other developed countries, Fong's manufacturing business would not have grown so rapidly. It is also true that the large scale of Fong's workshop enabled him to secure orders directly from foreign importers; but if the Hong Kong economy had not been characterized by the expansion of exports in the 1970s, Fong could not have secured more orders by going overseas. It is true that the competitiveness of Fong's workshop lay in his ability to retain and motivate his skilled workers; but if there was not a vast pool of cheap labour made available by the influx of economic and political refugees from mainland China in the early 1950s, and if the flexible arrangement of the labour was not made possible by the depoliticization orientation of the colonial government in general and the corresponding laissez-faire policy in particular, Fong would not have been able to expand his production through his subcontracting network.

All of this points to the fact that Fong's logic of maximizing production did not *automatically* enable him to expand his manufacturing regime from a small workshop through wholesale business to an exporter. It was the *conjunctural* situation, in which Fong's difference-makings – his logic of maximizing production – acquired *significance* which made Fong an *entrepreneur* and determined the course of his entrepreneurial path.

The opposite is also true. There was nothing in the broader growth of the local jewellery industry or the macro political economy of Hong Kong that required Fong to become an *entrepreneur* and to take his *specific* entrepreneurial path. The latter simply does not logically follow the former. What we intend to argue here is that the effect of Fong's entrepreneurial activities was not determined by either his micro-idiosyncratic business logic or the socio-economic-political dynamics; it rather depended on the way Fong's idiosyncratic business logic was taken up by the socio-economic-political dynamics at the macro level, which is never the only one possible. The determination of his difference-makings as meaningful and important *entrepreneurial* activities and the effect thereof were the result of the mediation between Fong's difference-makings and the broader growth of the jewellery industry as well as the macro political economy of Hong Kong.

There are two major implications of this chapter. The most obvious one is that neither the individual-centric nor environment-centric approach can be seen as a good explanation for Fong's entrepreneurship. Second and more importantly, entrepreneurship is relatively defined according to contexts. Looking at Fong's entrepreneurial process from the macro socio-economic perspective, Fong's manufacturing business was a typical industrial story of post-war Hong Kong. Fong's workshop did not really deviate from the Hong Kong industrial model. The workshop engaged in the labour-intensive production, the competitiveness of which lay in its ability to produce the jewellery products cheaply and efficiently, which was sustained by the availability of the vast pool of skilled workers, the cheap labour cost and the flexible arrangement of the labour. Fong was not a lone wolf when he started to engage in the export trade either. He followed the broader trend when the Hong Kong economy was characterized by the expansion of exports in the 1970s. In other words, Fong did not do anything new but followed the 'Hong Kong model' closely. Fong's course of business expansion therefore can hardly be understood as entrepreneurial if it is seen from the macro socio-economic perspective.

But Fong's story was not just another typical case if we see it from the perspective of the local jewellery manufacturing industry. Although the rise of Fong's workshop largely followed the typical Hong Kong model and the macro-economic trend, there was something special about Fong's case because very few, if not none, of the jewellery workshops expanded in a way like Fong's. Most of the workshops remained small in scale, not to mention that they would not attempt to engage in the wholesale and export businesses directly. Fong's own specific motivation, encounters, and decisions played a significant role in shaping the course of his entrepreneurial process. First, Fong's adherence to the maximization of production logic – which was a product of his early biographical experience – enabled him to expand his workshop aggressively. Second, Fong's aggressive expansion of his workshop in turn caused overproduction and overstocking which forced Fong to engage in the wholesale business and to get involved in the export business directly. Finally, these engagements were different from the business nature of his original workshop: provision of OEM services to local retailers/traders. This is akin to what Shane (2003) calls 'new means-ends relationships', the essential element of his definition of entrepreneurship. The expansion of Fong's business therefore should be understood as *entrepreneurial* from the perspective of the local jewellery manufacturing industry. In other words, the determination of any difference-making as an *entrepreneurial* activity is relative to the context in which such a difference-making occurs. We will return to the relativity of entrepreneurship in the Conclusion.

Note

1 As we will show in Chapter 7, Fong, as the founder of the company, was obligated to compensate his employees not just with immediate and practical monetary reward but, more fundamentally, a sense of security. Apart from the *'faat cin hon'* mentality, the obligation to take care of the livelihood of his employees by continuously expanding the company was another major motivation for Fong's persistent entrepreneurial effort.

5 Beyond manufacturing

The development of Fong's showroom business

In this chapter, we shall examine how Fong branched out into the showroom business in the 1970s. We argue that the success of Fong's showroom business was the result of the mediation between Fong's entrepreneurial move into the showroom business and the political economy of the local tourism industry as well as the complex relationships among overseas travel agents, local tour operators, and retail shops. In the first part of this chapter, we shall offer an ethnography of Fong's showroom to identify its characteristics. It is then followed by a brief history of the development of Fong's showroom business, showing why and how Fong started and developed his showroom business to the extent that it has become a 'cash cow' for Fong's company. But such a successful business demands an explanation. We therefore move to analyze the various ways Fong operated his showroom, exploring major factors that enabled Fong's success in his showroom business. We shall argue that the primary reason behind Fong's active diversification was directly related to the problems caused by the production-driven model of his workshop. In the final part of this chapter, we will argue that it was neither Fong's entrepreneurial move into the showroom business nor the political economy of the tourism industry in Hong Kong in addition to the complex relationships among overseas travel agents, local tour operators, and retail shops *alone* can account for the success of FBL's showroom business, but the mediation among them. We shall begin with an ethnography written by Chau, one of the authors of the book, who conducted fieldwork in the showrooms in 2013 when she was working at FBL.

One day in the showroom

On an early morning of 2013, I arrive at the office earlier than usual. Just as I do every day, I get to the lobby of the office through the 'bat cave', a nickname for the back entrance to FBL that is mainly used by the employees. I have some trouble finding the staff card in my bag, which is necessary for me to get through the entrance gate. Every FBL employee is supposed to enter the office through the gate, although some senior executives simply ignore it and got in through the door next to it; for part-timers, they have to punch in manually.

'Beep!' I put my staff card on the sensor of the gate and go through. I glance at the small monitor, it reads: 08:45. 'Oh, watch out!' A lady screams. I am almost knocked over by her, although I am more worried about my coffee and sandwich. The lady wears a light-pink blouse, a pair of black pants and shoes. 'I am really sorry!' she says. Then she continues to rush off in another direction. 'She must be someone who works in the showroom, because all of them wear the same uniform,' I murmur. She just walks out from a staff lounge right next to the gate. The 'lounge' basically is just a small pantry. There is a table and a few chairs. I always see a couple of employees eating and taking a rest there every morning.

When I am walking to the lift area, I see that a group of tourists has already arrived at the showroom, which is located on the right side in the lobby hall. Outside the showroom, some salespeople are introducing the products to another group of tourists. The opening hour of the showroom is 9:00 a.m. 'It seems that we will just cater to the tourists right after they arrive anyway,' I think. 'The lady might just be hurrying to get ready to welcome the unexpected guests.' The lift comes; I get in and press '2' to get back to my office.

It has been arranged for me to visit the showroom to observe operations today. After settling some pending tasks, I am ready to kick off my little adventure. I take the lift to the ground floor again around 10:00 a.m. When the door of the lift opens, I am shocked by all the clatter, bustle, and chaos of the scene. The lobby hall is now filled with people; to be exact, it is surrendered to the people. There are tourists idling on the staircases, tour guides going back and forth between the showroom and the lobby hall and FBL's showroom guides escorting group after group of tourists into the showroom. The whole atmosphere has completely changed.

The ten-minute tour

I struggle to pass through the crowd, as I am walking against the flow to get to the reception area at the main entrance of the company, which faces Man Yue Street.[1] 'Who are you? What are you doing up here?' The employees at the reception survey and question me carefully. Since Lee Wing Tat, the person in charge of the operation of the showroom, has already informed the managers about my visit a few days ago, after I briefly explain the case, the employees suddenly become much more relaxed and allow me to stay there to observe their work. I am shocked by the employees' suspicious attitude towards me because I had assumed that the showroom must be a very 'open' place as it receives so many different tourists every day. But from the suspicions of the employees there, I come to realize that it is not what I have assumed. The showroom is actually a highly secretive business. Strangers will immediately be spotted and questioned. I attempt to get more information about the showroom from the employees. 'We have altogether four showrooms here [in the headquarters]. They are located on the ground floor and first floor respectively,' one of them replies. 'The showrooms on the first floor receive non-mainland Chinese tourists exclusively. They are subdivided into the Korean hall and the Thai hall.' I then ask about the functions of the employees at the showroom. 'There are two groups of us. One group is salespersons, another is our company's showroom guides,' she explains to me. 'Salespersons are those who are responsible for selling FBL's products inside the showrooms. The major duty of our company's showroom guides, on the other hand, is to conduct a tour of the showroom for the tourists.' It seems to me that the employees at the reception are all FBL's guides. One of them looks like a leader, because she is holding a form to check with the tour records all the time.

When we are chatting, we notice a coach has just parked in front of the entrance. The employees suddenly look very serious as if a switch to combat mode had been made. I wait for a while before the automatic door opens. A middle-aged woman enters first. She greets the employees with a very confident, almost awe-inspiring smile. The employees are very polite to her as if she is a VIP. It seems that they are quite familiar with each other. 'Twenty people, Jiangsu,[2]' the woman tells the leader at the reception, after returning the greetings. When the leader is jotting down the information, a FBL's guide has already gotten up from her seat to get ready for the tour. 'We will take turns conducting a tour for the guests. When one is finished, we have to hurry to get ready for another tour,' one of the FBL's guides tells us later. 'We don't have a fixed lunch hour. It all depends on the arrangement and order of the leader. Usually we simply finish our lunch as quickly as possible to make sure that there are enough people to do the tour.' Then, the middle-aged woman signals a group of tourists to move forward. At this point, the identity of the woman is no longer a mystery to me: she is a tour guide from a local tour operator. During the tour, she stays at the back of the group, checking the phone, observing and monitoring every move of the tourists.

A FBL guide takes over the group of tourists from the tour guide. She first welcomes the tourists in perfect Mandarin. Then she leads them to stand in front of a few giant display boards near the reception and starts to introduce the development of FBL. She particularly emphasizes the story of Fong and the honours he has received. She then points to the brooch with the Chinese word '*jau*' (good quality) on her blouse. 'Our showroom is a Quality Tourism Services (QTS) Scheme-accredited shop,'[3] she says in a proud voice. 'Please enjoy your shopping here as your purchase will be guaranteed.'[4] Then she signals the tourists to wait for a moment at the spot. 'I am really sorry that we have too many tourists today,' she says. "We need to wait for the previous groups to move before we can continue the tour.'

A minute or two later, the FBL guide escorts the tourists through a passage in front of them. 'Every year, our showroom receives over one and a half million tourists from all over the world,' she speaks while she is passing through a jewellery-making workshop. 'Please look on your left-hand side, that is our workshop.' She stops for a little while before briefly introducing the function of the workshop. 'The products sold here are all hand-made,' she emphasizes. 'The masters have to go through three to five years of training before they can actually "get into the field".' She also gives a short introduction of several high-tech machines used in the workshop, such as the laser machine and the polishing machine. The tourists are only able to observe the operation of the workshop through a wide window.

The tourists do not really have time to get a closer look at the workshop, since the FBL guide keeps walking forward. 'I am really happy to let you know that we've got a big promotion today. Most of the products are 20 per cent off. Some products are even sold at half-price. You can get a free gift if you spend over $5,000 and an FBL watch if over $8,000,' she explains. 'It's completely free to resize the jewellery pieces. The masters at the workshop will be able to resize the products you choose within an hour.' And now the FBL guide has already led the tourists to stand in front of a big screen. 'It is now playing the latest commercial of FBL. The title of the series is "To love is to persevere",' she says. The FBL guide, however, adds hastily, 'The commercial is also being shown in China, so I am not going to waste your time here.' Then, she takes a right turn and ushers the tourists through a passage filled with ads to get to the entrance of a jewellery showroom. A lot of tourists are already there, so it is extremely noisy. Even though the FBL guide uses a portable microphone, one can hardly hear her voice. She tries very hard to raise her voice to attract the fading attention of the tourists. She points to the posters and introduces some of the featured products of the showroom. She also explains to the tourists in detail how they will be protected under the Quality Tourism Services scheme and the return policy of the company.

Afterwards, she pushes the glass door of the showroom and escorts the tourists in. There is a 'no photo' sign near the entrance. After the tourists start to scatter in the showroom, the FBL guide then leaves via the entrance and prepares to receive another group of tourists. The whole tour lasts only around seven or eight minutes.

Inside the showroom

The atmosphere inside the showroom bustles much like the streets outside. There are several groups of tourists in the showroom at the same time. When we get inside the showroom, the salespersons, who have already been waiting behind the showcases, greet us passionately. Each of them has with them a calculator, some forms and a plastic bag. The tourists usually walk around in groups. Sometimes, several salespersons stand together to try to help each other to promote a product to a tourist. A tour guide tells her tourists that they must stay at the showroom until 12:30 p.m. (it is 10:30 a.m.), then she goes to the exit of the showroom and stations herself there. In fact, quite a few tourists gather at the exit. The tourists can only get out of the showroom with the permission of their guides.

I spot a senior manager in the showroom. 'Why do the salespeople all gather behind the showcases near the entrance? Aren't they supposed to scatter and take care of different showcases?' I ask curiously. 'The salespeople do not follow the showcases, they follow the customers instead. That means, they go wherever the customers go,' the manager explains. 'Every showcase displays different products. In other words, our salespeople have to familiarize themselves with the details of every single product sold here.' When we are chatting, a middle-aged woman approaches the manager. I cannot hear their conversation clearly, but it seems that the woman is reminding the manager to pay more attention to the situation around instead of chit-chatting with me. 'She [referring to me] is from the Office, so I have to take care of her,' the manager tells the woman. The manager then turns to me and explains, 'The middle-aged woman is a tour guide from a local tour operator, we know each other very well. She helps and supports us a lot.'

Since the showroom is extremely packed, I can hardly observe anything. So, I struggle to push through the group of people gathering at the exit of the showroom and return to the lobby hall. There is another showroom on the other side of the lobby hall which sells only pure gold items. There are slightly fewer tourists in this showroom. I run into a very nice FBL guide and ask her, 'So the customers will go to the pure gold showroom right after visiting the jewellery showroom?' 'The movement of the tourists here is all decided by the tour guide,' she replies. 'We basically have no control.' I enter the pure gold showroom and decide to stand next to a showcase to observe the tourists. At that time, a couple are thinking of buying a gold bracelet. 'It's cheaper to buy gold in Hong Kong,' a salesperson keeps persuading them. 'The price is also standardized, a very fair deal indeed.' While the couples are hesitating and about to give up, another female tourist joins the conversation and asks the salesperson to give her some bracelets to try on. The couple do not leave, they stand nearby to observe. Later, the woman leaves, but the couple decide to buy a bracelet. They follow the salesperson to the cashier. An enormous poster of '100% return guarantee' is hung on the wall near the cashier.

At the same time, some tourists are shouting and complaining. I cannot follow the details, but it seems that they are angry that their tour guide does not allow them to leave the showroom. 'Just buy a little bit more, then we are done,' the tour guide keeps telling the tourists. 'Get some more good things to show the customers,' the tour guide orders the sales staff. 'Be quick, quick, quick!' The salespeople immediately take out some trays of jewellery to show the customers. I leave the showroom and return to the reception area at the main entrance.

Non-Chinese tourists

When I get back to the reception, the FBL guides there are still very busy. Then a male tour guide walks towards the reception area. He does not look like a Chinese. He gets a pile of shopping cards from the leader. 'It's a Korean tour. I have already called our showroom guide from the first floor to come down immediately,' the leader tells me. The male guide then distributes the shopping cards to the tourists. 'What's that for?' I ask, pointing to the cards. 'We use the cards to identify the shopping record,' the leader tells me. At the same time, a FBL female guide is walking quickly towards the group of tourists. She looks like a Korean. Her uniform is not the same as other FBL guides I met earlier: she wears a black suit, this makes her look more professional and senior.

Although I do not understand Korean, I still attempt to follow her tour. At first, the route of the tour seems to be the same. She first introduces the display board near the reception, then she points at the 'Quality' brooch and says something. She also takes the tourists to have a look at the workshop. But she does not lead the tourists to walk towards the big screen; instead, she guides them back to the staircase next to the workshop. There is a display board featuring the products of the Chinese zodiac series. She stops there and says a few words. Then she leads the tourists to go upstairs to the showroom on the first floor.

The environment upstairs is completely different from the showroom downstairs. It is extremely crowded and noisy downstairs, but the showroom upstairs is very quiet. In fact, this group of Korean tourists are the only visitors in the showroom. Once the tourists enter the showroom, the salespeople try to promote the products to them passionately in Korean. As there are so few customers in the showroom, my presence suddenly becomes very conspicuous. I am immediately questioned by the salespeople. I try to explain my case, but it seems that they are not very convinced. I do not want to make any trouble, and because I cannot understand the Korean language, I decide to leave the showroom and return to the reception area on the ground floor.

The drama

When I return to the reception area, only the leader is there as other FBL showroom guides are having their lunch break. It is around 11:30 a.m. 'The morning shift is done! Well, if you are interested in staying, you can keep me company for lunch,' the leader says. 'Thank you very much for your invite!' I say. 'But I guess I am almost done here as well, I have seen enough I guess.' I thank her and say good-bye. I walk through the passage and return to the lobby hall. A lot of tourists are still in the showroom, but some tourists are sitting on the staircase. They look extremely bored and are just killing time there. They seem to be waiting for other tourists to finish the shopping so that they can move on to the next destination. When I am about to walk upstairs to go back to my office, I hear some loud noises outside the jewellery showroom. I decide to stop and observe what happens. A female tour guide is pointing at a couple of tourists sitting on the staircase. 'You bought nothing! Haven't I told you all? I won't force you to buy anything in the evening! It's okay if you buy nothing in the evening. But I have told you before that we have to reach the target this morning!' she scolds the tourists loudly. 'The hotel rooms that you are staying in, and all other things all depend on this!' Some of the tourists still refuse to give way and insist on not buying anything. 'You see how cooperative other tourists are? They have helped me achieve the target right at the beginning!' the tour guide keeps screaming. 'And you? You bought nothing! I have already told you, you can return the goods after you buy them. We just need a figure! Do you really want to make the whole group suffer?' The tour guide keeps bombarding the tourists. Eventually, two female tourists can no longer bear it and follow the tour guide to the showroom. Suddenly, it becomes much quieter. As the drama is put to an end, I also return to the office.

Some observations of FBL's showroom

The ethnography mentioned earlier demonstrates why FBL's showroom business cannot simply be understood as an ordinary form of retail business. First and foremost, Fong's showroom only received tourists who were members of a packaged tour offered by a local tour operator. Usually the tour operators – who have signed a contract with FBL – would send the information of the incoming tours to the managers of the showrooms in advance. On the actual visit day, the FBL guides at the reception area would crosscheck the information with the tour guide. The tour guide would then distribute the shopping cards to the tourists so that they would be entitled to discounts. In fact, the shopping cards helped the showroom to identify and record the transactions of each tour. Based on the records, the showroom then calculated the amount of commission to be paid to the tour operators and tour guides. It follows that neither walk-in customers nor tourists whose local tour operator had no contract with FBL would be able to visit and shop in FBL's showroom.

Second, the tour guides of local tour operators played an extremely significant role here. They oversaw the schedule of the tourists, deciding how long the tourists will stay at the showroom and which showroom they will go to. They were also responsible for managing the tourists' behaviour in the showroom. For instance, as shown in the ethnography, the tour guides prevented the tourists from exiting the showroom. The FBL employees did not intervene; they instead focused on selling products to the tourists.

Finally, the visit to Fong's showroom was simply a shopping activity. As we can observe from the ethnography, the tour conducted by FBL's showroom guides was very brief. The main purpose of the tour was not to introduce the production process of jewellery – not even to promote FBL – but to encourage the tourists to buy more products in the showroom. FBL's guides explained the return policy and the QTS services to reassure the tourists that they would be well protected when they shopped in the showroom; they showed the jewellery-making workshop to the tourists in order to convince them that the quality of jewellery pieces displayed in the showroom was good and that the masters could help amend their jewellery pieces; and they emphasized repeatedly that discounts were offered to the tourists in order to make them believe that the products were really a good bargain. All of this was done to persuade tourists to spend as much money as they can on purchasing jewelry products from the showroom.

Taking all these together, we can conclude that Fong's showroom business was a special type of retail business that was embedded in the tourist industry of Hong Kong. But why did Fong start the showroom business?

The development of Fong's showroom business

In fact, no one in the company including Fong himself could tell us exactly when the showroom was established. From all the relevant information we collected, we estimate that Fong's showroom business probably started in the mid-1970s. In Chapter 3, we have illustrated that Fong had to relocate his workshop from Tsim Sha Tsui to Hung Hom in the early 1970s, as the government attempted to prosecute him for operating a workshop in a residential premise. Fong eventually found a new site for the workshop in an industrial premise. He set up a workshop that was over 10,000 square feet on the eighth floor of an industrial building. But new problems emerged. Fong explained to us:

> The workshop at the building was big even though I already had several hundreds of workers at that time. I had to think of some ways to make full use of the space and get enough jobs for the workers. Another problem was that it took some time to travel back and forth between Tsim Sha Tsui and Hung Hom. The jewellery stores were all located in Tsim Sha Tsui, it was inconvenient for us to deliver the products.

The expansion of the workshop and the inconvenient location of Hung Hom propelled Fong to explore new business opportunities. As Fong recalled:

> After we moved to Hung Hom, some friends of mine working for local tour operators visited my new place. They suggested that they could take some tourists to the workshop to buy the jewellery. I thought it was a good idea. So, I recruited people to help start and run a showroom to sell our products to the tourists.

This is how Fong began his showroom business. Since the showroom was set up on the eighth floor of an industrial building in Hung Hom, all the customers were brought in by the travel agents or tour guides; no individual tourist or local shoppers would be expected. 'We were the first jewellery company to set up a showroom in Hung Hom,' Fong emphasized. However, another problem emerged as Fong recalled:

> But it's not very convenient [as it was on the eighth floor], I thought we should further develop the showroom, it's gonna be a big business. So later we moved to the current site.

Fong bought several factory units in a nearby building in 1977 and established a showroom on the ground floor. Fong continued to recall:

> I thought it's good to have the [units on the] ground floor. At first, I just bought a half of it. After I moved in, I kept buying more and more units.

Of course, making full use of the space was not the only reason that Fong decided to start the showroom business. Nor could the fact that Fong believed that his friends' suggestion was a good idea alone account for Fong's decision. Fong's attempt to branch his business out into showroom retailing was mainly motivated by the pressure caused by his production maximization logic mentioned in Chapter 4. That particular business logic had been pressing him to solve the overproduction problem and create more job opportunities for the ever-increasing labour force so that he could retain the much-needed workers.

Fong's showroom business turned out to be very successful. At the time of our fieldwork, it still accounted for around one-third of the total sales of the company.

Desmond Chen, the former Deputy Chairman of FBL and who once oversaw the operation of the showrooms, told us:

> I'd say that, to the company, the showroom business is like a lifebuoy. Since we own the factory units here, we don't have to pay for the rent. The operation of the showroom involves a rather low fixed cost.

In other words, the showroom business is like a 'cash cow' for the company.

Fong then further expanded his showroom business. Two more showrooms were established in Aberdeen on Hong Kong Island in 1988 and 1990 respectively. Three more showrooms were added in the headquarters building in 1995 and 1998 respectively.[5] What enabled the success of Fong's showroom business? We argue that the growth of the showroom business was closely related not only to Fong's successful adaptation to the trend of the development of the tourism industry in Hong Kong but also to the way Fong operated his showrooms.

The operation of FBL's showrooms

The market focus of Fong's showroom business largely followed the developmental trend of the tourism industry in Hong Kong. As Wing Tat explained to us:

> You notice that there are a lot of coaches on Man Yue Street, right? Because there are many jewellery showrooms around this area. You can hear almost only Mandarin around because most of the tourists are from mainland China. People think that it's always the case, but of course it's not. The showroom business has kept changing.

Wing Tat further explained that Taiwanese tourists were the major customers of the showroom between the end of the 1970s and the early 1980s. From the 1980s to the early 1990s, the street was flooded by the coaches full of American and Japanese tourists. But tourists from mainland China started to replace their American and Japanese counterparts at the end of the 1990s.[6] As Wing Tat recalled:

> It's hard to imagine, right? The peak of mainland tourists coming to Hong Kong was between 1998 and 1999. At that time there were some so-called 'train tours'. Coaches would be arranged by tour operators to accommodate a whole train of tourists from the same province. One train required like 60 to 70 coaches. During the peak days, our showroom received around 300 coaches of tourists a day. But of course, the purchasing power of the tourists was much lower than those who visit Hong Kong today.

Since the sources of tourists had been changing from time to time, Fong's showrooms must adapt to the trend quickly in order to accommodate different customers. First, the showrooms were coded and each of them specialized in catering to a specific market. For instance, as shown in the ethnographic note, the two showrooms on the ground floor catered to mainland Chinese tourists while the showrooms on the first floor mainly received tourists from Korea, Thailand, and other Southeast Asian countries. The showrooms in Aberdeen, on the other hand, targeted Western tourists.

Second, the product mix of the showroom also took the taste of different origins of tourists into careful consideration. In the Korean showroom, in addition to typical jewellery pieces, pearl products were also being sold because Korean tourists were particularly interested in pearl products; *feng shui* related jewellery pieces such as accessories shaped like a windmill were featured in the Thai showroom; and the Chinese zodiac series products targeted the Western tourists as they loved to buy souvenirs with an 'oriental flavour'. The tourists from mainland China, we would like to point out, were not a homogenous group. They were broadly categorized along the north-south division. The visitors from northern China generally preferred diamond and karat gold jewellery while those from the south, especially from the Guangdong Province, preferred pure gold jewellery. Fong therefore established two showrooms on the ground floor to satisfy the different demands of tourists from mainland China. In addition to pure jewellery products, the showrooms also sold some Hong Kong related souvenirs.

To facilitate sales, Fong also employed salespeople and showroom guides with different nationalities to accommodate the specific groups of tourists. As shown in the ethnographic notes, FBL's guides and salespeople spoke the languages of the tourists perfectly. In fact, many of them were not local Hong Kong Chinese but came from other countries. In short, Fong attempted to tailor-make the showrooms in every detail to accommodate the demand of the tourists in the hope of increasing the sales.

Of course, the key issue in running the showroom business was to make sure that tour guides would take their tourists to visit the showroom. Fong employed business promoters who were responsible for liaising with local tour operators to invite them to take tourists to the showrooms as a part of the itinerary. In return, the tour operators would get commissions from FBL. The commission to the tour operators was calculated on the head count basis plus a percentage of the sales generated by the tourists they brought in. Usually, FBL would also give commissions to tour guides in the hope of boosting the sales. Tour guides, as we shall show later, played a crucial role in shaping the travel experience of the tourists. That is why the employees of the showroom in our ethnography were very polite and nice to the tour guides as they understood that it was the tour guides who controlled the itinerary and could motivate the tourists to shop. That also explains why many retail outlets like Fong's showrooms were willing to pay extra commissions[7] to the tour guides, who were more than happy to accept because the commission from retail shops, as we shall show in a moment, was the major source of their income. In short, paying legal or illegal commissions to the tour operators and tour guides was the only way for the showroom to secure customers.

Fong also had to pay commissions to the business promoters and the salespeople in the showroom. The business promoters played a key role in the showroom business as they were the middlemen between the showroom and the tour operators. The number and type of customers that the showroom eventually got largely depended on the referrals of the business promoters. 'In the past, the business promoters had to go to nightclubs, saunas and spas with the managers and bosses of the tour operators. That involved a lot of entertainment fees,' Wing Tat recalled. 'Now everything has become much more institutionalized. There are no longer so many under-the-table deals.' Business promoters could get commissions from FBL for the sales that they helped generate.

The commission was also an important part of the salary of the salespeople working in the showroom. Fong was especially keen on motivating the salespeople. As he explained:

> In the early days, I invented an incentive system modelled after auto racing. The salesperson who got the largest amount of sales would be granted the pole position.[8] It means that he would be the first one to receive the customers.

Fong cited Wing Tat as an example of the pole sitter:

> He [Wing Tat] has worked at FBL for many years. I guess it's his first job. His elder brother worked here as well. He [Wing Tat] was our top salesperson. To get more sales, he would rather work instead of taking leave. So, he got five more working days in a month than others did. He got the 'pole position' because he worked so hard.

The commission system outlined earlier explains how Fong was able to get customers to visit the showrooms in Hung Hom, a remote industrial area. However, according to Aaron Chow, Director of Showrooms at FBL, the commission rate was in fact very high. Why then was Fong still able to earn a profit given the high commission rate? Fong was able to yield profits from the showroom business mainly because of the pricing of the products sold in the showroom. The price of the products sold in the showroom, according to Wing Tat, was at least 50 per cent higher than those sold in the retail shops.

Although the showroom business remained one of the major sources of revenue for FBL at the time when we conducted research, it was facing enormous challenges. One of the major challenges was that it faced stiff competition from other jewellery retailers who followed Fong and started to build showrooms in the same area. It follows that Fong must pay a higher commission rate than his competitors did in order to attract the tour operators to take customers to his showrooms. The showrooms also had to deal with another challenge as tourists had less and less incentive to join a package tour, for two major reasons. First, tourists could obtain information from the Internet, guide books, and travel magazines so that they could research very carefully what they wished to buy from which shops before they actually came to visit Hong Kong. Second, more and more tourists had become dissatisfied with the 'arranged shopping' organized by local package tour operators because not all of them were interested in shopping; even if some of them would like to shop, they preferred shopping by themselves because they could avoid the over-enthusiastic attention of the sales staff in the showroom.

The management of the showroom was also a very complicated issue. Fong himself did not actively engage in the operation and management of the show-room. He adopted similar strategies with those in his export business in that he recruited people who had connections with the tourism industry to help him set up and manage the showrooms. In fact, the commission system in the tourism industry involved a lot of under-the-table and confusing transactions. As Aaron explained, 'To run the showroom in a "modern" and transparent way is really like asking a gentleman to play streetball. The operation is very complicated. It involves so many stakeholders.' The showroom business, due to the problematic commission, once caused a huge crisis at FBL that we will discuss in detail in Chapter 8. At the time when we conducted research, FBL was still struggling to transform its showrooms into a sustainable business.

We are, however, tempted to ask the question: why did this kind of travel-disguised shopping tour attract tourists and generate profits for the tour operators, tour guides, and ultimately Fong's showrooms? In order to answer this question, we must contextualize Fong's showroom business in the political economy of the tourism industry in Hong Kong in general and the complex relationships among overseas travel agents, local tour operators, and retail shops in particular.

The political economy of the tourism industry in Hong Kong

Since the 1960s, the growth of the tourism industry has been remarkable. The number of tourists visiting Hong Kong was 103,055 in 1958 (Hong Kong Tour-ist Association, 1959, p. 15). The number reached 927,256 in 1970 (Hong Kong Tourist Association, 1971, p. 3). By the end of the 1980s, it reached five million (Hong Kong Tourist Association, 1990, p. 1). The number surpassed ten million by the mid-1990s (Hong Kong Tourist Association, 2001, pp. 2–8). The tourism industry has become one of the three major industries and made a substantial con-tribution to the economy of Hong Kong whether in terms of its contribution to the GDP or the number of jobs the industry created in the 1980s.

One of the major reasons for the rapid growth of the post-war tourism indus-try is that Hong Kong was able to attract different tourists at different stages. Throughout the post-war period, the source of foreign tourists in Hong Kong gradually shifted from the West to the East. Before the 1960s, most of the tourists visiting Hong Kong were from the United States and the British Commonwealth. In the 1970s, the United States, Japan, and Australia were the most important countries of origin of foreign tourists in Hong Kong. Japan became the top source in 1971 and remained so for the following 20 years (Hong Kong Tourist Associa-tion, 2001, pp. 2–8). During the same period, the number of tourists from South-east Asia also increased rapidly. Taiwan and South Korea emerged as important sources of foreign tourists between the end of the 1980s and early 1990s. Taiwan even surpassed Japan to become the top country of origin in the tourist market in Hong Kong in 1990 (Hong Kong Tourist Association, 1991, p. 4). Around the same time, the Chinese government gradually relaxed its control on overseas travel and foreign currencies. For the first time in 1993, the Hong Kong Tourist Association (HKTA) included mainland China in the survey on foreign tourists (Hong Kong Tourist Association, 2001, pp. 2–8). A year later, mainland China became the largest source of tourists in Hong Kong and has since dominated the tourism market in Hong Kong, especially after the implementation of the Individual Visit Scheme[9] since 2003 (Hong Kong Tourist Association, 2001, pp. 2–8).

Despite the substantial contribution of the tourism industry to the local economy, the Hong Kong government, however, was reluctant to get directly involved in the development of the industry at least before Hong Kong was reverted to China in 1997. In Chapter 2, we have examined how the Hong Kong government adopted a series of depoliticization measures to avoid creating an image of a strong colonizer because the government worried that such an image might give rise to a national sentiment among the people of Hong Kong. The same principle operated in the domain of economy in which the Hong Kong government was determined to adopt the so-called positive non-intervention policy. Of course, this positive non-intervention policy also gave a good excuse to the government which was not willing to invest its already limited financial resources in Hong Kong's major industries including the tourism industry. In this regard, the establishment of the HKTA is particularly illustrative.

The HKTA was established as a semi-governmental corporation by the Hong Kong government in 1957. 'Semi-governmental' corporations here referred to those organizations that were established by the government outside the official government structure to carry out its policies, because the government believed that semi-governmental corporations could implement their policies more flexibly and efficiently than the official government bureaucracy (Okano and Wong, 2004, p. 120). We want to add that the establishment of semi-governmental corporations to carry out government policies could save the government's financial resources. The HKTA was initially funded by the annual government budget but that was soon replaced by the revenue generated by a newly introduced hotel accommodation tax. This new hotel accommodation tax was imposed on incoming tourists who stayed in any hotel in Hong Kong. In other words, the HKTA was in fact funded by the tourists themselves rather than by the Hong Kong government (Okano and Wong, 2004, p. 120).

The non-intervention government policy and the semi-governmental nature of the HKTA had two important consequences. The first was the limited role of the HKTA in the Hong Kong tourism industry. The HKTA had never had the financial resources 'to engage in large-scale production of tourism facilities and attractions' (Okano and Wong, 2004, p. 120). The statutory status of the HKTA as a semi-governmental corporation also deprived it of 'the authority to legislate or enforce tourism policies' (Okano and Wong, 2004, p. 120). The role of the HKTA therefore 'has been limited to making recommendations to the government on tourism policies, persuading the tourism industry and the private sector in general to invest in facilities, and convincing the government and private investors of the merits of tourism in Hong Kong' (Okano and Wong, 2004, p. 120). Consequently, what the HKTA had been doing was to produce and advertise tourist products including organizing events and conducting some domestic tours, promote Hong Kong to overseas markets, and conduct research, the results of which could be used to give advice to the government and the industry (Okano and Wong, 2004, p. 120).

Second, the limited power of the HKTA together with the free market policy of the colonial Hong Kong government made the tourist market – especially the inbound tourist market – almost undisciplined if not chaotic. Before 1997, there was no specific law that regulated the inbound tourist market and as a result, any investor who was interested in joining the market as a tour operator could do so if they applied for the ordinary commercial license from the government. The easy market entry made the inbound tourist market very competitive. In order to survive, many local tour operators were willing to take packaged tours from overseas travel agencies at below cost. Again, this was possible because the Hong Kong government, due to its non-intervention policy, was unwilling to set the minimum price for local tour operators to take packaged tours. Obviously, these local tour operators had to find other ways to compensate for their loss. One of the major ways was to incorporate shopping into their sightseeing tours because the commissions they received from retail shops where they took their tourists to shop could not only cover the loss but also bring them profit. Those retail shops were not ordinary retail establishments that received both tourists and local customers but special shops that catered *only* to the tourists on package tours. In other words, the local tour operators were the link between the local tourism and the retail industries. Following closely Okano and Wong (2004)'s discussion on Japanese package tours to Hong Kong in the 1970s and 1980s, we would like to illuminate the operation of the local tour operators.

Okano and Wong (2004) pointed out that Hong Kong was one of the most popular destinations among Japanese tourists in the 1970s and the 1980s. This is confirmed by the fact that Japan, as mentioned earlier, had overtaken the United States as the top country of origin of foreign tourists in Hong Kong in 1971 and remained there for almost 20 years. Many Japanese tourists at that time chose to visit Hong Kong through package tours because of the lack of tourist information about Hong Kong and more importantly their inexperience in overseas travel. They joined the packaged tours organized by Japanese travel agencies, which then subcontracted the package tour to the wholesale travel operators at a discount price. The wholesale travel operators would then further subcontract the service to the local tour operators in Hong Kong (Okano and Wong, 2004, p. 140). The local tour operator usually would employ a tour guide to look after the package tourists.

Okano and Wong (2004, p. 141) further argue that the hierarchical relation between Japanese travel agencies and local Hong Kong package tour operators was the key to understand the business model of the latter. Recall that the inbound tourist market in Hong Kong was basically a free market that any investor could join. As a result, there were always local package tour operators available in the market for Japanese travel agencies to choose from and this gave the latter considerable bargaining power over Hong Kong package tour operators because '[i] f one is not satisfied with a particular operator, they can always look for another' (Okano and Wong, 2004, p. 141). The power enjoyed by Japanese travel agencies enabled them to force local Hong Kong package tour operators to take packages below cost. Those local tour operators therefore had to find a way to make other sources of income to bring a profit. According to Okano and Wong (2004, p. 141), local Hong Kong package tour operators had three major sources of income. The first was to sell souvenirs, cosmetics, chocolates, and so on in the coach that carried the package tourists around Hong Kong. Second, they could sell optional tours to the package tourists. The final but major source of income was the commission they received from the retail shops where the tour guides took the package tourists to shop (Okano and Wong, 2004, p. 141).

Interestingly, these three sources of income closely corresponded to the itinerary of a standardized three-night/four-day Japanese package tour. Okano and Wong (2004, p. 142) presented a typical itinerary of a standardized Japanese package tour (see Table 5.1). We can see from the table that the whole journey except the third day was conducted in a coach so that it would be convenient for the tour guide to sell souvenirs to the package tourists in the coach. The tour guide could also sell optional tours to his or her customers for the third day in the coach. The key day was the second day when the package tourists were taken sightseeing because the sightseeing was in fact organized around what Okano and Wong (2004, p. 141) call 'arranged shopping'.

According to Okano and Wong (2004, p. 141), a typical one-day sightseeing tour on the second day of the standardized three night/four-day Japanese package tour was heavily dependent on shopping:

> In the morning of a one-day sightseeing tour, they [the local Hong Kong tour operators] usually take tourists to one or two points of interest such as Victoria Peak or Repulse Bay. The whole afternoon, however, is dedicated to visiting various shops which sell such items as jewellery, leather and silk products, and Chinese medicine. The tour ends in the evening at the Duty-Free Shop where tourists are left to shop for an hour or so. The whole afternoon is thus spent on what can be termed 'arranged shopping,' from which

Table 5.1 A typical itinerary of a standardized three-night/four-day Japanese package tour in Hong Kong in the mid-1990s

Day	Itinerary
The first day	Tourists arrive in Hong Kong from Japan
The second day	One-day tour: visit two tourist points in the morning; dine at a Chinese restaurant; and visit up to five shops including the duty-free shop in the afternoon
The third day	Free day but tourists can join one of the optional tours sold by the tour operator
The fourth day	Return to Japan

Source: Okano and Wong (2004, p. 142).

the major portion of income is generated for both the local tour operators and their tour guides.

The income generated from the arranged shopping was the commission retail shops paid to tour guides and local tour operators for the purchases of the tourists whom they brought there. Special retail outlets including Fong's showrooms were virtually unable to attract any customers – due to their remote location or less well-known brand name – without having tour guides take tourists directly to their shops. The two, the travel operators and the special retail outlets, then clicked with each other. The former helped bring in customers for the latter and asked for commissions in return and the latter made profits from the purchases by tourists in their shops.[10]

According to our interviews with the people working in the tourism industry, the situation described by Okano and Wong (2004) was not confined to Japanese package tours; it actually reflected the ecology of the whole in-bound tourist sector at that time. Our intent of following closely the previously mentioned study by Okano and Wong (2004) is to point out that the situation they described was in fact the background against which the reasons that Fong started his showroom business at that time and the associated business model he adopted can be understood.

But what happened at the macro-level – the political economy of Hong Kong's tourism industry or more specifically the complex relationships among overseas travel agents, local tour operators, and retail shops – could not determine Fong's adventure into the showroom business or the way he operated his showroom. Recall that Fong started the wholesale and export businesses as he had to create demand for his products to overcome the problem of overproduction and to retain the labour force caused by his idiosyncratic logic of maximizing production. The same logic again forced Fong to branch out into the showroom business as he could not only create jobs for his workers by creating this new, special retail channel but also ease the problem of overproduction by absorbing the stock of the workshop. In fact, Fong was one of the few local jewellery manufacturers who was willing to branch out into the showroom business. As mentioned in Chapter 4, the development of Fong's workshop business in the 1960s did not really stray away from the typical subcontracting system prevailing in Hong Kong at that time. What distinguished Fong from other manufacturers was that he actively attempted to expand and diversify his business. In fact, at that time it was extremely rare for a small- or medium-sized workshop to take the initiative to take up the function of marketing, trading, and retailing, in addition to manufacturing. Many jewellery manufacturers, that had failed to upgrade and transform themselves, were closed in the mid-1980s due to the economic recession (Cookson, 1983, p. 2). Fong, however, succeeded in moving his company beyond manufacturing to the showroom business, a special form of retailing.

We are not suggesting that Fong's entrepreneurial move into the showroom business and his way of operating showrooms could account for the historical effect of his move either. For the latter did not logically follow from the former. Although Fong's idiosyncratic logic of maximizing production made the whole situation different, the logic itself could not determine the significance of his showroom business. We argue that Fong's idiosyncratic entrepreneurial pursuit acquired its significance – its meaning and importance – in the way his pursuit was taken up by the political economy of the local tourist industry and the non-interventional colonial policy. As mentioned earlier, Fong's difference-makings were made possible and meaningful and the significance thereof was amplified by the complex relationships among overseas travel agents, local tour operators, and retail shops. For if local tour operators could bargain a reasonable price from the overseas travel agents, they would not have had to organize arranged shopping, forcing the tourists who join a packaged tour to purchase from Fong. If the Hong Kong government did not adopt the non-intervention policy, local tour operators would not have been able to take packages below cost, which would have made the arranged shopping unnecessary. It follows that Fong's showroom business would not have been possible no matter how efficiently and effectively Fong operated his showroom.

We argue that the success of Fong's showroom business can be attributed to the fact that Fong's branching out into the showroom business happened to be at the right time *and* in the right place. Fong was in a conjunctural position that enabled his venture into the showroom business and determined the significance thereof. But it was the conjunctural situation – the complex relationships among overseas travel agents, local tour operators, and retail shops – that put Fong in such a conjunctural position. The success of Fong's showroom business in turn reinforced and even legitimized the complex relationships among overseas travel agents, local tour operators, and retail shops.

Seen in this way, we argue that the success of FBL's showroom business was the result of the mediation between Fong's entrepreneurial move into the showroom business and the political economy of the tourism industry in Hong Kong as well as the complex relationships among overseas travel agents, local tour operators, and retail shops in the structure of the conjuncture.

Conclusion: a successful transition

In this chapter, we have examined how Fong diversified his business in the 1970s to engage in the showroom business. We argued that the success of FBL's showroom business was the result of the mediation between Fong's entrepreneurial move into the showroom business and the political economy of the tourism industry in Hong Kong as well as the complex relationships among overseas travel agents, local tour operators, and retail shops. The success of Fong's showroom business could not be attributed to the former, while the latter could not account for Fong's success in his showroom business either. It is true that what made Fong successful in his showroom business was his capacity to move his business beyond production to engage in the showroom business; it is also true that the success of Fong's showroom business was related to the fact that Fong was a go-getter and risk-taker. He would rather take the risk to explore the unknown but potential market instead of sitting back to wait for luck. Fong did not really do any serious calculation or formulate detailed strategies before involving himself in the new fields. He simply responded to the opportunity his friends brought to him. Recall that Fong himself did not identify the showroom business as an entrepreneurial opportunity. It was his friends who worked for local tour operators who suggested the opportunity to him. More importantly, his friends also promised to take their tourists to Fong's showroom if he decided to branch out into the showroom business. In other words, the showroom business as an entrepreneurial opportunity was also made possible by Fong's friends.

But all of this could not have happened without the political economy of the tourism industry in Hong Kong as well as the complex relationships among overseas travel agents, local tour operators, and retail shops. As mentioned earlier, the hierarchical relation between Japanese travel agencies and local Hong Kong package tour operators enabled the former to force the latter to take packages below cost. Taking their tourists to 'arranged shopping' was the major way for local tour operators to make profit. But what made the relationship between overseas travel agents and local tour operators hierarchical in the first place? We argued that the positive non-intervention policy gave an excuse to the Hong Kong government not to interfere the local tourist industry. As a result, anyone who was interested could join the industry as tour operators, and as a result, the market was over competitive, and in order to survive, local tour operators were willing to take package tours from overseas travel agency below cost. More importantly, the Hong Kong government did not want to regulate the local tour operators even when they took package tours from overseas travel agencies below cost.

All of these macro factors, however, could not determine what Fong would do and how he would behave. Fong's decision to branch out into the showroom business was driven by his logic of maximizing production. We have demonstrated that Fong attempted to diversify his business because he wanted to sustain his manufacturing business by solving the overproduction problem and creating more job opportunities to the ever-increasing labour force so that he could retain the much-needed workers. In other words, Fong simply wanted to make sure that his business could survive and make more profit.

Another major reason was Fong's *faat cin hon* driven pragmatism. Fong would use whatever means and opportunities that seemed to fit in the specific circumstances. As we have demonstrated in this chapter, Fong's involvement in the showroom business, again like the development of his workshop, was not a well-planned decision. To Fong, it did not matter whether he was going to develop the export business or engage in the showroom business, as long as he could make a profit, he was keen on giving it a try. In a similar vein, Fong did not really care if he was in direct control of the operation and management of the business. If the employees could help him earn money, he did not mind giving them the power and freedom to run the business. Fong was pragmatic enough that he did not really look for a winner-take-all result: if he was able to generate more profit, he would be happy to create a win-win scenario. We must add hastily that Fong did not choose to be a trusting employer; he just had to be. Fong clearly understood this. Fong was quite easy with the mismanagement and even betrayal of his employees as he saw more benefits than costs in it. Fong's easygoingness in turn enabled him to attract talented employees to help him diversify and transform the business.

The 1970s was a period when FBL underwent significant transition. Especially with the experience of running the showroom business, Fong gradually shifted the company's focus from manufacturing to retailing. Since the late 1970s, Fong had turned his full attention to the development of the local retail business, as he saw that retail business could generate a higher profit margin. 'When I didn't have enough money, I could only provide OEM production for others,' Fong said. "When I saved enough capital, I would want to open a store of my own.' In the next chapter, we will examine how Fong was able to develop FBL into one of the largest jewellery retailers in Hong Kong since the early 1990s.

Notes

1 The building that houses FBL's headquarters and showrooms is located on Man Yue Street. Man Yue Street is known as a 'jewellery street' in Hong Kong as a number of jewellery showrooms including the FBL showrooms are located there. According to Fong, he was among the first to establish a showroom in Man Yue Street; others followed suit after he gained success in the showroom business.

2 The woman is reporting the number of tourists from her group and their origin – here in this case the Jiangsu province in mainland China – to the leader at the reception.

3 The Quality Tourism Services (QTS) Scheme is administrated by the Hong Kong Tourism Board (HKTB) to recognize merchants that meet the standard of product quality and service set by the HKTB.

4 At the time of the visit, FBL implemented a '100 per cent return guarantee' policy. Customers would be able to receive a 100 per cent refund if an item was returned within six months. This offer was applicable only to the purchases made in the showroom and not in the retail branches.

5 One of which was closed shortly in 1997.

6 We have some reservations about the accuracy of Wing Tat's account of the changing source of tourist groups visiting the FBL showrooms as his description does not match very neatly with the data released by the Hong Kong Tourist Association (HKTA) as shown later in the chapter. The United States and Japan, for instance, had long been the major sources of tourists visiting Hong Kong since the 1960s and the 1970s.

7 The commission to the tour guides is illegal if the employers of the tour guides, that is, the tour operators, do not consent or acknowledge the payment. We will explain this in detail in Chapter 8 when we discuss the lawsuit against Fong and his son.

8 In motorsport, the pole position refers to the most favourable starting position. The pole position is given to the driver with the fastest time in the previous races or trial sessions.

9 The Individual Visit Scheme was first launched in July 2003. Prior to the scheme, travellers from mainland China could only travel to Hong Kong on a group basis. Under the Scheme, individual mainland Chinese travellers are allowed to visit Hong Kong on an individual basis with a simplified visa application procedure. The introduction of the scheme resulted in the influx of individual travellers from mainland China to Hong Kong.

10 This system has remained more or less the same today even though the Hong Kong government has involved itself more directly in the industry since the beginning of the 2000s by establishing a government body, the Hong Kong Tourism Board (HKTB), to replace the HKTA. The HKTB has started to tighten control over the inbound tourist market.

6   From a manufacturer to a brand

The development of Fong's retail business

In the previous two chapters, we have pointed out that Fong had to diversify his workshop business in the 1970s to retain his ever-growing labour force and to cope with the problem of overproduction at the workshop. The immediate solution that Fong came up with was to engage in the wholesale and export trades with the hope of getting new orders and more opportunities to sell the accumulating stock. Later, he also developed the showroom business to tap into the booming tourist market in Hong Kong and to serve as a new sales channel for the products manufactured by his workshop. Around the same time, Fong began to venture into the local jewellery retail market.

At the initial stage, retailing was not FBL's core business activity. The retail outlets mainly served, together with the showrooms, as a platform for Fong to sell the stock of his factories. The retail business was established to support the production of the factories. In the 1980s, especially since the mid-1980s, FBL's retail business experienced remarkable growth. By the end of the 1980s, FBL's local sales volume became greater than that of the exports. FBL's retail business reached its zenith in the 1990s: FBL was no longer known as a jewellery manufacturer but as one of the major local jewellery brands in Hong Kong. In this chapter, we shall describe Fong's adventure in establishing and expanding FBL's retail business and identify the key features in the transformation of the FBL retail network.

From a newcomer to the local giant

In Chapter 3, we have illustrated briefly how Fong, after receiving the encouragement of his former client, the third-generation owner of a century-old goldsmith in Hong Kong, set up his first retail outlet in Ocean Centre, one of the most high-end shopping malls in Hong Kong, in 1977. In the same year, Fong also changed the name of his company from 'Fong Bou Lung Jewellery Arts Company Limited' to 'Fong Bou Lung Jewellery Company Limited' to mark the shift in the nature of his business. To promote the launch of his first retail store, recall that Fong also borrowed a rare pink diamond and displayed it in his store to create and present a grand image for his store. In fact, Fong even advertised the 'exhibition' of the pink diamond in local newspapers to attract visitors. Despite Fong's effort to promote the store, the business did not go well. As Fong recalled:

> I had been running the store for several years, but it didn't really yield any profits for me. I kept thinking of the solution. Then one day I thought, 'Why don't I just try using big sales to attract the customers?'

Later, Fong started to implement big sales from time to time to increase the foot traffic to his store. Fong continued to tell us, 'I am talking about really big sales, like 70 per cent reductions. My store got very crowded after I introduced the sales.'

At that time, Fong's primary concern was to attract as many customers as possible; he did not care much about the profit margin or the image of the store. As Fong said exultingly, 'Another strategy that I came up with was to sell the Krugerrands at a discounted price.' The Krugerrand gold coin produced in South Africa was popular in Hong Kong between the mid-1970s and the mid-1980s as a promising investment option. Gradually, Fong succeeded in getting more customers to the store, but Ocean Centre, as mentioned in Chapter 3, refused to renew his lease because the management of the mall, accordingly to Fong, was not pleased with Fong's big sales strategy as that created a 'low' image. In 1986, FBL put up advertisements to announce that the Ocean Centre branch would be closed, and a 70 per cent sale was being introduced. 'This explains why we still don't have any store in Harbour City today,' Fong said bitterly. 'After Ocean Centre kicked me out, I then tried my luck in Yau Ma Tei, where Chinese gold-smiths traditionally clustered.'

Goldsmith and jewellery store

In fact, shortly after Fong set up his first jewellery store in Ocean Centre, he also set up two more branches in Causeway Bay and Central. When Fong failed to get the lease renewed in Ocean Centre, he no longer confined himself to the retailing of karat gold jewellery. 'I was really angry that Ocean Centre did not want us to be there as they thought that we were low. I therefore moved my store back to the goldsmith area,' Fong said. In 1986, Fong, as mentioned in Chapter 3, established his first jewellery and goldsmith store on Nathan Road in Yau Ma Tei selling both karat gold and pure gold jewellery products.

It seemed that Fong chose to establish a jewellery and goldsmith store in Yau Ma Tei simply because he felt aggrieved at the decision of Ocean Centre, but this was not the whole picture. According to Reuben Cheung, who joined FBL in the early 1970s, Fong had thought about selling pure gold, but he had not yet acquired a gold license. 'You need to get a license to sell gold in Hong Kong,' Reuben said. 'FBL became a member of the Chinese Gold and Silver Exchange Society in 1986. After getting the license, then it started to sell pure gold as well. Jewellery and goldsmith stores were then set up in Yau Ma Tei.'

Becoming a major jewellery brand

The retail network of FBL expanded rapidly between the mid-1980s and mid-1990s. Fong was actively involved in the process as he directly oversaw the interior design of the stores and the site selection. As Fong explained to us:

> There were several location selection criteria that I strictly followed. First, I had to make sure that other big jewellery companies such as Chow Sang Sang (CSS) and Chow Tai Fook (CTF) had set up their stores nearby. Second, the site had to look spacious and could accommodate at least 80 ft-heigh showcases. I wanted to make sure that my stores were as grand as those of the big names.

The number of FBL retail outlets increased from three in 1986 to eight in 1987 when FBL went public. 'FBL had actually tried to go public several times before 1987,' Reuben said. 'The attempts all ended in failure because the volume of turnover was not big enough.' The desire of Fong to get FBL listed on the stock exchange might be one of the reasons for the rapid expansion of the retail network from 1986 to 1987. According to the prospectus, four out of eight FBL retail outlets were opened within the five months prior to the initial public offering. At the time of the initial public offering of FBL stock, in addition to the stores in Central, Tsim Sha Tsui, and Yau Ma Tei, FBL also established shops in Mong Kok and Kowloon City; it had even set up a store in Yuen Long in the New Territories.

In 1989, FBL briefly became the largest jewellery retailer in Hong Kong in terms of the number of retail outlets. In the following decade, FBL, on the one hand, maintained its presence in the major tourist and shopping areas such as Causeway, Central, Tsim Sha Tsui, and Mong Kok; on the other hand, it aggressively expanded its retail network into other local residential areas. For instance, on Hong Kong Island, FBL set up stores in North Point (1990), Quarry Bay (1990), and Shau Kei Wan (1991); in Kowloon, it added spots in Kwun Tung (1989) and Ngau Tau Kok (1990); in the New Territories, it landed in Tsuen Wan (1989), Tuen Mun (1990), Tai Po (1991), and Sha Tin (1994). 'After opening my first *gam pou* in Yau Ma Tei, I wanted to have my own stores in all 18 districts in Hong Kong,'[1] Fong said proudly. 'I achieved that goal within a few years.' Before the economy of Hong Kong was hard hit by the Asian financial crisis, FBL had altogether 21 retail outlets in Hong Kong in the financial year 1996–1997.

Jewellery for ordinary people

We argue that what made FBL stand out in the early phase of the development of its retail business was that Fong emphasized and promoted the idea of jewellery for ordinary people – jewellery that ordinary people could afford and would buy. This, however, does not mean that Fong consciously devised a clear branding concept strategy in advance. Fong in fact did not really think much about the concept behind it, he simply did what he thought would attract the customers. Fong offered his own perspective on the rise of the FBL retail business:

> How could FBL outperform others? The reason was very simple, because our pricing was very low! In the past, we all did not dare to go into a jewellery store. We thought that it was a high-class thing; it was a place where we, the ordinary people, simply did not belong. But my jewellery is not the same. I hope that everyone can afford to buy his or her own jewellery. When the price of the jewellery is set very high, who dares to buy? I hope that at least office ladies are able to buy jewellery to reward themselves or to mix and match with their clothing. I was the first among my peers to launch big sales. When jewellery products became cheaper, locals began to buy the jewellery, it has then become a habit for ordinary people in Hong Kong. It didn't really matter that I earned less as long as I was able to attract the customers. When our shop had promotions, I would put a full-page advertisement in the newspapers. In the advertisement, we would show the picture of the jewellery products on a table and show the price clearly. The price range was around two to three thousand dollars.

It is hard to tell if Fong was the first person, as he claimed, to bring about the 'massificiation' of jewellery in Hong Kong, but it is true that Fong's positioning of his retail stores did enable him to draw the attention of the local customers and exploit the potential of the growing local market. Low pricing was, as Fong stated straightforwardly, the trademark of early FBL.

Fong's emphasis on big sales as a means of marketing and promotion was also innovative. As Harry Mak, a long-serving employee of FBL who joined the jewellery industry in the 1970s, commented:

> The concept of 'sale' in the jewellery industry was really made popular by Mr. Fong. During the sales, some diamonds were sold at extremely low prices that FBL could only earn 1 per cent profit from. It seemed crazy as the company didn't earn much, but through offering these extreme sales, Mr. Fong did attract a lot of customers to the stores.

In addition, Fong also tried to change the typical perception of jewellery; he attempted to convince local Chinese people that jewellery was not something unreachable for the masses, but a kind of affordable everyday accessory. An advertorial on FBL in 1978 succinctly captured the key features of Fong's idea of affordable, everyday jewellery (excerpt; translation ours):

> Wearing jewellery is no longer the exclusive right of rich women. In the past, it seemed that only rich people were qualified to wear jewellery, but today, jewellery has become an indispensable accessory to clothing. . . . Jewellery is like the clothes that we wear; it's a means to demonstrate your character and taste. . . . As long as you have good taste and make a wise choice, a piece of jewellery costing only a few hundred dollars will make you look stunning. . . .

If you are a modern women who loves dressing up and jewellery, then you should visit FBL jewellery company.

Marketing jewellery for ordinary people

Fong himself was well aware that emphasizing the new perception of jewellery as a kind of affordable everyday accessory had to be matched by the corresponding marketing strategy that focused on the pricing, which can be illustrated by the printed advertisements for FBL in the local newspapers during the 1980s. The signature of the early FBL ads was that most of them featured the big sales at the stores in a straightforward but dramatic way. For instance, the large Chinese character *gaam* (meaning 'reduction') was printed on the ad followed by a couple of words in a very big font size saying (translation ours):

> Every
> FBL
> Unprecedented
> Big Sale
> Up to 60% off

In another ad, several large words were printed (translation ours):

> FBL
> An Avalanche of
> Stocktake Sale

In a similar vein, in another ad, the title was printed extremely large (translation ours):

> FBL
> Shocking and Startling
> Stocktake Sale

Another signature of the early FBL ads was that they very often showed the details, the original price, and the discounted price of the selected products clearly, especially when the company was launching a big sale. For instance, in the last advertisement mentioned earlier, a list of five facts was provided for each of seven products. In each of the figures, the description of the product, the size of the diamond, the crossed original price and the 'stocktake' price were laid out clearly along with a photo of the product. In an advertisement in 1986, again, the lists of information featured the original and new prices of the products shown clearly together, with an emphasis on the size of the diamonds. In this advertisement, altogether 12 products were shown with each set in a square box containing the detailed information. This kind of table of products appeared very often in the early FBL ads. Instead of creating and promoting a general brand image, the advertisements of FBL emphasized bluntly, if not focused solely, on the low pricing of the products.

More interestingly, the messages of the early FBL advertisements were always delivered in a straightforward way, mainly through colloquial texts. Not infrequently, exaggerating if not shocking texts were used to underline the scale of the sale offers. In one of the advertisements, for instance, the upper part of the bold text states (translation ours):

URGENT ANNOUNCEMENT
FBL Jewellery
Ocean Centre Branch
Removal Sale
Brought about Shopping Rush
A Lot of People Were Disappointed
Please Accept Our Apology

A photo showing a crowd of people gathering in front of the FBL store was inserted in the ad. The text below states (translation ours):

Now, To Facilitate the Crowd Flow
The Central Branch
Is Offering a Big Sale as well
All are 70% off

Another example is even more dramatic. The big words on the 1988 advertisement state:

FBL
Made Hong Kong dollar
Totally appreciated
Because . . .
Bou Lung diamond jewellery
Are All 70% off

Examples like these are ample. In another advertisement in 1986, for instance, the upper bold text states (translation ours):

How can you Say No To
FBL's
Annual
Eighty Million Dollar
Diamond Sale?

Beneath the bold text is a photo featuring a glittering diamond. The first sentence in the small caption below the photo states, 'The answer is: Absolutely impossible'. The blunt, dramatic way of marketing in these advertisements was aimed at demonstrating that the jewellery of FBL was a good value for money. The straightforward and colloquial language of the advertisements reflected the fact that FBL attempted to appeal to the mass market.

These sale-and price-oriented advertisements of FBL with direct messages delivered by the signature giant, bold texts created and promoted a new image of jewellery and jewellery stores. With the overwhelming straightforwardness and emphasis on the low pricing in the advertisements, FBL established itself as a jewellery store that was approachable to ordinary people, and one that understood and shared their concern about the price of the products. The refreshing image of FBL became obvious when we compare the advertisements of FBL with those of the other major local jewellery stores.

The advertisements of FBL's competitors, for instance, attempted at either creating an aesthetic and glamorous image of the brands or emphasizing the professionalism of the companies. Two advertisements from two competitors of FBL in the 1980s, for instance, both feature a beautiful lady. One of the advertisements did not contain any text at all, featuring only a glamorous woman wearing jewellery accessories. The title of another advertisement was, 'The Presence of Attractive Gold Light'. The advertisement was to promote a set of vouchers named 'Gold Dating'. This type of advertisement usually featured beautiful or symbolic figures and poetic titles, which were aimed at constructing a grand, luxurious and high-end brand image. The advertisements of FBL, by contrast, were not subtle; their messages were straightforward and the image that they constructed was good value.

Other jewellery companies, on the other hand, might have hoped to create a professional image through advertising to enhance the trust and confidence of the customers. The advertisements of another competitor to FBL in the late 1970s, for instance, attempted to emphasize the jewellery knowledge and expertise of their staff in the advertisements. The winning formula of FBL to attract customers, however, was the emphasis on big sales and low pricing. Other jewellery companies in fact also advertised their promotions and sales, but rarely did they give as much details about the sales as FBL did. None of FBL's major competitors, for instance, clearly specified the information or price of the promotion items in the advertisements as FBL did.

The style of marketing at FBL turned upside down the stereotypical image of a jewellery store, which had been associated with luxury, glamour, and rich-people-only. Fong did not bother with maintaining the 'standard' brand image. Instead, he attempted to unveil the mystery around jewellery and presented it as an everyday necessity, which everybody could afford. The advertisements of FBL spoke directly and frankly about the price of the products, as this was what had previously prevented people from thinking of getting their own jewellery. The advertisements also used easy-to-understand titles and texts to bridge the distance between the jewellery store and the people. The central message that FBL attempted to convey was that jewellery could be affordable, and affordable jewellery could be as good as expensive jewellery.

Contribution club

Apart from printed advertisements in local newspapers, Fong also made effective use of the traditional concept of the 'contribution club' to make jewellery products affordable to ordinary people. What Fong came up with was the FBL Wong Tai Sin Gold Club. Members of the Club contribute a certain amount of money on a regular basis, which they could then redeem against the prices of products after a certain period. Reuben emphasized that the Club was not an innovation of FBL, but a common practice in the industry. To FBL, there were two major functions of the Club: to get the cash and to establish and maintain the network of customers. As Reuben explained:

> The nature of the Gold Club was actually like a *kaifong* association,[2] we did not really gain much from running it. It provided a platform for the salespeople to socialize with the customers. The customers had to submit the application form and the contribution to the retail branches directly, very often they would then stay at the store for a while to chit-chat. It provided good opportunities for the salespeople to enhance the relationships with them.

In addition to shopping discounts, various social activities were organized to attract new members. The Gold Club, for instance, organized various local travel tours and worship tours to the Wong Tai Sin Temple.[3] The highlight was the annual dinner, an occasion which not only drew the salespeople and customers closer, but also enabled Fong to get closer to his employees and the customers. At the beginning, professional performers were invited to entertain the members at the annual dinner. Later, Fong became the major star of the event. Fong was very happy whenever he mentioned the annual dinner of the Gold Club as he recalled:

> I love singing. I would spend time practising before the annual dinner. The response of the customers was good. They always wanted to shake hands with me. Later I decided to run the show myself, I didn't think that we had to pay to recruit someone else. After all, it was not very common for a boss of a listed company to sing in front of his employees and the public and to interact passionately with the customers.

The previously mentioned positioning of FBL, we suggest, was very much related to Fong's own biographical experience. Recall that Fong had a very poor background – he lived in poverty until he became a master; and he also received little education. In other words, Fong was no different from other fellow ordinary people, and he understood very well the desire and anxiety of the ordinary people. Fong's own background might also explain why when the business of his first high-end jewellery store in Ocean Centre did not go well, Fong immediately decided to implement big sales to attract the customers. This decision was very important to Fong's subsequent marketing strategy as it revealed to Fong that he should differentiate his store from other typical jewellery companies by targeting and appealing to the mass market, something that he was very familiar with. Fong, who always described himself as *faat cin hon*, understood how money mattered in the eyes of the ordinary people, and how sensitive they were to the pricing of the products. Fong, who claimed that he knew no aesthetics and was a very practical person, also understood that ordinary people would be more easily attracted to clear, straightforward, and often dramatic messages that emphasized price reduction instead of subtle texts and abstract images. Gradually, Fong developed a retail brand that resembled his own style: pragmatic, approachable, and economical.

We can also find a similar pragmatic, approachable, and economical style in Fong's management of FBL's retail shops. Our visit to the FBL's retail branch in a new town in the New Territories was illustrative of the operation and management of FBL's retail stores.

An afternoon at an FBL retail branch

We arrive at the store around two o'clock in the afternoon on a sunny day in 2015. It is not difficult to find the store because it is located on the first floor of the shopping complex in the atrium. Interestingly, the stores of all the major local jewellery companies are located on the same floor, forming a cluster. There are three entrances to the FBL store. The layout of the store is neither rectangular nor square, as one normally expects; it is more like an irregular polygon. That is the first thing that catches our attention. When we see the escape routing plan of the store hung on the wall, we realize that the store is a pentagon, and in fact its layout resembles a diamond. 'Mr. Fong loves this layout very much,' Eva Ho, the supervisor of the store, tells us later.

At the main entrance, a showcase on the left-hand side displays pure gold jewellery; on the right-hand side, a bigger showcase displays karat gold jewellery set with diamonds. The left wall of the side entrance is occupied by a giant poster featuring a blond Caucasian woman wearing jewellery pieces; on the right-hand side, again, there are showcases displaying pure gold jewellery. Beside the giant poster is a much smaller signature with a title written in both Chinese and English, 'Happy Chinese Valentine's Day'. The signature relates to a promotion on this occasion.

When we enter the store, we notice that there are around four to five salespeople. One of them greets us. After we explain our purpose, she escorts us to a waiting area. There is a sofa and a coffee table. Several copies of magazines are tidily put on the table, and there is a Chinese candy box used during the Chinese New Year. At the time of our visit to the store, the Chinese New Year holidays have just finished. Shortly afterwards, Eva comes to greet us. 'It's great to have such a nice waiting area in the store. You even have a candy box,' we tell her. 'Yes, many regular customers love to come to have a chat with us. For our branch, we have quite a lot of local customers, many of them have become our regular visitors and friends,' she explains. Eva is willing to tell us more about herself and her experience in FBL with patience:

I have been working in FBL for more than ten years, when this branch was first opened. I was employed as senior salesperson, because I had already become a manager of a smaller jewellery company before I joined FBL.

We are very curious about why Eva left her original company and joined FBL just as a senior salesperson. She replies:

I was attracted by an FBL advertisement in the MTR station. In the advertisements, there were four very professional-looking people. The basic message of the ad was that if you joined FBL, you would have the opportunity to receive GIA [Gemological Institute of America Inc] training for free and I thought it was a very good chance!

In-between our conversations, a couple of Cantonese-speaking customers enter the shop to check out the products. Soon after that, a Caucasian woman enters. She wants to check out some diamond rings, but it seems that none of the products that the salesperson shows her are satisfactory. Eva then intervenes and attempts to ask for more details from the customer. The customer clearly has some specific designs in her mind. Eventually, the salesperson jots down some details, and asks the customer to leave her contact information so that once the salesperson finds a product that matches her request, she will contact the customer immediately. 'It's quite surprising to see that there are foreign customers,'[4] we tell Eva. 'Well, we actually get quite a lot of them; many of our customers live in Sai Kung,[5] they drive to here to do shopping,' Eva explains. 'That lady wants to find some thick rings. Foreign customers very often prefer thicker rings.'

'Why do you still stay at FBL? Please bear our bluntness, we mean FBL did go through some really bad times,' we ask Eva. Eva replies without hesitation, 'Because of *jan cing mei*[6] (literally means the taste of human warmth).' Eva further elaborates:

In 2003 when Hong Kong was suffering from the outbreak of SARS,[7] other companies simply reduced salaries and laid off a lot of people. Mr, Fong, by contrast, always reminded us to take care of ourselves. In fact, I also worked in other FBL branches before. But later I wanted to keep a better balance between the family and my work, basically I needed more time to take care of the family. Something good about working in FBL is that you can always discuss your problems with your supervisors and boss. There are always room for negotiation. Since I live nearby, I was allowed to relocate to work in this branch.

When Eva talks about Fong, she is full of gratefulness. 'Mr. Fong understands very well the mentality of ordinary *daa gung zai* (wage earners),' she continues to explain to us. 'He understands that when you stop working, you just stop earning money. He never delays paying our salaries.'

When we are talking, a middle-aged woman suddenly rushes into the store. The staff all greet her as if they know her well. 'I am rushing to do grocery!' she speaks to Eva loudly. 'I've already got it ready for you!' Eva replies in an equally loud voice. The woman leaves her credit card to one of the staff members and then disappears. 'What's going on?' we ask curiously. Eva then explains:

> She is my *suk haak* (regular customer). I got to know her when I worked in another branch. It's over ten years ago. Her husband owns a company. She told me before that her friends were going to get married, she asked me to help her to keep track of the gold price. She trusts me a lot.

When the woman comes back, she brings with her a lot of goods. 'Quick, get her some bags, and help her carry the stuff to the car park,' Eva urges her staff to help the woman. 'It's alright, it's alright, thanks a lot. You are always very considerate!' The woman says to Eva. Eva then shows the woman the pure gold jewellery that she has chosen for her: a pair of Chinese wedding bangles, the so-called '*lung fung aak*' (the bangles of dragon and phoenix), costing around $9,000. The woman does not really check the item carefully; she just tells Eva, 'Please just decide for me. I trust your choice.' Then Eva also shows her a neck-lace that the woman has not asked for. 'When I was picking the bangles for you, I also noticed that this necklace fit you well. So, I have kept it for you and want to let you try it on,' Eva explains to her. Then Eva helps the woman to try on the necklace. Eva says, 'See, it looks great on you!' The woman's mobile phone rings, she answers the call. After a while, she finishes the conversation, turns to Eva and complains jokingly, 'I told my husband that I am in FBL right now. He then said that I treat FBL as my home, and I will spend a lot of money each time I come here.'

Shortly afterwards, a young lady enters the shop and joins the woman. At that time, there is no other customer, as it is a weekday afternoon. Virtually the entire staff's attention is on the two females. The young lady, the woman, and Eva talk for a while, then Eva says to the young lady, 'I need to give a red packet to your daughter! I haven't given her one yet.' She then rushes to the back office. The woman replies, "No, you don't have to! Come on!" The three continue to talk for some time before the young lady and the woman leave together. The woman eventually buys the pair of bangles along with the necklace.

We are eager to ask Eva to explain the situation to us. Eva explains as if she really knows a lot about the family of the customer:

> My *suk haak* has one son and a daughter. The young lady you saw is her daughter-in-law who just gave birth to a girl. The baby girl is a lucky star to the family because when she was born, the company of the family also succeeded in getting listed on the stock market. The son of my customer inherits the family business while her daughter is a designer working in the United States. She has a foreign boyfriend! My *suk haak* and I have already become good friends. I remember one day she gave me a call. She asked me to prepare 12 rings, five for men and seven for women. Her father was very ill then, she was worried that she needed to prepare for the worst. She came

to pick up the products the next day and cried a lot. I tried my best to comfort her. Luckily her father recovered later.

Before we leave the store, Eva also shares with us her views on today's young staff:

> Well, you know, the world has changed, we cannot use the old method to teach the young people now. I am a mother myself; I understand that very clearly. You have to reason with them. You can't scold them in public. They are very vulnerable. Once they feel hurt, they will lose the motivation to work. Training the junior staff is really like educating children.

In fact, we hear throughout our fieldwork in the shop that Eva calls her young staff *aa zai* and *aa neoi*, meaning 'son' and 'daughter'. When we are about to leave, Eva proposes to exchange our WhatsApp contacts and she says warmly, 'Feel free to visit us again anytime!'

Several observations of FBL's retail business

Several observations can be made in light of the ethnographic episode in the previous section. The first is the close personal relations between the salespeople and the customers. Sales is the most important aspect of any retail business, but selling jewellery is particularly difficult because jewellery is a luxury product, which implies that the sale process usually takes a few hours, a few days or even a few months because the unit price of jewellery tends to be high and therefore the purchasing frequency of the customers is low and they tend to be choosy. This further requires a lot of sales talks and thus is quite time consuming. More importantly, customers tend to be concerned primarily about whether the jewellery products they are going to buy are genuine and whether the price quoted is reasonable. Given the lack of specialized knowledge about jewellery products, customers must rely on the creditability of the salesperson and the reputation of his or her company. Salespersons in jewellery retailing earn their creditability by convincing the customer that they are professionals, which further requires excellent product knowledge. As Zoe Tang, who joined FBL in the late 1980s to work in the retail branch, recalled:

> The sale of jewellery especially requires good product knowledge. Back in the 1980s and 1990s, jewellery was regarded as something mysterious. Ordinary people in general did not have any channels to get the relevant information. The salespeople were therefore considered jewellery experts. The trust of customers mainly came from the knowledge of the salesperson.

Harry, based on his extensive retail experience in jewellery retailing, added:

> Salespeople are supposed to provide information and knowledge about jewellery to the customers and to convince them that they are professional. Very

frequently, for example, salespeople have to educate the customers about jewellery care and identification.

However, as jewellery became popular among the customers of Hong Kong in the 1990s, professional knowledge alone was no longer sufficient in getting customers. As Zoe explained:

> Of course, many customers today will gather a lot of information before shopping for jewellery. The salespeople can no longer rely on 'professionalism' alone. We need to gain the trust of the customers by providing better after-sale service and by reputation.

In the cultural context of the Chinese society of Hong Kong, the ability to establish and maintain good relationships with regular customers is also a 'must' for a good salesperson in jewellery retailing. As clearly revealed in the earlier ethnographic episode, to maintain a close relationship with the customers is of utmost importance to the sales staff. As we mentioned, the trust of the customers depends largely on the knowledge that a salesperson possesses, his or her credibility, and quality of service. Once a salesperson establishes a close relationship with the customer, he or she is likely to return or recommend the salesperson to others. It is especially true among the local customers. In order to establish a close relationship with the customers, the salespeople must try their best to accommodate the demand of the customers, to think in their shoes, as Eva showed in the ethnography. Harry told us a lot of examples of the friendships between the sales staff and the customers. One of the stories is particularly illustrative:

> One day, a middle-aged woman came to our store. It was around eleven o'clock in the morning, we had just opened. The woman came with her son, I guess he was around seven or eight years old. They stayed at the store to chat with our sales staff. Around noon, she even ordered lunch for us, all on her! She continued to 'play' around until seven o'clock in the evening. At that time, I asked the salespeople to take turns talking to her, so that she could chat with different people; at the same time, our salespeople could also take care of other customers. After that, she became our *suk haak*; she had a close relationship with us. Whenever she came to our store, she would buy something. Later, when she could find nothing to buy, she would simply ask us to melt the gold and remodel it for her. Later, she just left all the orders in the store. Whenever she came to the store, she would ask us to think of some ways for her to place orders so as to help us boost our sales figures. The relationship lasted for three years, isn't it amazing?

This example demonstrates that it takes a lot of effort and patience from the salespeople to establish personal relationships with the customers. But once a personal relationship is established, it will bring many business opportunities to the salespeople.

Teamwork

Our second observation is the teamwork among FBL's salespeople. In fact, *gam pou* in Hong Kong operated in a very individualistic, hierarchical, and authoritative way. In this regard, Harry's personal experience is very illustrative. Harry started to work in a typical *gam pou* in the mid-1970s in Wan Chai on Hong Kong Island. He still vividly remembered the operation of the goldsmith. According to Harry, there were around ten people working in the shop, including the boss. The business hours were from 9:30 a.m. to 6:00 p.m. In some stores, there were residential masters. There was only one calculator in the cashier. The showcases of the goldsmiths were usually arranged in a 'U' or 'I I' shape (Figure 6.1) and the jewellery and pure gold products were displayed separately.

The salespeople were ranked, according to Harry, as the *tau gwai* (first case), the *ji gwai* (second case), the *saam gwai* (third case), and so on. The so-called '*gwai*' refers to the specific showcases to which the salesperson was assigned. The first case was also closest, spatially, to the entrance of the shop. The *tau gwai* was the highest-ranked employee in the store. Once a customer entered the shop, he was the first one who could approach the customer. 'Of course, the *tau gwai* could choose to give his customers to other *gwais*,' said Harry. 'He was like a *zoeng gwai* (shopkeeper), who had strong power over other employees.' The *mei gwai* (last case), on the other hand, mainly sold synthetic and artificial gemstones and other karat gold jewellery. Tam Chi Chong, who had also worked in a goldsmith before joining FBL, said:

> It's basically not possible for the *mei gwai* to get any business, since the customers had already been taken by other *gwais*. The promotion of the salespeople in the *gam pou* depended solely on the discretion of the boss. Normally the mobility was not very high as one had to wait for the previous *gwais* to leave so that one could take up his position or when the owner decided to expand the business.

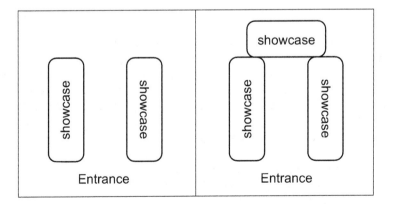

Figure 6.1 Floor plan of a typical *gam pou*

We have to point out immediately that the hierarchy of traditional goldsmiths determined not only the status of different staff but also who could get business first, which is further related to his or her income because the commission system was individual-based. The hierarchy and its associated individual-based commission system tended to encourage keen competition among different staff of the shop, which always resulted in hostile personal relations among the shop staff.

The FBL stores however abandoned this *gwai* system, as used in the traditional goldsmiths. Each FBL branch instead was divided into two teams, namely the 'attack' and the 'defence' teams. The 'defence' team at each FBL retail branch usually consisted of two staff members sent from the headquarters and therefore they followed the working hours of employees at the headquarters instead of the sales staff in the shop. The concept of 'defence', according to Stella Lam, who joined the company in the mid-1990s, was introduced to FBL's retail branches by Reuben. The 'defence' team was responsible for all non-sales tasks, among which the most important task was to conduct daily stocktaking before and after the business hours of the store. Nobody would be allowed to leave if the counts did not match. Obviously, the deployment of the 'defence' team was to 'defend' the interests of the company by preventing shoplifting by the employees in the retail branches; and that is also why the 'defence' team members had to be sent from the headquarters. As Reuben himself explained:

> For any jewellery store, you need to find someone to make sure that no product is stolen. Products, that is, the jewellery, are the most important assets of the branches and the company. The major duty of the 'defence' team was to protect these assets.

The 'defence' team also took care of other tasks such as assisting the branch managers to schedule shifts and holidays and deal with documents, answering calls, ordering products, and coordinating the transfer of goods between branches.

Sharing similar experience-based skills

The 'attack' team, on the other hand, was responsible for the sales. The hierarchy of the salespeople on the attack team was (beginning with the lowest): junior salesperson, salesperson, senior salesperson, sales supervisor, sales manager, and branch manager. We have to emphasize that FBL's salespeople were differentiated in the hierarchy not in terms of who should get the business first or the content of their tasks but by their status and product knowledge which were usually related to their relevant experience in the industry. Every salesperson at FBL's stores was encouraged, if not required, to take up various tasks.[8] That is to say, each salesperson had a chance to experience all the tasks involved in selling different jewellery products and learn various skills necessary for the operation of the shop. As a result, salespeople of different status at FBL shops shared similar experience-based skills. Wong (1999) conducted an ethnographic research on the sales floor of a Japanese supermarket in Hong Kong, demonstrating that experience-based knowledge shared by a team of salespeople could help sales clerks deal with uncertainties including changes and problems. The ability of handling uncertainties was particularly important given the fact that retail sales at FBL shops always involved a high proportion of changes and problems. One of the major uncertainties in FBL shops consisted of the customers, who demanded to be served whenever and wherever they presented themselves. Suppose, for example, a customer asks for service at the *gwai* that sells diamonds when all of the sales staff there are occupied by other customers, as is often the case on a busy day. Salespeople from other *gwais*, who are familiar with the diamonds sold at that particular *gwai* because they also possess the necessary knowledge of diamonds, and who are free at that time, can then serve the customer immediately.

The second typical type of uncertainties involved dealing with problems, the first and foremost of which were customer complaints. As mentioned earlier, the reputation of a jewellery retailer is very important to its survival. In order to maintain its reputation, FBL had to make sure that customer complaints were to be contained on the spot and answered immediately, otherwise customers might spread their complaints to their friends or even bring their cases to the media, which would definitely ruin FBL's reputation. The ability to deal with customer complaints quickly and satisfactorily was a 'must' to FBL's shop operations. Such an ability consisted of making accurate and rapid judgements on which side, FBL or customers, should be responsible for the case concerned. If it was the former, sales staff had to contain the complaint straightaway; if it was the latter, they must come up with a way to calm the customer down while at the same time avoid making unnecessary compensation. To be able to make a correct and quick judgement on customers' complaints required knowledge of a variety of patterns of complaints. Salespersons also needed to learn how to prevent the recurrence of mistakes that lead to customers' complaints by identifying the causes correctly and speedily in order to minimize financial loss and image damage. They also needed product knowledge and some knowledge of the overall operation of the shop to rectify the problem. Since FBL's salespeople were encouraged to develop similar experience-based skills, they appeared to be particularly efficient in dealing with uncertainties involving customer complaints.

We have demonstrated that the FBL mode of hierarchy could encourage its salespeople to take up various tasks that further fostered knowledge-sharing among sales staff. Such a significant extent of knowledge sharing in turn enhanced the ability of the salespeople to handle uncertainties on the sales floor from which FBL's retail business benefitted substantially because the effective and efficient handling of uncertainties was closely related to the efficiency of FBL's retail business. The question now is why FBL's salespeople were willing not only to take up different tasks but also co-operate with each other?

We argued that FBL's team-based commission system whereby commissions generated from sales would be shared by all the members of the sales team was crucial not only in cultivating team spirit among the sales staff at FBL's shops, but also in helping to avoid the hostile human relations among individual salespeople that had always been an essential part of the everyday life of *gam pou*. The sales supervisor of an FBL branch explained that she joined FBL because of its commission system:

> Before joining FBL, I had worked in another jewellery company. But I didn't like the way it did business and the individual commission system. I joined FBL in 1996 when it introduced the team-based commission system. It reduced internal politics and enhanced motivation in teamwork. I loved that.

The relative lack of hostile human relations was indeed quite often cited by the frontline staff as one of the reasons why they felt attached to the company. Many of the senior employees at the headquarters, who once worked as frontline staff in the branches, told us that they missed their time in the shops very much. 'Things in the shops were much simpler,' Harry said. 'We all fought for the same goal.' Stella, who was posted in the cashier's office of the branches, also shared the same view: 'The colleagues in the branches were very funny; our relationship was very good. We really had a great time back then.'

Kinship tactics

Another major reason for the willingness of the salespeople to cooperate was the eagerness of the senior staff members to frame the relationships among colleagues and between superiors and subordinates in FBL's shops in kinship terms. Recall that Eva referred to her subordinates as *aa zai* and *aa neoi*. Following Maurice Bloch (1971, p. 82), we contend that the kinship terms here were 'a judgement on people rather than a label – it is a moral concept'. They were used by the senior staff members of FBL's shops as a tactic (Bloch, 1971, pp. 82–83) to impose the moral obligations embedded in the kinship terms on the subordinates *as if* the latter were their sons or daughters. As a 'son' or 'daughter', the subordinates should be loyal to their 'mother' or 'father'. The senior staff members, in return, should protect and take care of their 'sons' and 'daughters'; provide them personal guidance in human relationships, personality, education, and career; and show emotional concern towards their 'children'. Despite its tactical nature, the use of kinship terms and the associated moral obligations helped cultivate a family-like atmosphere among the employees of FBL's retail shops. As a result, the relationship among employees, at least at the experiential level, was no longer just instrumental but also expressive, not only professional but also emotional, and not simply contractual but also human imbued with *jan cing mei*, an important topic we shall return to in the next chapter.

Within less than 20 years, Fong not only transformed FBL from a jewellery manufacturer into a retailer, but also made it a highly recognized jewellery brand in Hong Kong. However, Fong's idea of jewellery for ordinary people and his way of running his retail shops as described earlier *alone* could not be held responsible for the success of Fong's retail business. We argue that the historical effect of

Fong's marketing positioning and his management style is rooted in their mediation with the development of the jewellery retail market in Hong Kong in the 1980s which coincided with the emergence of a new shopping culture.

The development of the jewellery retail market in Hong Kong

Hong Kong society in the 1980s was marked by the emergence of a new shopping culture.[9] In the previous two decades, shopping, to most of the people in Hong Kong, was done for practical rather than entertainment purposes. For example, housewives of low and lower-middle class – who constituted the majority of Hong Kong's population – would shop for daily necessities in the ground-floor shops of their settlement blocks and fresh food in the wet markets close to their estates. On rare occasions such as Lunar New Year's Eve, they might do their shopping at *guohuo gongsi* – China department stores selling Chinese products – but only for their children who did not even have money to do any shopping. Only well-to-do customers could afford shopping in non-Hong Kong department stores in high-end core retail areas. In other words, most Hong Kong people *did* rather than *went* shopping in the sense that they did shopping for practical rather than leisure purposes. What they were most concerned with therefore was whether the merchandise was affordable or how long the products could last. In other words, price and durability of the products rather than the trends were the major criteria used by most Hong Kong people when they did their shopping at that time. However, thanks to the large Japanese retailers, especially Yaohan which established its store in Hong Kong in the early 1980s together with various factors including the increase in deposable income of the people of Hong Kong, the convenient public transportation systems such as the Mass Transit Railway and the electrification of the Kowloon-Canton Railway, and the emergence of shopping malls in both private and public estates, a new shopping culture emerged. The people in Hong Kong started to *go* rather than *do* shopping. What they were concerned with was no longer affordability or durability but fashion.

The jewellery retail market in Hong Kong also expanded along with the gradual emergence of this new shopping culture. The jewellery retail market in Hong Kong could generally be divided into the tourist and local markets. In fact, before the 1970s, tourists were the major customers of jewellery retailers in Hong Kong. Tai-lok Lui (2001, p. 25) argues that the early 'malling' and consumer culture of Hong Kong was driven by tourism; it was not until the 1970s that a local consumption culture arose due to the growing prosperity of the local population. According to Lui (2001, p. 26), the early major shopping areas in Hong Kong were in fact tourist areas – notably around the Ocean Terminal, a cruise terminal and high-end shopping complex which later became a part of the Harbour City, in Tsim Sha Tsui, and along Queen's Road in Central and near the waterfront of Wan Chai. At that time, shopping and consumption were not normal and day-to-day life activities of ordinary local people. Jewellery consumption was not common among the local people; it was mostly a tourist or expatriate activity. Even with the rise and growth of the local shopping culture in the 1980s, the jewellery retail market in Hong Kong had still been heavily shaped by the tourist market.

Jewellery consumption, however, had become more common among the local population since the 1970s. It was largely due to the increase of wages and wealth of the local people, which in turn gave rise to a new pattern and preference of jewellery consumption for the local people. We want to emphasize that in the traditional Chinese cultural context, jewellery is regarded as a luxury instead of a necessity. Pure gold products, on the other hand, are regarded as something with practical and specific uses such as the storage of value, investment, and gift-giving on bridal occasions. As Harry further explained:

> The Chinese housewives love to buy pure gold jewellery. They keep checking the gold price all the time; when the price is good, they will just buy some-thing – a gold ring, a gold necklace, a gold bracelet and so on. They want to leave something for their children, you know, sometimes they just want to keep something precious in case of any emergency. It is especially true for the generation of people who went through the war. They only believe in pure gold as it gives them a sense of security.

In the past, local Chinese people in Hong Kong mainly purchased pure gold jewel-lery as a value-storage medium. Later, they began to purchase and wear pure gold jewellery accessories to display their newly gained wealth. As Harry elaborated:

> Back in the 1970s, the local people loved to buy cheap gold jewellery acces-sories. Owners of *daai paai dong* (street food stalls), in particular, loved to buy gold pieces and ask the goldsmith to help them make heavy gold neck-laces. Striding in the 1980s, the local people, both men and women, loved to wear short, thick gold necklaces. The economy of Hong Kong developed very rapidly. The sex industry also experienced a big boom. The managers of nightclubs loved to buy a lot of gold jewellery to demonstrate their power and status. They could also convert the jewellery into cash easily when necessary.

It was in the 1970s that the local people also started to purchase more non-pure gold jewellery items such as diamonds. 'Back then, Hong Kong was in fact a very backward society,' Harry said. 'Jewellery had already become popular in Shanghai and Guangzhou before the [Second World] war. People in Hong Kong only began to buy jewellery from the 1970s and the 1980s.' All of this gave birth to a flourishing domestic jewellery market. Recall that pure gold products were regarded as practical things and jewellery as non-necessity luxury products by the local Chinese. The shift of the consumption pattern of the people from buying pure gold (for a practical reason) to purchasing jewellery (for leisure) reflected the broader change of the shopping culture in the Hong Kong society.

With this thriving domestic market, the jewellery retail industry in Hong Kong experienced remarkable growth in the 1980s. 'The 1980s' Hong Kong was a world of luxury and dissipation. An extremely poor guy could become a millionaire tomorrow, and vice versa,' Harry said. 'The business of the goldsmiths and jewellery stores was very good.' According to Harry, the goldsmiths and jewellery stores in Hong Kong underwent drastic changes between the 1970s and the 1990s. In the 1970s, many goldsmiths were small, independent stores. The scale of each goldsmith or jewellery company was not very big. Since the circle of the local jewellery retailers was rather small, it was not common for the employees to jump ship. The variety of products sold at the local goldsmith and jewellery stores was also relatively limited.

From the 1980s, big chain stores had gradually emerged to exploit the prosperous market. The demand of the customers became higher, so the stores started to pay attention to the style of showcase displays and the designs of the products. *Gam pou* also had to implement reforms to 'modernize' their stores to keep and attract customers. Harry recalled the time when he still worked at a goldsmith's as a sales manager:

> The 1980s was a period of great transformation. Everything was changing. We [the goldsmith] also had to catch up with the trend. We [the employees at the goldsmith] started to wear uniforms during work. It was my first time, so I remember that very clearly! The uniform was provided by our boss. It included a brown suit, a pink shirt – the collar was 4-inch-long, you can't imagine right, together with a brown Goldlion necktie.[10] At that time, I really loved to wear that suit, I loved it so much! I felt it was cool!

The local jewellery retail industry became more institutionalized in the 1980s, and in the 1990s it was dominated by a few big goldsmiths and jewellery companies, such as CTF, CSS, and FBL.

Another key feature of the transformation of the industry was the emergence of a new jewellery retail establishment that sold both pure gold products and karat gold jewellery. In Chapter 3, we have identified that local jewellery retailers were broadly divided into two groups: *gam pou* (traditional goldsmiths) selling pure gold products and *zyubou hong* (jewellery stores) selling karat gold jewellery usually set with diamonds. The former mainly targeted local customers and the latter mainly catered to tourists and foreigners. Gradually, jewellery retailers started to combine the two forms of stores to sell both pure gold and karat gold jewellery and to target both local customers and tourists, which resulted in the birth of a hybrid format of '*zyubou gam hong*' (goldsmith and jewellery companies). CTF was, among the big names, the first to establish itself as a goldsmith and jewellery company; it did so as early as 1960. It was in the 1970s, when both the local and tourist markets grew rapidly, that goldsmiths and jewellery stores started to transform themselves into *zyubou gam hong* to tap the dual markets.

We argue that the success of FBL's new jewellery retail establishments is also closely related to the identity formation of the new middle class. The identity of the new middle class was underlined by the cultural logic: 'in-between-ness' which has been shaping and shaped by the consumption of the people of Hong Kong for decades. Wong has made this unoriginal and banal argument too many times, but if we can just say it once more: the new middle class of Hong Kong considered themselves as neither Chinese nor British/Western, and by extension neither traditional nor modern.[11] They are an in-between generation, the in-between-ness of which functions to categorically demarcate the new middle class from their parents' generation who migrated from China and by extension from the people in China. In the event, the identity of Hong Kong people emerged. In other words, the 'in-between-ness' is the cultural logic of the formation of the Hong Kong identity. The *zyubou gam hong*, as mentioned earlier, also had an image of something that is between the 'West' and the 'East', the 'foreign tourists' and 'local Chinese', and 'modern' and 'tradition', a happy parallel to the cultural logic of the identity of the new middle class. Such a parallel made *zyubou gam hong* a totemic marker of the new middle class and thus made it popular among the new middle class because the more people shopped in *zyubou gam hong*, the more they became the new middle class.

We can now see how the advent of a new middle class in the Hong Kong society, the jewellery retail market in the 1970s and the 1980s, and the emergence of a new shopping culture in Hong Kong in the 1980s made possible, and facilitated, the rise and development of FBL's retail business. Of course, these macro-phenomena could not determine Fong's further branching out into retail business. In fact, under the same context, not every jewellery manufacturer could successfully transform themselves into retailers, and even fewer could eventually become one of the major local jewellery brands. The fact that Fong was trying to expand his business further is very crucial here because it made the whole different. Recall that Fong, due to his logic of maximizing production, set up a jewellery store in Ocean Centre in Tsim Sha Tsui, one of the major tourist and shopping areas in Hong Kong, in 1977 to help absorb the stock resulting from overproduction. Fong successfully promoted the new idea of jewellery for ordinary people. With an emphasis on big sales and low pricing of jewellery, Fong successfully turned jewellery into something more approachable, affordable, and local for the public to consume. The management of the FBL retail stores is also distinctive in the sense that it was characterized by the close personal relations between the salespeople and the customers, effective teamwork, a large extent of sharing similar experience-based skills, and kinship tactics. All of this helped not only enhance the efficiency of FBL's retail business but also cultivated among FBL's employees a sense of human touch at work and in the company. In short, we cannot deny Fong's agentive power.

However, Fong's idea of jewellery for ordinary people and his way of running his retail shops *alone* could not be held responsible for the success of Fong's retail business because they could not account for the significance they had, that is, they could not explain why ordinary people in Hong Kong were willing to spend money on something luxurious like jewellery or more fundamentally why they chose to buy jewellery in the first place. There is no sufficient relation between Fong's idea of jewellery for ordinary people and Fong's management style in the retail shops and the success of Fong's retail business because the latter does not logically follow from the former. Fong's marketing positioning and his management style had their own reason, that is, Fong's biographical experience; but their specific historical effect turned on the way they were taken up in the socio-cultural context of Hong Kong in the 1980s, a way that is never the only possible one. We have demonstrated how the emergence of a new shopping culture (from doing to going shopping) further encouraged the expansion of the local jewellery retail market. More importantly, we have argued that there was a parallel between the cultural logic of the identity of a new middle class and the image of FBL's retail stores as something in-between the traditional jewellery stores and the traditional gold-smiths that made the company a totemic marker of the new middle class and thus made it popular among the latter because the more people shopped in *zyubou gam hong*, the more they became the new middle class.

Conclusion

In this chapter, we have traced the development of FBL's retail business since the 1970s. We have argued that the success of Fong's retail business was enabled and facilitated by the advent of a new middle class and a new shopping culture in Hong Kong. First, the emergence of a new shopping culture and the ever-grow-ing tourism industry facilitated a bourgeoning market. To tap the growing local market, Fong transformed FBL's retail shops into goldsmith and jewellery retail establishments in 1986 to sell both pure gold and jewellery products. Second, Fong's new goldsmith and jewellery retail shops matched the cultural logic of identity for the new middle class, which further magnified the success of the new retail format. That is why the retail business of FBL expanded vigorously in the 1980s and the early 1990s.

We again are putting forward an argument which is in three terms: Fong's mar-keting positioning and his management style, the socio-cultural context of Hong Kong, and the historical effect, which is the relation between the first two. It fol-lows that we cannot *directly* reduce the historical effect of Fong's entrepreneur-ship to either his marketing positioning as well as his management style or the socio-cultural context of Hong Kong, although it is somehow determined by the two. The historical effect of Fong's marketing positioning and management style is found in their mediation with the socio-cultural context of Hong Kong in the 1980s. We shall now turn to the second part of the book to examine the character-istics of FBL as a Chinese family firm and the professionalization of the company carried out by Fong's son and daughter-in-law.

Notes

1 Hong Kong is divided into 18 administrative districts.
2 *Kaifong* is a Cantonese term meaning neighbours. *Kaifong* welfare associations are local mutual aid organizations in Hong Kong. They played an important role in provid-ing local-level social assistance to the people during the early post-war period.
3 The Wong Tai Sin Temple is one of the most well-known shrines in Hong Kong com-memorating Wong Tai Sin, a Chinese Daoist deity. The temple is also a popular tourist attraction. According to our informants, Fong was also a worshipper of Wong Tai Sin.

4 We did not mean or assume that the Caucasian customer is a 'foreigner' instead of a local Hong Konger in terms of citizenship. In Hong Kong, people often simply describe non-Chinese looking people as *ngoi gwok jan* (foreigners) during their daily conversations.

5 Sai Kung here refers to Sai Kung Town which has a thriving expatriate community.

6 We will discuss the concept of *jan cing mei*, a core feature underlying Fong's management style, in detail in the next chapter, Chapter 7.

7 The outbreak of the severe acute respiratory syndrome (SARS) in Hong Kong began in March 2003 and was only put under control in June. The epidemic resulted in 299 deaths and jeopardized the retail and tourism industry in Hong Kong.

8 Of course, junior sales staff would only be assigned to sell pure gold jewellery because selling pure gold jewellery did not require sophisticated product knowledge.

9 Wong has offered a thorough analysis of the emergence of a new shopping culture in Hong Kong in the 1980s elsewhere (see Wong and Yau, 2014), so we want to be brief here.

10 A popular brand in Hong Kong in the 1980s specializing in men's accessories, especially neckties.

11 Wong has discussed the emergence of the middle-class in Hong Kong in terms of the notion of 'in-between-ness' elsewhere, see Wong (2006, 2015a, 2015b), Wong and Hui (2005), and Wong and Yau (2012, 2014, 2015).

Part II

7   *Jan cing mei* management

In the first part of this book (Chapter 2 to Chapter 6), we have examined the entrepreneurial process in which Fong established his jewellery empire, starting as a manufacturer and subsequently engaging in the export, showroom, and retail businesses, taking him from rags to riches. We have illustrated how, over the three decades from the 1960s to the 1990s, the mediation between Fong's entrepreneurship and the changing socio-economic contexts of Hong Kong society enabled him to expand his business and transform his company into one of the most popular local jewellery brands. Fong's business reached its zenith in the early 1990s as the company established more than 20 retail stores in Hong Kong and other retail outlets in mainland China, Malaysia, Taiwan, and Macau.

This chapter marks the beginning of the second part of this book which focuses on Fong's management of FBL as a Chinese family business and its transformation. In this chapter, we will explore Fong's management regime, demonstrating how Fong applied the kinship logic to his relations with employees at FBL, which further explains the key characteristics of the management of FBL: ignorance of the organizational charts, autonomy and agency, and holistic relations. We suggest that Fong's management can best be captured by what his employees call '*jan cing mei* management' which, we argue, characterizes many Chinese family businesses. We will explain what '*jan cing mei*' means in Fong's management of FBL. In the conclusion, we shall highlight some major shortcomings of Fong's *jan cing mei* management style, which, as we shall argue in the next three chapters, is responsible for the two related crises of Fong and his company in the 2000s (Chapter 8), the nature of the transformation as a professionalization process initiated by Jackson and Emma, Fong's son and daughter-in-law (Chapter 9), and how and why the professionalization was possible at the beginning and what rendered it a failure in the end (Chapter 10).

Jan cing mei management

Until recently, FBL and Fong were almost inseparable – at least in the minds of the public in Hong Kong. The employees as well as Fong himself were perceived as one and the same. This was not just because the company bore Fong's name, but also because of Fong's active, high-profile social life, and his king-like presence in the company. Since the establishment of the company, Fong had remained the unchallenged king until he was forced to step down as FBL's chairman in 2000. Fong was not simply the 'founder' and 'chairman' of the company because these terms failed to depict the role and position of Fong in the company. Fong was the 'king' of his jewellery kingdom. Although the company had already gone public in 1987, FBL had been and essentially was a one-man company with Fong as the absolute arbitrator.

The concentration of power in the owner, who at the same time is the father figure, is one of the most frequently recounted features of Chinese family firms. During the interviews we conducted with the employees of FBL, when asked to describe the company, many of them immediately pointed out that FBL was a typical Chinese family business. When we asked for further explanation, not many of them, however, could describe very clearly the features of FBL as a typical Chinese family business. Very often, like Eva Ho, the store supervisor we mentioned in Chapter 6, they reiterated the keyword: *jan cing mei* (literally, the taste of human warmth). We attempted to press for clarification:

W&C: What do you mean by *jan cing mei*? We heard that very often from other interviewees.

INFORMANT: *Jan cing mei*, well, that's it, you don't understand? You feel the warmth here. The colleagues have close relationships. They're not just colleagues, they're like friends and family members.

W&C: So *jan cing mei* means close human relationships?

INFORMANT: Yes, and the work environment is not rigid, there is always room for negotiation.

W&C: We don't get it.

INFORMANT: The rules are dead, but people are alive, right? In a [Chinese] family business, the human relation counts more than the rules.

The management of Chinese family businesses is conventionally understood, to draw an analogy, as a kind of 'rule of man' vis-à-vis the 'rule of law' in modern corporations. In the sections that follow, we shall examine and explain how Fong's *jiaye* (family business) is organized and governed around human relationships instead of contracts and regulations. But in order to understand Fong's management of FBL as a *Chinese family business* (*jiaye*), we have to examine the *Chinese family* first.

Chinese family[1]

In a recent article, Wong (2017) attempts to answer the question: what Chinese kinship is and is not. He argues that Maurice Freedman's functionalist paradigm of Chinese kinship, which has been widely considered by many Western anthropologists of Chinese families and lineages as *the* paradigm, simply cannot explain the way Chinese people have constructed their kin groups, according to their *own* interests, values, and purposes (Wong, 2017). To simplify enormously,

Freedman's functionalist paradigm emphasizes functional factors, especially landed estate, as the essential element of Chinese kin groups. Without shared landed estate, there are, according to Freedman, hardly any Chinese kin groups. In other words, Freedman and his followers tend to emphasize functional factors, especially landed estate in defining Chinese family.

Citing a symbolic analysis of two native concepts of kinship, *fang* and *jia-zu* (Chen, 1986), Wong (2017) argues that Chinese do not understand their family *functionally* but *genealogically*. Literally, *fang* refers to the bedroom of 'a married son and his wife' (Chen, 1986, pp. 55–56); it emphasizes the son's conjugal status, designating 'the son himself, the son and his wife as a unit, or all his male descendants and their wives as a kin set' (Chen, 1986, p. 64). Metaphorically, *fang* thus takes on the meaning of the *genealogical* status of the son as a conjugal unit in relation to his father. *Jia-zu* is a blend of *jia* and *zu*. *Jia*, as we will discuss in a moment, refers to a co-resident, commensal group, whereas *zu* is a genealogical notion referring to the sets of agnates and their wives regardless of their functional aspects (Chen, 1986, p. 64). Taken together *jia-zu* refers to the genealogical aspect of Chinese family.

It is important to point out the differences between the functional and genealogical aspects of Chinese family because Chinese always emphasize the continuity of the latter rather than that of the former. In this regard, the native concept of qi^2 can further help us understand the genealogical nature of *fang/jia-zu* and thus its differences from the functional aspect of Chinese family. According to Shuzo Shiga (1978, p. 123), *ch'i*[3] literately means 'breath', which 'refers to the formless life itself, which is extended through the male reproductive function to sons and grandsons'. The concept of *ch'i* thus implies a patrilineal principle that the formless life flows from the father to the son, who will then pass it to his sons. Shiga (1967, p. 35) characterized the father–son relation with a phrase, '*fu-tzu chih ch'in, fen-hsing t'ung-ch'i*' from a Chinese classical text, *Nan Shih Chuan*, which Allen Chun (1985, p. 97) translated as 'with respect to the relation of father to son, there is a distinction of (corporeal) form but a commonality of ch'i'. According to this phrase, the father is connected to his sons by *ch'i*, which flows from the former to the latter, which is also to say that the son is the extension of his father's life, while the father is the origin of his son's life (Shiga, 1967, p. 35). It follows that father and son share the same life (*ch'i*) which Shiga called '*fu tsu t'ung ch'i*' ('share the same vital life essence between father and son'). If the son is the extension of his father's life, it logically follows that his brothers, who are the sons from the same father, can also be seen as *t'ung ch'i* (share the same vital life essence) (Shiga, 1967, p. 37, 1978, p. 123).

While *ch'i* as 'shared substance' characterizes the relationship between the father and the son and among brothers from the same father, it, however, does not apply to the relationship between the father and the daughter. In other words, the daughter cannot inherit *ch'i* from her father, which is also to say that the daughter is not considered to be the same *kind* of person as her father and brothers. What a daughter can do is to get married to a man through which she comes to share the *ch'i* of her husband. Through marriage, women and their husbands become *t'ung ch'i*; and they are the same *kind* of person. That is why when a married woman passes away, she will be buried in the same grave with her husband (Shiga, 1967, p. 37).

Shiga argued that the *t'ung ch'i* between the father and the son, the husband and the wife, and among sons from the same father defines the membership of *tsung-tsu* as a genus of persons who share the same *ch'i*; and these three relationships constitute the basic relation of *tsung-tsu* (Shiga, 1967, p. 37). We have to point out immediately that Shiga's *tsung-tsu* is equivalent to Chen's *jia-zu*, referring to the focal ancestor and all his male descendants and their wives.

The concept of *qi* helps us make an important point: *fang/jia-zu* or *tsung-tsu* is genealogically defined; its existence is not dependent on any functional factors such as shared landed property. More importantly, *fang/jia-zu* constitutes a basic framework whereby Chinese organize their domestic life as we shall see in the case of *jia*.

Jia can be seen as a co-residential group and is thus functional at the domestic level. Unlike *fang/jia-zu* which includes all the male descendants of the focal ancestor and their wives *only*, in addition to *fang/jia-zu* members, *jia* could also include non-*fang/jia-zu* members such as unmarried female descendants (including daughters and sisters) or even their uxorilocal husbands who are related to the *fang/jia-zu* through their wives, which is also to say that while a daughter is not a *fang/jia-zu* member, she is nonetheless a *jia* member. We have to add hastily that *jia* membership could include not only non-*fang/jia-zu* members such as sisters, daughters, sons-in-law, but also anyone who is personally related to the members of *fang/jia-zu* such as servants.

The difference between the genealogical *fang/jia-zu* and the functional *jia* can also be seen in the way Chinese family property is divided. Chinese family property is the accumulated surpluses left over from the *jia*'s budget. Shiga (1978) argued that the financial management of *jia* can be understood as a 'joint-account' which can be characterized by what David Graeber (2014, p. 67) called 'everyday communism' in that the relationship among *jia* members 'operates on the principle of "from each according to their abilities, to each according to their needs"'. In more concrete terms, the *jiazhang* (head of the *jia*, usually the male head of *fang/jia-zu*) or his wife allocates money to *jia* members for daily use. In return, all *jia* members are required to contribute financially to their *jia* (Shiga, 1978, p. 113). Behind this is an ideal of unselfish sharing among *jia* members: just as *jia* members are required to support one another unconditionally, they must share with others all they have, because *jia* will offer financial help to any member when situations require.

Not all members, however, have a right to the family property because the ownership of Chinese family property is defined *only* by the *fang/jia-zu* membership (Chen, 1986, p. 130). In fact, Chinese family property should be understood as *fang/jia-zu* property. As members of *fang/jia-zu*, sons can equally share the *fang/jia-zu* property, especially landed estate, when their father decides to pass the family property to them, while non-*fang/Jia-zu* members such as daughters or daughters-in-law, no matter how much they contribute financially to the *jia*, are not entitled to *fang/jia-zu* property. We can now see how the genealogical *fang/jia-zu* is fundamentally different from the functional *jia*; and Freedman's etic is *not* the Chinese people's emic. The Chinese kinship system, as Chi-nan Chen concluded (1986), is genealogically understood by the Chinese people rather than functionally defined by Freedman & Co.

Chinese familial ethics

The fact that the Chinese kinship system is genealogically understood rather than functionally defined helps us further understand two related major Chinese family ethics which are particularly relevant to the context of this book. First, the continuity of the *fang/jia-zu* line is the single most important imperative of Chinese family (Chen, 1986, p. 80). The *fang/jia-zu* line flows from the father to his son who, once he becomes a father, passes the line on to his son, and so on. It is through this successive father–son filiation that a Chinese family attains its eternity because if there is at least one single son born to the *jia-zu* in every generation, the life of the focal ancestor of the *jia-zu* can last forever because the life of a son, as mentioned earlier, can be seen as the extension of that of his father. That is why there is always an intense pressure on Chinese men to bear a son because only a son can continue his father's *qi* by creating a *fang*. A man without an issue is regarded as the most miserable fate in Chinese society because his *fang* line is threatened with termination or his life (*ch'i*) is endangered (Chen, 1986, p. 102).

It follows from this that the continuity of the *fang/jia-zu* line is more important than the continuity of any functional kin group including *jia*. In fact, *jia* is expected to be terminated, while *fang/jia-zu* is supposed to continue in Chinese societies. For example, upon the division of *jia*, each son will establish a new *jia* and the original *jia* will be terminated, while each *jia-zu* is *genealogically* divided into *fang*s according to the number of sons; but the original *jia-zu*, unlike the original *jia*, does *not* vanish.

The primary importance of the continuity of *fang/jia-zu* over that of *jia* can also be seen in the case of the *kuo-fang* (agnatic adoption) practice.[4] In the *kuo-fang* practice, the adopted son does not necessarily change his *jia* membership, which is also to say that he could still live with his original parents in their *jia*; but he is rearranged genealogically to become the son of the deceased man who is the member of another *fang* of the same *jia-zu* so that the deceased man's *fang* line can be continued. The adopted son is entitled to the deceased man's *fang* property while the former is also required to worship the latter as his *father*. Chen (1986, pp. 174–191) argued that the major purpose of *kuo-fang* was to continue the deceased's *fang* line rather than his *jia*. Chen (1986, p. 174) also added that *kuo-fang* can highlight the primary importance of the continuity of *fang/jia-zu* over that of *jia*, which is the second major Chinese family ethics.

Jia as the organizational form of Chinese family businesses

Despite the fact that the continuity of *jia* is less important than that of *fang/jia-zu*, the former rather than the latter can help us understand the organizational structure of Chinese firms because Chinese entrepreneurs tend to run their family businesses through the organization of *jia* because running a family business is also an important function of a *jia* as we can see from the Chinese term *jiaye*. It follows that the dynamics of *jia* management can help us understand Fong's management style, to which we now turn.

The way *jia* is operated is totally dependent on the *jiazhang* who oversees everything about the *jia*. The membership of a *jia*, as mentioned earlier, is defined by each of its members' relationship with the *jiazhang*. The *jiazhang* is the centre of the *jia*, from which there is a series of concentric circles of social relations radiating outward. The first inner circle usually includes his wife, sons, and daughters-in-law. It is followed by the second tier of members which usually includes his daughters, sons-in-law, and other relatives, all of them are non-*fang/jia-zu* members. The third circle usually consists of his friends, classmates (*tongxue*), and people from the same origin of home with the *jiazhang* (*tongxiang*). The fourth circle may include his long-serving servants. The actual members of each circle and the number of circles can vary with circumstances but the general principle – people with closer and more significant relationships with the *jiazhang* will be in the closer circle and vice versa – remains unchanged. This picture is well captured by Fei Xiaotong (1992, p. 68) who points out that Chinese societies have a structure that he calls *chaxugeju* (the differential mode of association):

> like the circles that appear on the surface of a lake when a rock is thrown into it. Everyone stands at the center of the circles produced by his or her own social influence. Everyone's circles are interrelated. One touches different circles at different times and places.
>
> (Fei, 1992, pp. 62–63)

In other words, Chinese societies are generally characterized by egocentrism and organized by *chaxugeju*; everyone produces a series of concentric circles of social relations with the self at the centre. The farther away the circle is from the centre, the more distant and less significant the social relation is to the self. As Fei (1992, p. 65) summarizes:

> Social relationships in China possess a self-centered quality. Like the ripples formed from a stone thrown in a lake, each circle spreading out from the center becomes more distant and at the same time more insignificant.

Members of the first inner circle are related to the *jiazhang* through being a member of the same *fang/jia-zu* with the *jiazhang*. Since each of the life of the *fang/jia-zu* members is in fact an extension of the *jiazhang*'s life, the *fang/jia-zu* members must logically follow the decisions of the *jiazhang* because the former, as different embodiments of the *jiazhang*'s life, just implement the decisions *on behalf of* the latter.

The membership of *jia* for non-*fang/jia-zu* people, as mentioned earlier, is established through their *personal* relationship with the *jiazhang*. Daughters and sisters, for example, acquire their *jia* membership by being the daughters and sisters of the *jiazhang*. People of the third inner circle become a member of the *jia* by being the *jiazhang*'s *tongxue* or *tongxiang*. In short, it is the personal relationship with the *jiazhang* that gives non-*fang/jia-zu* people *jia* membership.

We have to point out immediately that the *jiazhang* in the Chinese *jia* tends to extend the same kinship logic to non-*fang/jia-zu* members. He sees non-*fang/jia-zu* members as the extension of his *qi*; he demands absolute loyalty and full submission from them; and he continuously evaluates their performance by the extent of loyalty and submission they display to him. In return, the *jiazhang* offers them financial security and protection. As we have mentioned earlier, the financial management of *jia* is such that every *jia* member is allocated money for their daily use and, more importantly, those members who need financial help will be taken care of by the *jia*'s common budget.

One distinctive property of the relations between the *jiazhang* and non-*fang/jia-zu* members is that the relations are potentially unstable because they are not the 'real' kin. The relations are not only continuously vulnerable to events but also ever subject to negotiation, which requires continuous confirmation and validation by both the *jiazhang* and non-*fang/jia-zu* members through the exchange of *li* (ritual propriety). The content of *li* can be various depending on contexts; it, for example, can be but is not limited to being a gift. One major *li* exchanged between the *jiazhang* and non-*fang/jia-zu* members of a *jia* is the exchange of care and loyalty. The *jiazhang* is required to take complete care of non-*fang/jia-zu* members of his *jia*, while the latter must show absolute loyalty and full submission to the *jiazhang*. To make the matter more complicated, some non-*fang/jia-zu* members work to move into a closer circle by strategizing their interaction with the *jiazhang* through showing more loyalty and submission to him, that is, through the presentation of self. In other words, the position of non-*fang/jiz-zu* members in a *jiazhang*'s *chaxugeju* is not fixed but subject to change. In fact, we can always find empirical cases in which servants or friends are included in the first inner circle.

Fong's management style

At the beginning of Chapter 1, we highlighted the fact that Fong's room was located at the end of the office area on the second floor of the head office. Occupying the second largest single room in the office (the largest one was, not without sense, the chairman's room), one could say that this arrangement underlined the important status of Fong as the founder and let him 'oversee' the workforce. But one might, alternatively, interpret it as a sign of his isolation, if not banishment, from the power centre of the company. The fall of Fong,[5] as seen in the eyes of many *lou san zi* (literally, old servants, usually used to describe long-serving employees in a company), was a miserable scene because Fong had long been, after all, the only centre of the company and the employees. Although Fong's company was incorporated as early as 1971 and listed on the Hong Kong Exchange in 1987, it was organized and governed in a way more like a *bong paai* (roughly translated as Chinese gang) set up in pursuit of business than a modern corporation.

The *bong paai* metaphor is used here to highlight one important feature that characterizes Fong's company: FBL is organized around personal relationships maintained by loyalty and dependence. As the founder and chief of a *bong paai* company, Fong was the unchallengeable centre in the sense that the *bong paai* company was an embodiment of his will – he was basically the sole decision-maker and the supreme arbitrator. It is in this sense that Fong's relationship to FBL is akin to a Maori chief's to his people who, as Johansen (1954, p. 180), cited in Sahlins (1985, p. 35), described, "'lives the life of a whole tribe,'" in that "he stands in a certain relation to neighbouring tribes and kinship groups," and "he gathers the relationship to other tribes in his person"'. Under Fong were a couple of key right-hand men who were trusted by the chief and had direct access to him. These men, in turn, had their own circles of followers/subordinates. The farther away one was from Fong, that is, the centre, the less power one had in the *bong paai* company, since the power was bestowed upon and disseminated from Fong, the chief. Fong's position was like the ruler in traditional Chinese society – he was like 'the North Star, which makes all the other stars surround it' (Fei, 1992, pp. 67–68). The major function of the employees was to follow the will and serve the need of the 'North Star' and the only way to enhance one's influence was to establish a close relationship with the 'North Star' to move towards the centre of his circle. As a result, Fong is like a king of greater Fujian states who

> is the condition of the possibility of community . . . no one [in the community] can stir abroad in the morning, no community life or work appears, until the sacred drink of kava is offered to the king or 'human-god' (*kalou tamata*): every morning, the king recreates the world.
>
> (Lester, 1941–1942, pp. 113–114; Sayes, 1982, cited in Sahlins, 1985, p. 36)

The relations between Fong and his followers

One effective way to become close to Fong was to demonstrate one's loyalty to him, which is also to say that one has to demonstrate that he or she always acted in Fong's interests. This, however, does not mean that employees could not have constructive objections or discretions. As long as their intention was to advance Fong's interests, they would often be given a free hand to deal with matters independently. The crucial point is that they had to demonstrate that they always put Fong's interest above those of others, including themselves, especially when there were conflicts of interest. Loyalty in the *bong paai* company therefore is the sacrifice of oneself for the sake of the founder-chief. Similar to Chinese religions, the more offerings and sacrifices one is willing to offer to one's God, the more pleasant the God will be and the more blessings one will receive from the God. Indeed, Fong was the God in FBL.

Followers who demonstrated their loyalty and faith to the founder-chief would, in turn, be rewarded. Fong compensated his followers not just with immediate and practical monetary reward but, more fundamentally, a sense of security and superiority. The *bong paai* company was an organization established specifically for the purposes of business and the pursuit of profits. The founder-chief, having assembled the followers, had to take up the responsibility to ensure that everyone would get a share from the fruits. Recall Fong repeatedly emphasized that his major concern was to guarantee the livelihood of the employees. The authority and supreme power of the founder-chief were primarily derived from his promise and actual competence for providing the means of living to the employees. The founder-chief would reward the most loyal followers not only with the largest share of the profit but also the biggest guarantee of their livelihood. The closer one moved towards the centre, the more attention and security one could get from the founder-chief. When there were limited resources, the founder-chief would *first* take care of the welfare of the followers in the closest circle. The founder-chief also did not intend to hide his favouritism and the hierarchy based on it – every sensible follower would be able to recognize, unmistakably, who were the closest men to the chief. Those who were far away from the centre would then approach and attempt to cultivate a good relationship with those in the inner circles in the hope of shortening the distance between themselves and the chief. This created a sense of superiority among the followers in the closest circle as they had profound influence in the *bong paai* company. But one should note that they did not actually own or share the power with the founder-chief, they just *borrowed* the power from him to exercise authority over others. The founder-chief remained, always, the one and only ruler in the *bong paai* company.

The *bong paai* company was maintained through the mutual dependence between the founder-chief and the followers. The founder-chief had to take care of the welfare of the community of followers, to provide them jobs and opportunities to earn more money. The followers depended on the founder-chief to provide them a secure life and social status in the company, which was sustained foremost by the guarantee of jobs, monetary reward, and power in the company. The extent of dependence experienced by the followers became higher as they got closer to the centre since the founder-chief was willing to increase his commitment to take care of the welfare of his closest men. The social relations in a Chinese family business very often extend beyond the work sphere. The cost for the followers to leave the founder-chief, who had created a comfort-zone for them, would become much higher if they were close to the founder-chief and worked in the *bong paai* company for a long time.

Lou san zi

Over the long course of serving their companies, many followers become *lou san zi*. *Lou san zi* or long-serving employees usually enjoy a special status in Chinese family businesses. The privilege is not simply derived from their seniority, experience or capability, but more fundamentally, from their manifested loyalty. The long service of *lou san zi* itself represents their loyalty to the *bong paai* company and, of course, to the founder-chief. *Lou san zi* might not be the smartest or the most competent employees, but they are, at least from the perspective of the founder-chief, the most trustworthy followers. *Lou san zi* are thus highly respected as they have each cultivated a long-term relationship with the founder-chief.

In Chinese family businesses, *lou san zi* are regarded as the elders or seniors in the founder-chief's *jia* as if they are the 'real' kin. In fact, the fictive 'kinship' principle in the business context can be reflected in the way employees are addressed in the company. The seniors are usually addressed in kinship terms by others as *suk* (uncle), *go* (elder brother) for males and *ze* (elder sister) for females, whereas juniors are referred to as *zai* (son) for males and *mui* (younger sister) or *neoi* (daughter) for females. The addresses, of course, are not fixed but positional in that they change according to the relationship between the individuals. For instance, current employees would address Chan Keung, Fong's first apprentice, as 'Keung *go*'. Even the heir of the company, Jackson Fong, had to respect Keung and address him as *go*; but to Fong, Keung was 'Keung *zai*'. The address used for Reuben Cheung, another *lou san zi*, also transformed from 'Yu *zai*' to 'Yu *go*' and finally to 'Yu *suk*', reflecting the elevation of his seniority in the company.

In the *bong paai* company, the social relations are all personal. The employee does not interact with people as 'Managers', 'Regional Heads' or 'Executives'; instead he deals with *specific* persons. In the *bong paai* company, the formal job titles and functions are not very relevant, what matters are the specific kinds of relationship one has established with others and ultimately with the founder-chief. The employees do not really work for the company but for the founder-chief himself. The loyalty to the founder-chief is personal, specific, and non-transferable (with the exception of the designated heir to fulfil the wish of the founder-chief). When a specific person is gone, the person replacing him to take up the same post usually will not be able to inherit his social relationships or his status in the *bong paai* company. The *bong paai* company is organized by specific social relations rather than a stand-alone organizational chart which composes faceless individuals. This explains why in Chinese family businesses, *lou san zi* do not always behave humbly in front of professional managers who are new to the company. In the eyes of *lou san zi*, the newcomers, despite their formal job titles and positions, are simply inferior to them in terms of the actual influence and status in the company.

Jan cing mei *management regime*

The '*bong paai* company' and 'founder-chief', we have to emphasize, are metaphors to help conceptualize the nature and organization of traditional Chinese family businesses. We, however, do not mean that every Chinese family business is like *a bong paai* company and the owner is necessarily like a founder-chief. Our major purpose is to illustrate that Chinese family firms are primarily organized and governed by a web of *specific* social relations, which is maintained by personal loyalty and mutual dependence, and with the owner at the centre. The owner is like the sun in the solar system with the other planets and objects orbiting it. The social relations are specific in the sense that they work in this system with the specific owner at the centre.

Specific social relations – which play a central role in the Chinese family business – are maintained by *jan cing mei*. But what does *jan cing mei* mean in a corporate context? Why did so many employees of FBL emphasize that they felt attached to the company because they thought that the company and the boss had *jan cing mei*? When we say that FBL has *jan cing mei*, we mean that a person is treated by Fong and his company as a *specific* person who cannot be reduced to any abstract category such as 'employee', which is also to say that to enjoy the sense of *jan cing mei* in FBL means to enjoy the sense of being treated as a specific person instead of just a faceless machine which has no agency and is made only to perform a certain task. The *jan cing mei* management regime is therefore a system which confirms, emphasizes, and even celebrates the *specificity* of a person. Of course, the specificity of a person in FBL is defined by his or her specific relation with Fong. The *jan cing mei* management of FBL was manifested in three major ways: ignorance of the organizational chart, autonomy and agency, and holistic relations.

Ignorance of the organizational chart

First, the organizational chart that specifies job differentiation, job demarcation, and job assignments was always ignored in the FBL context. Fong did not follow any organizational chart at all; he had in his mind a list of people whom he would summon on certain specific occasions. His choice was not determined by the job position the employees held, but by their relationships with him. Fong, for example, would ask the Director of Product Development to help him supervise the renovation of the flagship retail store and to make sure everything would be fine or ask the Director of Marketing to help him conduct research on his private investment. From Fong's perspective, he could mobilize anybody to accomplish tasks beyond his formal job duties at any time. Fong expected that the employees were there to help solve problems for *him* – whatever these problems were – instead of just performing a set of prescribed tasks. The golden principle here was not to put 'a right man in the right place' (Aoki, 1988, p. 12) but to get things done by a specific person who is assigned and entrusted by Fong to do the work.

This expectation also extended to other supervisor/subordinate relations in the company. One's actual job duties were not defined or circumscribed by formal titles and job descriptions, but by the interest of the boss/supervisors. To be a good employee at FBL meant not to perform *professionally* according to his or her position in the company but to perform *specifically* in the interest of one's supervisors, that is, to help them solve problems. Stanley Lee, who joined the company in the 2010s as a new director, explained how he was confused by the vague boundaries of work and the opaque relations:

> I have never worked in a Chinese family firm before. At the beginning, I was quite confused. I didn't know whom I should approach to get things done. When something went wrong, I asked the person in charge. A would say that it's not his decision. It's B's. I didn't understand why B would be involved

in it since that's not B's job duties. I'd then ask B and B would say that C, his supervisor, asked him to take care of this. C would defend himself saying that it's the order from above [Fong]. On other occasions, I found that my title alone had no authority. Some people simply did not 'give face' to me despite my supposedly higher position.

In the setting of FBL, where the chain of commands was not always followed, the actual power and social status of an individual in the company was not primarily determined by the formal job title/position but by his or her human relations, especially the good relations with *lou san zi* or Fong. Seniority, experience, and interpersonal skills rather than formal professional and education qualifications were sometimes even more relevant to the ordering of one's position in the company.

The fact that the specification of job assignments by the organizational chart was always ignored, however, created flexibility for the employees to take up different tasks in the company. It was not unusual for employees to be transferred to a new field or to take up new job assignments. Reuben was a typical example. Reuben joined FBL in the mid-1970s. At the beginning, he was assigned to work in the Billing Department. Then, he was asked to become a *hang gaai* (salesman). In the 1980s, Fong asked him to take charge of the operation of the retail branches and product development. He also represented the company to take part in many industry-related events. As one of Fong's key right-hand men, Reuben's actual job duties and functions were far beyond what his formal title, 'Director of Group Product Planning and Trading', prescribed.

The flexible job assignments also mean that the employees had relatively more chances to be transferred, if not promoted, to positions that they otherwise could hardly 'reach' in a formal setting. In fact, many employees told us that one of the best things about FBL was that the company was very willing to invest in the development of the employees. We have to hastily add that the 'development' was not just limited to formal training; it was also about the possibility for the employees to take up new responsibilities and to develop different expertise. The example of Natalie Wong, Senior Manager of Merchandising and Gem Supply, was very illustrative. Natalie joined FBL in the late 1970s when she was only 16 years old. She started as a salesgirl in the showroom and was later transferred to work in the retail section. She was subsequently promoted to manager of a retail branch and later the Regional Manager. In the 1990s, Jackson, Fong's son and the heir to the company, asked Natalie if she could leave the 'front line' and work in the head office instead. She recounted:

Jackson approached me and said that he would really like me to help him. In fact, I always enjoyed working in the front line as I could interact with my colleagues. We were like a big family with the same goal. I was happy to work in the stores. Jackson asked me to help him to design some new products. I told him that I was hesitant to take up this new challenge because I might not have the talent relevant to the new post. He told me not to worry because he trusted me. He even recruited coaches to teach me how to use a computer. Since then, I have been involved in the jewellery design work. I have a strong interest in it. I paid a lot of attention to the jewellery products when I was in the front line. After all, I had to understand the features of the products so that I could promote them to my clients. I also love reading fashion magazines. I love beautiful things [laughter]. I am very grateful that my boss gave me the chance to try something new, despite the fact that I didn't receive any formal training in this field [jewellery design] before.

Natalie showed us the visual images of her own designs and explained her ideas behind each of them. The jewellery products designed by Natalie bore special product codes signifying the identity of the designer. Natalie stressed that she just felt extremely flattered by the trust and recognition of the bosses (referring to both Fong and Jackson). The examples of Reuben and Natalie illustrated that the job mobility within the company was relatively high. The employees would not be confined to a particular position or a particular path of promotion due to the rigid job demarcation based on formal qualifications and organizational structure. They could break the glass ceiling if they succeeded in establishing trust with the boss through demonstrating their loyalty. In this respect, to say that the management of FBL had *jan cing mei* is to say that it provided employees the *possibilities* to take up different tasks in the company regardless of their job titles, positions, and relevant experience or educational background. In FBL's workplace, the employees were not simply a part of the machine that could just be set in a specific position but a mobile work force that could be deployed to tackle different challenges. To enjoy or to cope with the mobility, the employees, in turn, had to possess strong generic skills which enabled them to deal with unprecedented occasions.

Autonomy and agency

The second feature of the *jan cing mei* regime of FBL was that it encouraged the agency of the individual employees. The employees were given the autonomy to solve problems without being restrained by formal job duties. A salesperson who had worked in an FBL retail store for five years explained to us the relationship between *jan cing mei* and autonomy:

W&C: What attracts you to stay here [FBL]?
INFORMANT: I think that people here in general have more *jan cing mei*. The colleagues are quite nice.
W&C: Can you further elaborate? We mean how about other jewellery companies? They don't have *jan cing mei*?
INFORMANT: I can't comment on others. But I did hear from my friends who worked in other [jewellery] companies. They were just like vending machines.
W&C: Vending machines? What do you mean?
INFORMANT: The hierarchy was very rigid. Everything had to go through the manager first. You couldn't just *zap sang* (literally means to improvise to cope with the contingency). Take an example. I am in charge of the showcases in

this area [pointing at the showcases in front of us]. If there is a customer who needs help in that area [pointing at the showcases at the back] and all my colleagues just happen to be preoccupied, I will just go over to offer help without hesitation. It's like you help cover your teammates in a ball game, right?

W&C: Yes, that makes sense. We will do the same too.

INFORMANT: But my friends told me that they were not allowed to do so. They just couldn't leave their assigned area/position without prior permission. If the same situation happens there, they will have to ask their supervisor first if they can go over to that area. Of course, they won't ask. The supervisor doesn't like them to be so 'active'. They are just expected to perform the assigned tasks. *Zap sang* is an ability to deal with contingency, but if you *zap sang* there, you will be perceived as a troublemaker. Aren't they just like vending machines?

The view of the interviewee largely echoed the comments made by a jewellery master we interviewed in another FBL retail store. At the time of the interview, the master had just joined the company for a couple of months. He had worked in another major local jewellery company for a long time. We were curious why he would choose to leave the original company. He explained the reason behind his decision:

The company [the company which he previously worked for] has changed. It has become so highly corporatized. They requested us [the masters] to work in the new plant in Shenzhen. I hated it as they just treated us like workers in the assembly line. I didn't have any autonomy. So, I just quit. I have been here [FBL] just for several months. I can't comment much since I haven't stayed here long enough. But so far, I feel good. At least I have more freedom and feel more respected as a human being.

Both the salesperson and the jewellery master we interviewed emphasized that working in FBL made them feel 'human'. The *jan cing mei* management regime of FBL allowed if not encouraged the employees to *zap sang*. The crucial point was that the employees in FBL were given the autonomy to improvise. They were not just like vending machines, as the salesperson we interviewed told us, who could only respond to specific orders in a regulated way and who were not expected to do something not prescribed in the 'manual'.

In fact, Fong appreciated one's ability to *zap sang*. He could not stand people who could only follow the written rules and show no flexibility in dealing with contingency. Fong himself believed that one of the factors contributing to his success was his own flexibility, the ability to follow and accommodate the changing trends and to bypass formal restraints to get things done. When commenting on the performance of Jackson, Fong said, 'He's hardworking. I won't deny that. But he is not *shingmuk* (smart) enough. He's not flexible, he just knows how to go by the book.' Consequently, the employees of FBL enjoyed a high degree of autonomy in the daily operation of the company.

The employees' autonomy was further encouraged by Fong's down-to-earth attitude: the result is more important than the process. As we illustrated in the previous chapters, Fong was a very practical entrepreneur, who was simply concerned about whether the employees could help him solve problems. He did not bother to intervene in the process, or to be exact, he generally had no interest in learning how things were done. At the same time, Fong was willing to delegate power to his employees, as he believed if he provided enough monetary reward to the employees, they would try their best to meet the targets. In Fong's mindset, incentives rather than rules regulate most effectively the behaviour of the employees.

The management of FBL, as a result, resembled the Japanese method of organizing work at the shop-floor level discussed in Masahiko Aoki's (1988) work. Aoki (1988) compares the ideal way of organizing work in typical Japanese firms and the traditional unionized American auto plants. As Aoki (1988, p. 10) summarizes:

> Whereas American industrialization has generated an exceptionally high degree of job differentiation and attached a high value to specialization, the Japanese work organization seems to rely more on the versatility of workers and flexibility in job demarcation. In the Japanese work organization, problem-solving tasks – such as coping with absenteeism, malfunctioning machines, and defective products – tend to be entrusted to a team of operating workers, whereas in the American organization they are entrusted to specialists. . . . In the American firm, coordination between different jobs as well as different shops has itself become the 'specialized' function of supervisors and managers, and has helped to make professional hierarchical control more sophisticated. In contrast, the Japanese firm seems to rely on a less hierarchical structure that facilitates coordination through horizontal flows of communication among peers and among shops (the well-publicized decision making based on consensus is but one such phenomenon).

That is to say, the American model is characterized by a high degree of job differentiation, clear job demarcation, rigid job assignments, and sophisticated professional hierarchical control. Workers were assigned to a specific position to perform specific tasks. They were expected to take care of those tasks *only*. That is why when an operating worker in the American plant spots a problem and even knows how to fix it, he is not expected to solve the problem immediately by himself. Instead, he is supposed to report the problem to the supervisor before any action can be taken. Interestingly, the worker himself or herself is also unwilling to fix it because 'doing so might have jeopardized the machinist's job security by making him appear redundant' (Aoki, 1988, p. 18). As Aoki (1988, p. 13) pointed out:

> Each operating worker is required to perform a specific task assigned by a supervisor, according to formal or customary rules, operating manuals, or a supervisor's directives. When something unexpected occurs . . . remedies

are usually sought, under the direction of the supervisor, by the appropriate specialists. . . . Operating workers are normally not responsible for coping with unexpected emergences, as is evident from a long-standing custom at the American factory that prohibits the worker from stopping the production line on his or her own initiative, even when an event takes place that makes it desirable.

The Japanese model, on the other hand, is characterized by simple job differentiation, ambiguous job demarcation, flexible job assignments, and less hierarchical control. Under the Japanese model, individual workers are expected to contribute to the work of the whole team, to cover the work of the team members and to actively spot and solve problems to enhance the performance of the team. It is not unusual to observe in the Japanese factory that '[w]hen a high number of defective products are found, the cause of and the solution to the problem are sought on the spot before calling in help from outside' (Aoki, 1988, p. 14). In the Japanese model, developments of multiple skills and a cooperative attitude are prioritized while specialized skills and individual responsibility are underlined in the American model.

Resembling the Japanese model, the *jan cing mei* management regime of FBL gave the employees an intense sense of job satisfaction through providing them autonomy as well as imposing on them holistic responsibility at the same time. The employees would have a feeling that they were respected because their own agency, judgment, and ability were 'trusted' by the employer as they enjoyed the freedom to *zap sang* without being restrained strictly by formal organizational hierarchy or regulations.

Fong's *jan cing mei* management, however, is different from the Japanese model in one fundamental aspect: while the Japanese model usually occurs in a teamwork framework which is still a part of the overall organizational chart and therefore still constrained by the organizational structure, the previously mentioned practices of *jan cing mei* management are dependent on Fong's idiosyncratic if not totally arbitrary decisions. Fong's *jan cing mei* management can be more or less flexible than its counterparts in Japan; outcomes would be totally contingent on Fong's mood.

Holistic relations

There is one more thing which made the employees of FBL feel that the company had *jan cing mei*: a *holistic* relationship between the employer and the employee. What we mean here is that the relationship between the employer and the employee was not simply a work-specific relation, the boundary of which ended at the entrance/exit of the workplace. A holistic relation is not just an extension of a 'work-ship' to a 'friendship', in which colleagues become personal friends, either. A holistic relationship is a relationship which blurs the public and the private, integrating different categories of relationships – employee–employer, comrades, friend, family – into one, which is maintained through exchanges of *li*.

In other words, a holistic person is also a concrete as well as a real person who maintains holistic relations with other similar concrete and real people.

When individual employees established relations in the company with their colleagues, supervisors, and even the boss, they would be treated like a *jia* member in that their public (work) as well as private (personal) life would be taken care of. Keung, for instance, recalled how Fong helped him with his wedding:

> It was back in the 1970s. I wanted to get married, but I didn't have money. You know, weddings are always costly. I remember very clearly that Mr. Fong just simply lent me $3,000 without saying a word.[6] I really respect him as a boss and as an elder brother. He is willing to help you when you're in trouble. He never turns a blind eye.

Fong was very familiar with the family situation of his employees (of course limited to those who were close to him). He could, without any difficulty, recount their life stories. Fong did not mind sharing his private moments with his employees either. Whenever he was on a business trip in China, according to Fong, he would first take his staff to a karaoke box or massage parlour to relax and have fun together. We noticed that many employees, at least among the *lou san zi*, also maintained off-work relations. They knew about the personal lives of their colleagues. They could describe to you the situation of the sons and daughters, the parents and the spouses of their colleagues. The different families might hang out together outside the workplace. As we mentioned in Chapter 6, the managers in the retail stores usually called their subordinates as *zai* (son) and *neoi* (daughter). This was not simply a gesture to enhance intimacy. Very often, the manager did take care of the subordinates as if they were really his/her own sons and daughters. They would try to understand their personal background, listen to their personal problems and try to offer guidance.

The crucial point here is not just about the people getting close to each other to become friends or even 'family members', but more about the integration of the public and personal spheres. It would be socially acceptable, and in fact desirable, for your boss/supervisor/colleague/subordinate to cross the work boundary to show interest and get involved in your personal sphere and life. Within FBL, the social relationships must be holistic by nature, otherwise they would simply fail to be qualified as proper relationships. No clear roles and responsibilities can be defined in these holistic relations as one can be the colleague, the family member, the friend, the benefactor, and the beneficiary at the same time. The holistic relationship is not governed simply by the relational position, but by the endless chain of reciprocal exchanges of *li*. To maintain the relationship, both sides are expected to give and return *li* in both the private and public spheres. The content of *li* is contextually dependent; it might include the demonstration of kindness, such as offering you a slice of cake; the demonstration of care of your friends and relatives, such as offering a red packet to your son and daughter; the demonstration of favouritism, such as giving you convenience at work; the demonstration of trust, such as giving you some insiders' information and so on. We can see that the content of *li* is never confined to gift-giving only. In fact, the *content* of *li* is not important, what matters is the *exchange* of *li*. *Jan cing* thus refers to the proper way *li* is recipro-cally exchanged whereby the holistic relationship among employees and between the founder-chief, *lou san zi*, and employees is maintained and reinforced. The proper reciprocal exchange of *li*, in turn, is the way to maintain *jan cing*.

To say that the relationship is holistic further implies that one cannot distin-guish clearly the means and ends of maintaining the relationship. Wong and Yau (forthcoming) point out that it is methodologically difficult, if not impossible, to distinguish whether the creation and maintenance of social relationships in Chi-nese society is motivated by *jan cing* or practical calculation of benefits. They contend that it is a mixture of both, which, they argue, is culturally distinctive because the interpersonal relationships in Chinese societies tend to be holistic. Friendship, for example, is defined by both instrumentality and expressivity. The ontological nature of friendship prescribes that friends are not only the ones from whom Chinese seek emotional support; they are also the ones who are expected to offer their assistance when Chinese need practical help. That is to say, Chinese people would turn to 'close,' rather than so-called 'instrumental' or 'ordinary' friends for practical (especially financial) help, because the 'closeness' of friend-ship is *the* base for asking for such practical help.

The same can be observed in the FBL context. While no one would fail to recognize that Fong ultimately was the boss and employer, Fong did not simply interact with the employees only as a boss/employer. Certainly, the larger-than-work relationship, in part, reflected Fong's effort to motivate the employees, to gain their trust, and to create a loyal army of workers. While it is true that Fong's actions were motivated by some very practical and strategic reasons, one cannot fully explain or understand Fong's behaviours from a purely utilitarian perspec-tive. In addition to lending Keung $3,000 for his wedding, Fong also allowed the employees to borrow money from the company in the 1980s to settle the down payments for their houses as Fong wanted to help his employees to have a 'settled' life as soon as possible. Recall that Fong repeatedly emphasized that he thought he had a responsibility to take care of the welfare of the employees. The 'welfare' here did not simply refer to the salary; as a boss, Fong believed that he had the responsibility to help his employees to have a better life. The motivation might be practical, but it is equally normative and thus cultural.

Once the holistic relationship is established, it becomes extremely difficult to be cut off from the relationship completely. Many employees thought that Fong had *jan cing mei* because he did not tend to fire people, especially those who had worked for him for a long time. Even though some *lou san zi* might appear redundant, in the eyes of the newly joined employees, due to their relatively low productivity, Fong still strived to reserve a place for them to make sure that they could work until they no longer wanted to. A notable example is the case of Fun.[7] Fun had been serving as a cleaning lady in FBL for three decades. She was forced to retire by the Human Resources Department when she turned 70. Although Fong no longer had any real power in the company, he still tried hard to fight for Fun's case. Fong complained to us:

She has been working here for such a long time. Three decades, man. She can still work, and she wants to work. She comes from a very miserable family; she needs the money. Why don't they let her work? Is it so hard to be flexible? She has worked for us for so long. We just ask her to go now, that's cruel, showing no *jan cing mei* at all.

Given Fong's down-to-earth attitude, he should have fired the employees immediately when they became less productive. He, however, tried to tolerate and protect those who had worked for him for a long time. Once he had established a holistic relationship with his employees, he did not simply evaluate them and relate to them only in the workplace context. The personal and emotional factors also weighted heavily. Kate Tse, the Regional Branch Manager, told us how Fong became extremely emotional when he had to fire a few employees due to the debt crisis. 'He actually cried. He felt so guilty that he had to fire people. He was so worried that they couldn't find another job quickly. Did you ever meet such a boss who cares about the employees so much?' Kate recalled.

Of course, the holistic relationship is fundamentally based on the work relationship. Fong would not really treasure employees who were not useful at all or who did not devote themselves to the company. The key point here is that one can hardly calculate precisely the costs and benefits in such holistic relationships. Both sides are forever indebted to each other. They can only keep exchanging *li*, in both public and private spheres, and be bound to each other as a form of practical expediency as well as an inescapable emotional attachment.

Conclusion

The idea of this chapter is basically very simple. Our core argument is that in order to understand Chinese family firms, we have to understand Chinese families first. The Chinese family includes the functional (*jia*) and genealogical (*fang/jia-zu*) aspects from which we can derive two major Chinese family ethics. The first is the overriding importance attached to the continuity of the *fang/jia-zu* line. Second, the continuity of the *fang/jia-zu* line is more important than the continuity of any functional kin group such as *jia*. We further argued that *jia* is the organizational vehicle whereby the *jiazhang* of *fang/jia-zu* managed the domestic life of his *jia* including family business.

In managing the family business, the *jiazhang* tended to apply the kinship logic to his personal relations with non-*fang/jia-zu* members. The key term governing the interpersonal relations in a Chinese family business is *jan cing*. We have demonstrated how Fong's management was characterized by *jan cing*. We, of course, do not attempt to argue that the *jan cing mei* management regime of FBL represents all the cases of Chinese family businesses for each Chinese family business have their own peculiarities. The features of FBL management, however, are not uncommon in the Chinese family business context. Under the *jan cing mei* management regime, which focuses on the specific social relations instead of the formal organizational structure, we find (1) a general ignorance of the organizational chart; (2) autonomy and agency of individual workers; and (3) holistic relations between employee and employer as well as among employees themselves. We argue that the *jan cing mei* management regime tends to offer the employees a sense of 'humanity', from which they can derive a higher sense of job satisfaction.

All of these are not novel, nor are they our own discoveries as many management scientists have already identified these characteristics of Chinese management in their research (Redding, 1990). The insight generated from this chapter is that these characteristics of Chinese management cannot be attributed to the abstract, general Confucianism. As we demonstrated, these characteristics are closely related to the concrete features of the Chinese family.

But why did the employees of FBL feel that they were treated as 'humans' under the *jan cing mei* management regime? Why did they think that the FBL management has *jan cing mei*? Or what *jan cing mei* means to them? The answer lies in the way individual employees were treated in the company. As we have demonstrated, the specificity of a staff member in FBL is not defined primarily by their formal job titles and positions but by their own characters and specific sets of social relations developed in the company, which is also to say that he or she is a concrete person. As Sartre (1963) effectively argued, a concrete person who is not reduced to any abstract concept such as 'employee', 'manager', or 'supervisor' is a real person. Within FBL, an employee is not only remembered as a 'junior sales' or a 'manager' but also as a *real* person.

A real person is also one with agency. Employees cannot be reduced to fixed parts of a machine, which can only operate according to the guidelines and are locked into a fixed hierarchical position; instead they have their own perception of, affection towards, and action towards, the problems. They are given the autonomy and freedom to respond to the problems in their own specific ways. Without a clear demarcation of private/public realms, the employees are also perceived as holistic individuals who are specific and thus real. They are not forced to become purely passive instruments, the utility of which is measured only by their performance at work.

All of this speaks to the fact that under the *jan cing mei* management regime, employees of FBL are given more room for free-form creativity and improvisation because the employees are comparatively less subject to rules, regulations, and fixed procedures than people working in a bureaucracy. The contrast between the *jan cing mei* management regime of FBL and a bureaucracy is point-to-point similar to the difference between 'play' and 'game' observed by Graeber (2015). Contrasting 'play' with 'game', Graeber (2015) argues that game simply denotes rules. Games are clearly confined in time and space, and thereby cut off from *everyday life*, which is also to say that any place, person, action that falls outside the game is peripheral. Game also has rules, which define precisely what players can and cannot do; and more importantly what players must do to win the game. In other words, game is *inhuman* because it does not exist in everyday life; it is also *constraining* because it is always rule-governed. Any bureaucratic environment is likewise limited in terms of time and space and cut off from normal life. Within this temporal and spatial limit, certain people are involved and given certain roles. There are rules which define precisely what people therein can and cannot do in that specific limit. Not unlike game, there are also clear ideas of the rewards, of what to do to extract the greatest benefits from it (Graeber, 2015, p. 190). In short, games are rule-governed which serves to sweep away all these uncertainties and ambiguities. The game-like bureaucracy, however, suggests that the life inside a bureaucracy, not unlike playing games, is inhuman.

Play, according to Graeber (2015), implies free-form creativity as it allows and enshrines freedom. Although the arbitrariness of play suggests uncertainty, ambiguity, and even threat or destructiveness because we do not know where it leads, play is real and human, but this exactly is why the employees working under the *jan cing mei* management regime of FBL felt that they were treated as humans not as parts of a big machine, which reminds us of the humanistic management recently promoted by some management scholars and practitioners in the West (Acevedo, 2012; von Kimakowitz et al., 2010; Whetstone, 2002, 2003).

Fong's *jan cing mei* management, governed by social relations instead of formal regulations, no doubt creates an intense sense of attachment, if not identification, with the company among the employees. In the early entrepreneurial process, this management style helps create a flexible, creative, efficient, loyal, as well as largely result-oriented work force. While the success of Fong's entrepreneurial pursuit, as we have already discussed in the previous chapters, is the result of the mediation between many factors including the broader development of the post-war Hong Kong economy, Fong's own characteristics, and his management style that undoubtedly helped him draw, retain, and motivate a large pool of loyal workers who were devoted to driving the development of the company.

The *jan cing mei* management, however, was not without problems. The major problem of FBL is that its fate is just too closely associated with Fong, the founder-chief. All the power is in Fong's hands and all the social relations are centred upon him. The result is that there is no effective governance in the company. The employees are, ultimately, accountable only to Fong, not to their assigned job duties or to FBL as a public company. Although FBL became a public company as early as 1987, the management of the company still resembled that of a *bong paai* company. Fong remained the unchallenged supreme leader of the company who enjoyed absolute power in the company. The company was not subjected to the strict control and monitoring of the Board of Directors nor the shareholders because Fong remained the absolute largest shareholder of the company until he went bankrupt. More importantly, the mentality of Fong did not change at all. He still regarded the company as his *own jia*; he was ignorant of risk management, not to mention procedural regulations, and was concerned only about the end results; and he was not interested in governance and only fixated on generating more profits. Despite the fact that FBL had become a publicly listed company, Fong still acted like the founder-chief of his *bong paai* company.

As FBL grew in scale, the problem became more salient and fatal. On the one hand, the ever-enlarging organization became a confusing labyrinth of complex social relations. The lack of formal organizational structure increasingly jeopardized the efficiency of the operation. On the other hand, Fong found it increasingly difficult to get to know the actual situation of the ever-enlarging empire. He had to rely heavily on subordinates to rule over the vast territory. FBL in fact gradually lost its flexibility due to the rapid expansion, but the decision-making process remained the same – it remained spontaneous, personal, and authoritarian by nature. The failure of FBL to transform itself into a modern corporation paved the road for its own demise. As we shall show in Chapter 8, since the late 1990s, these problems had gradually become more serious and eventually turned into a series of crises, which further led to the downfall of Fong and the near collapse of his own jewellery empire.

Notes

1 Some paragraphs included in this section are drawn, in amended and abridged form, from the article entitled 'What is Chinese Kinship and What is Not?' written by Wong (2017).
2 There are variations in the transliteration of this native Chinese term *qi*. We use the Standard Chinese pinyin here. Scholars whom we quote in this chapter such as Chen (1986), Chun (1985), and Shiga (1967, 1978) used another pinyin system and the term becomes *ch'i*. We will follow their transliteration of the term when we quote them. However, in our own discussion, we will use the term *qi*.
3 Refer to the previous note. *Ch'i* here is the same as *qi*.
4 *Kuo-fang* is defined by Chen (1986, p. 174) as 'a genealogical re-arrangement of an agnate's *fang* filiation within the same *chia-tsu* [*jia-zu*]' (underline original).
5 The detail of Fong's fall will be discussed in Chapter 8.
6 The monthly salary of a schoolteacher was around $1,000 in the 1970s.
7 We do not know Fun's full name as she was just addressed as Fun *ze* in the company.

8 The crises

In Chapter 6, we have illustrated how Fong developed the retail business of FBL and transformed the company into one of the largest local jewellery retailers in the early 1990s. Since 1998, the Fong family and FBL, however, have gone through a series of crises. First, the company faced a serious financial crisis that endangered Fong's control over his company. Then, Fong was ordered to declare bankruptcy. Later, the senior management of FBL including Fong and his son, Jackson, were arrested, prosecuted, and sentenced to prison. Within a decade, FBL had gone from a reputable brand into a failing company on the brink of collapse.

In this chapter, we shall examine the events leading to the crises and explain the reasons for the outbreak of the crises in order to provide a historical background against which the professionalization of FBL initiated by Jackson's wife, Emma, after she took over the management of the company should be understood. Second, we aim to explain how the crises of FBL as a Chinese family firm are fundamentally related to the logic of the Chinese family as understood by Fong and his son. We shall demonstrate how the failure of the company was related to Fong's obsession with real estate, the formation of the speculative culture in Hong Kong, the cultural meaning of landed property in Chinese societies, and more fundamentally, the problems resulting from Fong's running of FBL as his own *jia* and his '*jan cing mei* management' regime. The problems include the unrestrained *jiazhang* and the abuse of discretionary power by some major members of the company's senior management team. At the end of this chapter, we argue that the Chinese family ethic that gives priority to the interests of *fang/jia-zu* rather than those of *jia* is the fundamental cultural reason for most of the problems associated with the operation of FBL in particular, and of Chinese family businesses in general.

The crises

The economy of Hong Kong went through a period of frenzied speculation in the 1990s. The real estate market and the stock market rose remarkably in 1991. The government had to introduce regulatory measures in 1994 to alleviate the overheated real estate market (Lee, 1999, p. 29). Housing prices fell slightly after the measures were introduced, but soon rose again and reached a peak in 1997 (Lee,

1999, p. 64). Speculating on real estate and the stock market became an important part of daily life for the Hong Kong people, who expected that the prices would just keep rising.

Fong was no exception. Under his chairmanship, FBL actively joined the game of scrambling for real estate deals one after another. The company purchased a 17-storey commercial building in Tsim Sha Tsui at a price of $500 million in May 1997, which caught media attention. However, following the outbreak of the Asian financial crisis, the stock market and real estate market in Hong Kong experienced a great crash in late 1997. Property prices plummeted by 50 per cent and only became relatively stable again from early 1999 (Lee, 1999, p. 199). The unexpected property market crash brought about a widespread negative equity disaster in the city.[1]

FBL's financial crisis

FBL also became heavily indebted due to the crash. The company had to sell off its properties hastily to reduce its debt burden between 1998 and 1999. The company suffered great losses from the transactions as it was forced to sell the properties at a time when the property market had slumped. FBL also launched an unprecedented 'one billion diamond sales' campaign to increase its cash flow, selling its jewellery products at significantly discounted prices in May 1998. The campaign lasted for three months. As Fong recalled:

> We had to bargain away our products for cash to repay the debt. It's easy to convert gold into money, but it's not the case for jewellery and diamonds. Some products were sold nearly at cost prices. All we wanted was cash.

The unprecedented big sale campaign, however, failed to alleviate the financial predicament of the company. The financial situation of the company was indeed very dire.

To make the situation even worse, Fong personally also encountered a serious financial problem due to his own losses in the stock and real estate markets, which unavoidably had further financial impact on FBL as Fong was the controlling shareholder of the company. In September 1999, a European multinational invest-ment bank, JOI,[2] filed a petition for bankruptcy against Fong. Fong originally owned 49.7 per cent of the shares of FBL but he pledged all his shares to JOI to secure a loan facility of $150 million in July 1997. After Fong had failed to return the debt as requested, JOI decided to take legal action against Fong.

The impact of Fong's financial difficulties on the company was manifested in two major ways. The first was that Fong's own financial debt aggravated the finan-cial situation of FBL. For example, FBL entered an agreement with an investment fund which included a special term that the fund had the right to demand for the early redemption of the shares with a value of over $170 million if the controlling stake of the Fong family in FBL fell below 40 per cent. Since Fong might lose 49.7 per cent of the shares of FBL because he could not repay his loan with JOI,

FBL, according to the agreement, was obliged to redeem preferential shares from the fund. The early redemption of preferential shares would therefore aggravate the financial problems at FBL. By the end of the year of 1999, both Fong and his company were on the brink of bankruptcy.

Second, if Fong was finally forced to hand over his shares of FBL to JOI, Fong's own controlling position in FBL would be threatened, which might lead to a change of management at the company. Fong therefore made a series of arrangements to keep his shares. One month after JOI filed the petition for bankruptcy against Fong, Zebra, a consortium led by a former CEO of FBL, Tsang King Pang, purchased JOI's equity stake in FBL along with the rights and interests of the loan facility to Fong in October 1999.[3] Market insiders generally thought that Zebra was a white knight to help the Fong family. In January 2000, FBL announced that King Pang was appointed as Vice-chairman and Executive Director of the company. Surprisingly, Fong's son, Jackson, filed a lawsuit against King Pang and Zebra in April 2000 to ask for the return of the FBL shares as Jackson claimed that King Pang was only an agent holding the shares on his behalf. The two parties reached an agreement in the end. Jackson agreed to settle a debt of three million dollars in total to King Pang, and in return, King Pang gave back the shares along with the rights and interests of the loan facility to Icrop,[4] a company owned by Jackson.

According to a former senior employee at FBL, King Pang originally agreed to help the Fong family but later refused to return the shares, and that is why Jackson had to go to court to get back the shares. After Jackson got back the shares, he had replaced Fong as the controlling shareholder of the company since 2000. Since then, Fong had never been able to return to the Board even after his bankruptcy order was revoked in 2004. We shall get back to the feud between the father and the son in a moment.

Fong's bankruptcy and the unintended succession

Fong's loan, however, was not just with JOI. He told us in our interview that he bore in total around $200 million of debt to a dozen banks. Following the petition of JOI in September 1999, a local bank, one of Fong's creditors, also filed a similar petition in March 2000. When the local bank cancelled its petition after negotiating with Fong in July, another investment bank filed another lawsuit against Fong for his failure to repay a loan. Fong was eventually ordered bankrupt by the court on 25 September 2000. He owed creditors around $230 million in total. Fong was forced to step down as the chairman of FBL. He, however, remained as involved in the management of FBL as he did before. He was employed by the company as a consultant and he still kept his own secretary. When Jackson took over the leadership of FBL, the company was in such a dire financial situation that FBL only had funds to support its operations for four months.

Jackson therefore endeavoured to solve the debt problem of the company, consolidate the controlling stake of the Fong family in FBL, reform the company, and most importantly revamp FBL's brand image after taking up the chairmanship. In

2001, Jackson filed a case to prevent the Official Receiver's Office from redeeming Fong's shares in order to ensure that the shares of FBL would remain in the hands of the Fong family. In 2004, Jackson succeeded in attracting one of the world's largest diamond trading companies to invest in FBL. With the injection of new funds, FBL was able to redeem the $200 million loan from four creditors, thereby significantly reducing the total debt of the company.

In 2004, 22 days before the expiry of Fong's bankruptcy order, the Court ordered the revocation of Fong's bankruptcy record as he had reached an agreement with his creditors. Fong paid back $13.8 million to his creditors out of a total of $230 million. Fong became a 'free man' again. When Fong told us about the clearance of his bankruptcy order, he was still very emotional. He kept all the newspaper clippings and showed them to us:

> I was very happy, as if I had walked out from a black hole. You see, this [the revocation of his bankruptcy order] was covered in different newspapers. I don't understand why people keep saying that I was bankrupt! I had returned the money and the bankruptcy order was already revoked. I could have left the bankruptcy order as it was so that I didn't need to return any money to my creditors, but I still chose to pay back the creditors because I am a man of my word. If I were given another chance, I would not return the money!

In November that year, a debt restructuring proposal was passed in the annual shareholders' general meeting of FBL. The debt ratio of the company was reduced to 50 per cent (the ratio once reached 600 per cent). After the stock consolidation arrangement, the Fong family controlled 73.9 per cent of the total shares of the company. The controlling position of the Fong family would no longer be threatened, although the majority of FBL shares was owned by Jackson rather than by Fong. We can see that the transmission of Fong's FBL shares did not take place according to the *fang/jia-zu* principle which prescribes that the property of Fong's family be divided between his two sons, Jackson and Joseph. This is obviously due to the unusual situation of the company described earlier.

Arrest and prosecution[5]

It seemed that the Fong family and FBL had overcome the many difficulties of the previous years and were ready to start a new page. The Fong family and the company, however, were struck by another and a far more fatal crisis in 2005. In April, Fong, Jackson and an FBL employee were arrested by the Independent Commission Against Corruption (ICAC) over allegations of illegal commission, misappropriation of the company's funds, and tax evasion.[6] In the so-called 'Pearl Operation,' the officers of the ICAC raided the FBL headquarters and took away all relevant documents. The arrest sent shock waves through the jewellery and tourism industries and became headline news. In addition to the people associated with FBL, the ICAC also arrested several employees of a travel agency. They were suspected of receiving illegal commissions from

FBL to provide advantages to the company by bringing tourists to the FBL showrooms.

The employees of the travel agency were released two days later without charge, however. Eventually, the ICAC prosecuted five former and then incumbent employees of FBL including Fong and Jackson. The hearing of the case took place between August 2007 and March 2008. The judgement was passed in April 2008. All five defendants were convicted and sentenced to jail a month later. Fong's sentence was the lightest while Jackson's the heaviest.

Table 8.1 shows the list of defendants, their position in FBL at the time of prosecution, and the sentences they received. We are not going to go through every detail of the court case due to the limited space; instead, we aim to outline a general picture of what happened and to identify the major wrongdoings of the defendants. To simplify enormously, there were four major charges in the case in relation to: (1) bribery; (2) false accounting; (3) embezzlement, and (4) defrauding the Inland Revenue Department (IRD). Most of the charges (1, 2, and 4) were related to the invention and implementation of the illegal commission system concerning FBL's showroom business. In order to understand the case, we have to first understand the problems with the commission system of the FBL showrooms.

The James Bond Project

The story can actually be dated back to February 1996. At that time, the ICAC visited the FBL showrooms to search the offices and interview several FBL staff to investigate alleged illegal commission payments made to the employees of travel agencies. After the ICAC visit, the senior management of FBL immediately convened meetings to discuss the solution. As we have discussed in Chapter 5, FBL's showroom business depended on tour operators to arrange tours for visits and on the tour guides to convince the tourists to shop. In return, FBL paid them commissions for their service. The commission payment itself was not illegal; but the commission system of FBL was problematic because FBL failed to get receipts for payments of commission from the staff of the tour operators and freelance agents. More importantly, some payments were made to the employees of the tour operators and freelance agents without the consent or acknowledgement of their employers or their principal travel agents, which constituted acts of bribery.

Table 8.1 List of defendants in the FBL court case

	Name	Position in FBL at the time of prosecution	Sentences
D1	Fong Bou Lung	Founder, Former Chairman	3 years 3 months
D2	Jackson Fong	Chairman, Former Chief Executive Officer	5 years
D3	Mandy Wong	Former Finance Director	3 years 9 months
D4	Otto Schneider	Chief Executive Officer	3 years 9 months
D5	Terry Lai	General Manager (Showroom Division)	4 years 3 months

Since the showroom business faced fierce competition, if FBL stopped paying the problematic commissions, business would be severely affected. The senior management therefore came up with a scheme called the 'James Bond Project'. Under the scheme, FBL would enter an agreement with an overseas company which would help procure tourists for the FBL showroom. In return, FBL would pay the company for its service on a headcount basis. In reality, the overseas company was just a money transfer vehicle: it provided no real service to FBL. The payment sent by FBL to the company were channelled back to Hong Kong and distributed in cash to the staff of the showroom, who would then give the money to the employees of the tour operators.

For this purpose, the company then classified the commissions into two types namely 'Commission A' and 'Commission B'. 'Commission A' referred to those commission payments which had proper accounting documents while 'Commission B' were those payments paid secretly to the staff of the tour operators with no accounting record. To make the scheme possible, the company set up a separate computer system to cater to the Commission B paid to the overseas company. False documents were also prepared to make the transactions between FBL and the overseas company look genuine. The arrangement brought commercial advantages to FBL on two aspects. First, the agents 'would be more disposed to patronize the showrooms of FBL than the showrooms of other companies who were not prepared to offer this advantage'; second, FBL could claim tax relief on the payments made to the bogus overseas company. The recipients of the unrecorded commission would also have tax advantages. Between 1996 and 2003, three overseas companies were used for the money transfer purpose.

Two FBL staff members at that time played a crucial role in the scheme. The first one was Paul Chung, who was the Executive Director of the company overseeing the operation of the showrooms. The second was Steve Chow, who was business promotion manager in charge of three showrooms. Steve came to know Fong around 1980 and helped him to set up a finance company. He joined FBL as the business controller of the showrooms around 1984 and was senior to Paul who also joined the company around the same time. Paul and Steve, after being granted full immunity from ICAC, became the major prosecution witnesses in the case. According to their testimonies, Steve was arranged to resign from FBL to set up the first bogus overseas company. Paul would prepare the false invoice to the company and withdraw the money and channel back to Hong Kong. He would then distribute the money by himself or through Terry Lai, the General Manager of the showroom division.

PROJECT B

When the bogus overseas company was established, the senior management of FBL decided to devise another scheme to disguise the problematic commissions since the sum of monies to be transferred by the overseas company was too large. Some of the commission payments were then disguised as payments of promotional commissions to 11 staff members of the showrooms. The staff members were instructed to sign false invoices. The scheme was known as 'Project B' and the payments to the overseas company were known as 'Project A'. 'Project B' was terminated in October 1997, while Project A was to continue through the setting up of a new bogus overseas company by Paul. The company was in fact controlled by Paul's brother.

In August 2000, Mandy Wong joined FBL as the Deputy Chairman and Finance Director. In September, Jackson became Chairman and CEO of the company after his father's bankruptcy. Paul gave a detailed briefing to Jackson and Mandy about the 'Commission B' system. In May 2002, Mandy proposed to Paul that another bogus overseas company should be set up as the large payments to the bogus company might attract the suspicion of auditors. Paul's brother, again, was arranged to help control the new company. The total amount of commission payments made through the 'Project A' and 'Project B' exceeded $116 million.

The court documents also revealed that Paul and Steve made advantages for themselves through the 'Commission B' system. They stole commission money from FBL. Paul also never disclosed to FBL the involvement of his family in the overseas company and the benefits they received.

THE ROLE OF FONG AND JACKSON

According to Paul's testimony, most of the meetings leading up to the invention of the Commission B system were attended by him, Steve, the then Finance Director, and the then Company Secretary. The then CEO of FBL also attended some important meetings to discuss some crucial matters. Paul also told the Court that Fong said in a meeting that 'they should do their best to maintain the showroom business'. Paul also agreed that Fong 'left it to the senior management as to how this goal was to be achieved'.

Fong and Jackson might not be very clear on the details of the scheme, but they were aware of the scheme and were being kept informed of its development. For instance, Fong signed the minutes of the board meetings in respect to the appointments of the two bogus companies to provide services to FBL with Jackson's initial. Later, Jackson signed the minutes of the board meetings in respect to the appointment of the new bogus company to provide services to FBL with Mandy's initial. Jackson was also given a briefing on the system by Paul after he took up the Chairmanship of the company.

Embezzlement

In addition to the bribery charges, Fong and Jackson were also convicted for stealing money from the company for their own benefit through the commission system and disguised bonus to staff (Charge 3). As Paul testified in the court, Mandy told him around February 2002 that Fong wanted some money urgently from the company, but she could not find a way to help Fong. She however indicated that she might be able to help Fong through the commission system of the showroom as it was 'a bit loose'. Mandy suggested that the company issue Terry $100,000 per month in the guise of a bonus payment. Terry retained $15,000 per month to meet his tax liability and paid the balance to Paul who would then pass it on to Fong.

Paul talked to Terry about Mandy's idea. Terry told him that 'since they worked for the company they should work according to instructions'. At the end, five payments, each for $100,000, were prepared and approved by Jackson and Mandy. At the end, a total of $500,000 was taken from FBL for Fong.

In June 2002, Jackson approached Paul. This time, Jackson himself wanted money from the company and he told Paul that he was in a financial difficulty. According to Paul, Fong asked him to discuss with Terry to see if $100,000 could be arranged to be paid to Jackson monthly. At the end Paul and Terry suggested making use of the loophole of the showroom's commission system again.

Between August and December in 2002, FBL paid five sums of promotion fees, totalling more than $1.7 million to the business promoter of one of the FBL showrooms, half of the money was in fact destined for Jackson. Jackson admitted receiving $600,000 from the business promoter, but he insisted that it was a loan.

In fact, earlier than that, Jackson had already conspired with Mandy to take money from the company under the disguise of a bonus payment made to a resigned employee, Samuel Chan. Samuel was the President of the China Division of FBL. Due to health issues, he resigned in October 2001. Under his employment contract, Samuel was entitled to 3.5 per cent of the net profit of the China division. Samuel, however, said that he did not expect any bonus payment.

On 27 March 2002, FBL convened the first meeting of the Remunerations Committee to discuss the bonus issue of Samuel, which Jackson proposed. The attendees included Jackson, Mandy, and two independent directors. After the meeting, Jackson and Mandy agreed a bonus due to Samuel totalling around $1.9 million. Mandy, however, contacted Samuel and gave him a cheque of $100,000. Samuel was informed he was not entitled to any bonus but $100,000 would be paid to him as an appreciation of his service to the company.

Then in April 2002, Jackson approved three payment requisitions on the purported bonus payable to Samuel. Jackson received the money in cash in Hong Kong dollars. In July, Mandy gave Jackson a cash cheque for around RMB150,000, the last of the four payments in respect of the purported bonus for Samuel. Samuel, after receiving the $100,000 cheque from Mandy, did not hear anything further about his bonus until December 2002 when Jackson approached him.

In December 2002, Jackson set up a meeting with Samuel. Jackson was accompanied by Fong. Jackson told Samuel that 'he had used his name to obtain some money from the company' and suggested that they share the money. Samuel said that he needed time to consider the matter. After consulting his solicitor, Samuel told Jackson that he did not wish to receive any money. Jackson later repaid the money to FBL via his solicitors in January 2003. Jackson wrote to FBL to explain that he had received the bonus for Samuel, and he had delayed the handling of Samuel's bonus because he was very busy between July and November 2002. He said that he later contacted Samuel, but he refused to accept the bonus.

Board room disclosures

The Commission B system and the conspiracies of embezzlement first came to be known to the Board of FBL in December 2002. Jackson was the one who revealed all the wrongdoings. On 14 December 2002, Jackson visited the home of George Land, a director of a company which served as a financial adviser to FBL. George recalled that Jackson was in an emotional state and was very worried about the future of the company. George said that Jackson revealed to him that his father and he had received cash from the company. Jackson also told him the use of overseas companies in relation to the commission payments and he received the money supposedly due as a bonus to a colleague. George said that 'by the end of the meeting Jackson had become hysterical and was in a flood of tears'.

George arranged a meeting on 16 December attended by himself, Jackson, and another director of the financial adviser. What Jackson had told George at his home was repeated at the meeting. George said that Jackson agreed to make full disclosures to the FBL Board and the FBL advising team. A full board meeting was arranged on 18 December. During the meeting, Jackson told the Board what he had told George. The meeting was concluded with several resolutions. First, four independent non-executive directors of the Board were appointed to form an independent sub-committee conduct investigations and prepare an 'appropriate report on the Company's affairs'. Second, NER,[7] an auditing firm, should be commissioned to conduct a forensic investigation into various issues disclosed by Jackson and the use of the overseas companies in relation to commission payments. Third, Jackson was to step down as the CEO of FBL and be replaced by Otto Schneider. Jackson was to remain as the Chairman.

Fong had no idea about Jackson's decision to make disclosures to the Board. He only learned about it from Paul, who told the Court that Fong called him the night before the meeting and asked if a Board meeting would be held the following day. Paul told Fong that Jackson was going to disclose everything including the embezzlement. Paul said that Fong told him that Jackson had become 'crazy by believing in Jesus too much'.[8]

On 19 December 2002, Otto was appointed as the CEO of FBL. Shortly after his appointment, Paul told Otto the real purpose of the overseas companies. Otto asked Paul to prepare a flowchart to explain the system to the NER forensic investigators. Paul gave the flowchart to Otto, who helped to correct the English. Paul submitted the flowchart to the NER forensic team.

On 28 February 2003, the NER forensic team sent its confidential report to Jackson, Mandy, Otto, the team of FBL advisors, and the independent directors. The report concluded that 'the overseas companies used by FBL were money transfer vehicles without any legitimate commercial purpose'.

FBL made a public announcement on 2 October 2003 in respect to the NER forensic reports and in particular to the commission payments and the transactions which Jackson was involved with. The announcement pointed out that 'this [commission payment] system was examined by NER Forensic in the context of the Review and during that process certain internal control weaknesses in particular in connection with payments were identified'. The announcement stated that the Board had introduced new internal control measures to address the issues. FBL 'notes that notwithstanding the historic weaknesses in the system, there is no evidence that it resulted in any losses or liabilities'.

Regarding Jackson's transactions, the announcement stated that the company 'has introduced new internal controls in relation to salary/bonus payments made to employees'. But the Committee concluded that there was no clear evidence that there had been any wrongdoing involved:

> The Committee has concluded that in circumstances where there is no clear evidence either that the Company has suffered any losses or that there has been any wrongdoing, no further action is required by the Company.

All the problems seemed to have been settled. In fact, FBL did not suspend the Commission B system, however. Paul told the court that after he told Otto about the illegal commission payments, Otto said that 'this was a normal arrangement which appears in other trades'. The payments to the bogus foreign companies therefore continued until May 2003 when the management decided to pay the secret commission to local business promoters instead of overseas companies after Paul, Jackson, Otto, and Terry had discussions over the commission payments. Between May 2003 and March 2005, a sum totalling around $44 million was paid to the three local promoters including secret commissions.

Defrauding the Inland Revenue Department

The commission payments of FBL caught the attention of not only the ICAC but also the Inland Revenue Department (IRD). The large amount of commission payments drew the attention of the IRD as early as 1999. In 2002, FBL appointed MJS[9] as its tax representative to negotiate with the IRD. However, Paul, Steve, Jackson, and Otto told another version of the story to MJS. They insisted on the genuine nature of the overseas companies in providing business promotion service to the FBL showroom.

MJS then submitted a report to the IRD to explain the operation of the promotion fee payments. FBL attempted to convince the IRD through the document that the foreign companies were used for legitimate commercial purposes. In fact, the information provided by FBL to MJS was very different from that provided to the NER forensic report. The NER report was never shown to MJS.

Throughout the interviews and bargaining with the IRD, Paul, Steve, Jackson, and Otto repeatedly lied to stress the genuine nature of the business promoters in the hope that the IRD would allow FBL to claim tax relief for the commission payments and promotion fees paid. In the verdict of the court, the judge concluded that '[a]fter the introduction of the commission B system, lying became a matter of FBL corporate policy'.

Discussion

The conviction of Fong and Jackson dealt a serious blow to the Fong family and FBL. The criminal records have left a lasting imprint on the lives of the father and his son. The company was on the verge of collapse as its reputation was severely damaged. The public lost their confidence in the company and many senior executives left the company due to the court case. The court case also brought about a family feud between Fong and Jackson. After Fong served his prison term, he immediately filed a lawsuit against Jackson, his own son, with an attempt to get back his FBL shares. Fong claimed that the FBL shares that Jackson purchased from 2000 to 2004 belonged to him. Jackson just helped to retain the shares on his behalf. However, Jackson later refused to return the shares to Fong as previously agreed. In fact, the relationship between Fong and Jackson had become very bad after Jackson made disclosures to the FBL Board without giving Fong a notice in advance. Fong reportedly had a heart attack and needed to be hospitalized after learning of Jackson's plan. Fong finally dropped the lawsuit after the mediation of other family members.

We have to point out that the two major crises of the Fong family and FBL in the decade since 1998 – the financial crisis and the ICAC prosecution – were closely related to each other. The financial predicament of the company and of the Fong family prompted Fong and Jackson and their collaborators to take part in the conspiracies to sustain the illegal commission payment systems of the showroom, to misappropriate company funds, and to defraud the IRD. Although the illegal commission payments system had been established before the collapse of the property market, the worsening financial situation of the company explained why Fong and Jackson did not have the incentive to fix the problematic system. Since the showroom revenue represented a third of the total turnover of the company and provided a steady cash flow to the company, FBL could not afford to curtail the competitiveness of the showroom business especially at a time of financial difficulties. This explains why Jackson still clung to the faulted system even after his revelations at the Board meeting and the release of the NER forensic report by using local companies to replace the foreign companies to process the commission payment.

On the other hand, Fong and Jackson were motivated to misappropriate company funds as they also encountered personal financial problems due to the losses caused by Fong's speculation in the property market. Fong himself went bankrupt while Jackson was under huge mental and financial pressure to negotiate the restructuring arrangements with the creditors of the company and to get back the shares Fong pledged to the creditors. Both Fong and Jackson told us that they had a very difficult time back then. Fong told us that he did not want to go out during his bankruptcy:

> I think it's [the bankruptcy] a shame. I had a feeling that people were looking at me and gossiping, 'Look at the guy, he's broke!' My doctor said that I got anxiety disorder.

Jackson also told us that he had a very hard time dealing with the financial situation of the company:

> The company simply didn't have enough money. I had to keep looking for potential investors to raise funds. At the same time, I had to attend rounds of meetings to deal with the creditors and to negotiate with them. I was under tremendous pressure. It was a very hard time.

The court case thus cannot be studied as an independent event. It was closely related to the financial crises of FBL and the Fong family which took place between the late 1990s and the early 2000s. The financial crisis itself, as mentioned at the beginning of this chapter, was largely a consequence of Fong's obsessive speculation in the real estate market. There was no doubt that Fong bore the major responsibility for leading the company in that fatal direction. His speculative activities in the mid-1990s directly led to the financial crises of FBL and of himself. We must examine Fong's obsession with real estate so as to understand the failures of the company. We will argue that Fong's obsession with real estate and his tendency to speculate in the property market should be understood in terms of his own biographical background, the meaning of landed property in the Chinese cultural context, and the formation of the culture of speculation in post-war Hong Kong.

Fong's obsession with real estate

The great loss that Fong and his company suffered in the property market was by no means a singular incident. Fong had a long, if not notorious, record of speculating in the property market. Prior to the speculation in 1997, he had already used his company's financial resources to invest in real estate in the early 1980s and early 1990s. All of Fong's attempts to get a share of the lucrative property market, however, ended in failure and brought losses to the company. The negative impact of Fong's speculative activities on the company in the 1980s was clearly pointed out in the prospectus of the company issued in 1987 when it went public:

> the previous property speculation and gold trading activities undertaken by Fong's other companies had caused substantial loss to the Group. In 1986, it was decided to reorganize the organizational structure and business of the Group, especially to focus the resources of the Group on the core business – the jewellery business. The Group will not engage in property-related business and participate in the investments which are unrelated to jewellery.

The company had to make such a declaration to gain the confidence of the investors. The pledge, however, was soon broken as Fong resumed speculating in the property market in 1990 which led to the increase of debt level for the company. During the financial year of 1990/1991, Fong's debt-shareholder fund ratio reached 144 per cent. Fong had not learned from the previous lessons partly because the profit of his jewellery business could always offset the losses he made in the property market. Another major reason was that Fong did not agree that his investment in the property market was a speculative activity to make quick money. As Fong defended himself:

> I hate people saying that I speculated in the property market hoping just to make fast money. I bought real estate in the interest of the company. For retailers like us, rent is a big burden. So, I want to purchase as much real estate as possible so that our shops don't have to pay rent. I once bought a piece of land hoping to convert it into a big jewellery centre. Then the disputes over the political future of Hong Kong between the British and Chinse governments emerged. What a bad luck! The market slumped so I had to sell it off. Another guy took the land and built a commercial centre.

It is true that Fong purchased properties to help the company to alleviate the rent burden, but this does not mean that Fong was not speculating as he claimed. In fact, Fong admitted on other occasions that he simply could not let go of the golden opportunities of making money through the property market. The property market, in the eyes of Fong and of course many others, was simply like the goose that laid the golden eggs. 'All those rich guys got rich because of [investing in] real estate. When you have money, there is no reason not to join the game,' Fong once said.

But why did Fong keep failing to control his impulse to speculate in the property market despite the repeated failures? He blamed others for encouraging him to stay in the game:

> People around me, my friends and business partners, kept encouraging me to invest [in the property market]. It's not just me, you know. Everyone was crazy, buying and selling houses like they were just some daily necessities. The banks, especially, just kept asking if I would like to borrow money every day! Back then, it was too easy to get a loan. You could get mortgage up to 90 per cent of the price of the property. It was very tempting. The banks were bad. They tempted you to borrow money when the market was good, but when things started to go wrong, they immediately turned back on you. When I had difficulty, they just backed me into a corner.

Although Fong himself should be responsible for the losses he made in the property market, he did point out the prevalence of a speculative culture in the society which played a significant role in creating the property market bubble in Hong Kong in 1997. Fong's frenzy speculation in the property market and his failures, we contend, should be understood in the broader context of the speculative culture in Hong Kong.

The speculative culture in Hong Kong

We have to emphasize that Fong was one of the many people in Hong Kong – including rich businessmen, middle class, and other ordinary people alike – who suffered a great loss as a result of the collapse of the property market in 1998. The economy of Hong Kong entered a period of deep recession. In 1998, the real GDP of Hong Kong shrank by 5.1 per cent making it the largest economic contraction of the city since 1961 (Liu, 1999, p. 40). Reports of people declaring bankruptcy and even committing suicide due to their heavily indebted status appeared on local newspapers from time to time during the period. The Asian financial crisis is often cited as the reason for the bursting of the property bubble and the economic downturn of Hong Kong. However, studies have already shown that the crisis could only be regarded as a catalyst instead of a fundamental cause for the collapse of the property market (e.g. Liu, 1999; Wong, 2010).

Chi-shing Liu (1999) elaborates on how the formation of the speculative culture in Hong Kong along with the property related policies of the government and the tendency of banks to provide property loans helped create the property market bubble. A bubble, according to Liu (1999, p. 15), is formed when people become over-optimistic, believing that the prices of the properties will keep increasing. The property market is increasingly led by psychological factors instead of genuine demand, resulting in unreasonable prices which do not actually reflect the real values of the properties (Liu, 1999, p. 58).

The speculative culture in Hong Kong, Liu (1999) points out, is the key to the formation of the bubble. We have argued in Chapter 2 how the policy of the colonial government in Hong Kong contributed to the extremely materialistic ethos of Hong Kong society. The materialistic mentality gave rise to a speculative culture underlined by the fervent desire for making fast money. The Hong Kong people were enthusiastic about speculating on anything ranging from stocks, real estate to toys and vehicle registration marks. They did not purchase the products for their own use but for reselling. In other words, it was the anticipated market price instead of the intrinsic values of the products which mattered to the people. Properties, in the eyes of many Hong Kong people, were thus only instrumental tools to be traded to gain profit. The high demand in the market did not reflect the real demand for housing but the high expectation that the prices of the properties would keep rising.

The high land price policy of the colonial government was also one of the factors creating such expectations. The sale of land was one of the major sources of income to the government. The high land price was maintained by the government through its control of the supply of land. The property developers, in turn, would transfer the cost to the consumers to maintain the high price level of the properties. Liu (1999) also argues that a series of home ownership schemes implemented by the government, along with the ever-increasing property prices, led to the strong belief of the people that they should invest their money in the property markets as real estate was the best hedge against inflation. The increase in demand then further drove the prices of the properties up which in turn caused higher demand due to the anticipation of future increase in prices.

The boom of the property market was also boosted by the tendency of banks to provide easy loans. The tendency could be traced back to the early 1980s. According to Liu (1999, p. 35), the growth rate of property loans grew from 34 per cent in

1979 to 56 per cent in 1980. Banks became more prudent in property-related lending after the crash of the property market in the early 1980s which subsequently led to a wave of bank failures (Liu, 1999, p. 36). However, they soon became aggressive again in property lending. According to Liu (1999, p. 36), 44.2 per cent of the total bank loans went to the property market in 1997. In accordance with Fong's account, with the ease of mortgaging, buyers would need to pay only 10 per cent of the total price of the property. The presence of easy finance encouraged the speculative activities and boosted the prices of the properties.

The inflow of international hot money further drove property prices to a peak. Since the property market was supported by the anticipation of the people instead of a sound foundation, when the Asian financial crisis set in, foreign investors started to withdraw money leading to a drop in the property prices, which triggered a domino effect. The middle class was most fatally affected by the slumping property market. The assets they bought with their life-savings became liabilities overnight. It was reported that around 100,000 private flats became negative assets in September 1998 (Liu, 1999, p. 41). The collapse of the property market led to the largest contraction of the Hong Kong economy ever during the post-war period.

The meaning of land in Chinese society

Fong's obsession with real estate was not only economical but also cultural. Chinese people in general have a special attachment to real estate for they believe that it provides the ultimate source of security against changes. Owning a house and even a piece of land is the foundation of living a good life in Chinese societies. Fong is no exception. This kind of mentality is clearly reflected in the design of the logo of his company. Fong explained to us his idea:

> The logo of FBL looks like the word Chinese character *tin* (field). It's I who designed that logo. It means *jau tin jau dei* (having fields and lands). We are Chinese, it's important to have one's own properties. When we have our lands, we can then flourish. They are our roots. I use the money earned from the jewellery business to buy properties, and through buying properties to expand the company.

This also explains why, as mentioned in Chapter 7, Fong was willing to lend money to his employees to help them buy their properties. Fong believed that nothing was more important than owning one's own house. The employees, he believed, could only have a secure life after acquiring their own houses. Helping the employees to buy their own houses, from Fong's perspective, was thus one of the best ways of expressing his care to the employees, to show that he, as a boss, was willing to help the employees to achieve one of the most important missions in life.

Recall that Fong had a very rough childhood and had to leave home to live with a goldsmith when he was only 13 years old. Even after he started his business, for most of the time, he basically lived in the workshop. With this background, it is not difficult to understand why Fong placed such a strong emphasis on owning one's own real estate. It provided a sense of security to Fong, who had undergone a very long period of hardship and changes, since it represented the tangible form of his achievements. This explained why Fong had a wish to buy all the flats in the building where the FBL headquarters was located, so that he could rename the building 'Fong Bou Lung Building'. The desire was by no means a result of pure economic calculation; instead it reflected the symbolic values of real estate to Fong.

We, however, argue that we need to investigate the relationship between the landed property and the family to understand the symbolic values of real estate in Chinese societies. Adopting H. Franz Schurmann's insights about the meaning of landed property in Chinese societies, Allen Chun (1985) contends that landed estate in Chinese societies cannot be seen as wealth but a medium for creating wealth. As he argues, '[s]ocial production creates values on the land, and the products derived from it are manifestation of wealth proper. Land then is merely a medium for creating value rather that the valued commodity *per se*' (Chun, 1985, p. 85; underline original). We are convinced that although speculating in the property market in contemporary Hong Kong could be very profitable, the nature of land as a medium for creating wealth helps explain culturally why the Chinese of contemporary Hong Kong were so keen in speculating in the property market because they were culturally made to see landed property as a major medium for creating wealth. But Chun (1985) hastily adds that the keen interest of Chinese in investing in landed property cannot be considered as being motivated by individuals' self-interest; it is instead driven by the need to maintain social solidarity among family members. Chun (1985, pp. 86–87) repeats what Schurmann emphasized:

> the transmission and management of property by the family and clan were subject to sanctions in ideological terms and that these ideologically sanctioned values, as manifested within divine ownership, ancestral obligations, filial piety, sacredness of the family tomb and the centrifugal nature of kin solidarity, served an essentially conservative function, the absence of which would have given rise in China . . . quite possibly to the dissolution of these social groups as well.

We therefore argue that Fong's speculative impulse in the property market of Hong Kong can be attributed to the interest of his family rather than his own. But we have to add immediately that the family here refers not to *jia* but the *fang/jia-zu* of Fong. Recall that the surpluses from the *jia* as a joint-account become *fang/jia-zu* property, the ownership of which are defined not by *jia* but *fang/jia-zu* membership which only includes sons (Chen, 1986, p. 130). Sons can equally share the *fang/jia-zu* property, especially landed estate, when their father decides to pass the *fang/jia-zu* property to them. More importantly, the interest of *fang/jia-zu* is more important than that of *jia* to the extent that the latter could be sacrificed for the former. That is why Fong did not hesitate to risk FBL's (*jia*)'s interest for the sake of his *fang/jia-zu* by continuously speculating in the Hong Kong property market. We shall return to this in a moment.

Running the public company as a jia

The fundamental factor contributing to the failures of FBL, we contend, is that Fong continued to run FBL as his *jia* even after FBL was publicly listed on the Hong Kong Stock Exchange. One characteristic of *jia* that is relevant to our current discussion is that, as we discussed in Chapter 7, *jia* members share a common budget and all members are required to contribute financially to their *jia*. Financial resources are then allocated to members according to their needs by whoever controls the financial budget of the *jia*; but usually money is distributed by the *jiazhang* or his wife who is delegated by the *jiazhang* to manage the *jia* budget. For the *jiazhang* has the absolute power over the management of the *jia* and its financial budget. Seen in this way, we can now understand why Fong turned to FBL when he needed money because it is very natural for Fong to get money from his company for he considered FBL as his *jia*; and as the *jiazhang*, Fong had the absolute power to decide how the *jia*'s financial budget is distributed and spent. That is also why Fong could repeatedly use FBL's financial resources to speculate in the property market in the 1980s and the 1990s; and why Fong used the company's money to pay back his personal loan, to which we shall return in a moment. For to Fong, FBL's financial resources were his *jia*'s money which was under his control. We can also understand why Fong ordered his staff to get money from FBL's account for his son when Jackson was in financial difficulties because Fong had the power to distribute the *jia*'s financial resources to the *jia* members according to their needs. More importantly, one of the core values of *jia* is an ideal of unselfish mutual sharing of financial resources among *jia* members as well as unconditional financial support of each other when circumstances require. This core value helped to legitimize Fong's decision to get money from the company's account for Jackson.

The unrestrained jiazhang

As the *jiazhang*, Fong had the absolute power over the management of FBL. In Chapter 7, we have already explained that the organization of FBL was based on the web of specific social relations with the chief at the centre. The relationship between the chief and his followers was sustained through the continuous presentation of loyalty to the chief by the latter and through the continuous provision of security, in terms of money and welfare, to the latter by the former. To present their loyalty, the employees must demonstrate that they always put the interest of the founder-chief above those of others including their own.

Following this logic, it is not hard to understand why Fong and Jackson were able to get help from the employees to get money from the company. Fong and Jackson actively approached their staff to come up with a solution to solve their personal financial problems. The staff helped them to identify the loopholes in the accounting system, to issue false documents, and even to arrange the payments. Despite the fact that these actions clearly hurt the interest of the company and obviously were illegal, the staff still tried their best to entertain their bosses. Recall that Terry told Paul that 'since they worked for the company they should work according to instructions'. In their mindset, similar to their bosses, they did not distinguish FBL from Fong, or to a lesser degree, Jackson. They did not perceive themselves hurting the interests of FBL as a public company as they were actually helping their bosses.

This further explains the weakness of the internal control of the company. The employees tended to follow the instructions of their superiors as long as they understood that it was the order of the boss. In fact, quite a few of employees of the company were involved in the operation of the illegal commission payments system. Even the Board failed to monitor and prevent the wrongdoings. Paul, who played a key role in all the conspiracies related to the court case, was himself a Board member. The other Board members also had little disciplinary power over the behaviour of Fong and Jackson. After Jackson's disclosures and the receipt of the NER forensic report, the Board still stated that 'there is no clear evidence either that the Company has suffered any losses or that there has been any wrongdoing'. In fact, it was not the first time that the Board 'tolerated' the wrongdoings of the controlling family.

Back in the time of the financial crisis in the late 1990s, the auditor of FBL was not able to reach a conclusion about the accuracy of the financial statements submitted by the company partly because of a deposit paid to a potential business partner in China in the 1999/2000 fiscal year. The deposit was later revealed to be used to offset Fong's personal debt owed to a PRC Company. FBL announced in July 2000 that the company had already reached an agreement with Fong, who promised to return the money to FBL within five years and the company would not further pursue the matter.

In a similar vein, the Board also failed to stop the speculation of Fong in the property market. The nature of the relationship between the owner and the employees in FBL brought about fundamental weaknesses on the internal control mechanism of the company.

The abuse of discretionary power

In Chapter 7, we show that the *jan cing mei* management of FBL was characterized by the high level of autonomy and agency of the employees in the sense that they were granted great discretionary power for two reasons. The first is Fong's pragmatic attitude. As demonstrated in previous chapters, Fong was only concerned about getting things done; he had no interest in learning how things are done. Therefore, he was willing to grant discretionary power to his employees to help him identify solutions and solve the problem.

The second reason is related to Fong's own limitations. In fact, especially after the company grew and went public, Fong had to rely on the employees to handle the situation as he could not master the complexity of managing a modern corporation. Sharing the discretionary power with the employees was in fact a result of necessity. For instance, we believe that Fong was not very clear about the concept of a public company neither was he able to comprehend the critical difference between public and private companies. Recall that we have described in Chapter 3 Fong's motivation to make the company public; as he told us:

> My friends told me that if my company was listed on the stock market, it's easier to raise funds and to expand. One dollar could be easily turned into ten dollars. So, I set it [to go public] as my target and I finally achieved the goal. I didn't know much about the procedure. I just found some people to help me with this.

Obviously, Fong could not understand the implications of FBL's going public. He was not aware of the fact that a public corporation no longer belongs to a single individual or company since a certain percentage of the shares is required to be circulated in the stock market. Even the controlling shareholder like Fong is supposed to be only *one of the owners* of the company and thus to be responsible for the interests of other shareholders/owners of the company. In Fong's understanding, to go public was simply a means for him to get more money. The notion of public ownership was completely absent in Fong's mind. He simply didn't regard the company as something 'public' but as his *jia* and he operated the company in the same way he ran his *jia*. We do not mean that Fong did not understand the basic difference between public and private companies; what we want to point out is that Fong might not comprehend the boundaries between public and private companies. Recall that Fong received very little formal education and knew no English. He could only rely on the professionals to deal with the day-to-day management of the public company.

When we asked Fong about the court case, he repeatedly emphasized that he just followed the advice of the experts:

> It was all about the tax arrangement. We followed the advice of the consultants and accounting firms to set up overseas companies to get tax reductions. I don't know how that works, but they are supposedly the experts, right? It's even stranger for the commission part. I still don't understand why paying someone is illegal!

Of course, we are not suggesting that what Fong told us is all true and that he was not aware of his wrongdoings. What we want to point out is that sometimes Fong might not really have comprehended the details and possible implications of the arrangement on the corporate level. Recall that in the court case, Paul also mentioned that Fong just 'left it to the senior management as to how this goal [to continue the commission payment] was to be achieved'. Reuben Cheung, who worked in the company since the mid-1970s, also pointed out that Fong very often signed documents, the content of which he did not know or could not understand. What we are suggesting is that Fong increasingly lacked the capacity to evaluate the advice and action of the employees and the possible implications in the complex corporate setting.

Fong's heavy reliance on his staff, however, made it difficult, if not impossible, for him to monitor the behaviours of the employees and to prevent them from abusing the autonomy they enjoyed. This explained why Paul and Steve could make use of the freedom given to steal the commission money of FBL and why they did not receive any punishment. Fong and Jackson had to rely on them to operate the illegal commission payment system. As the company grew, the management style of FBL became more problematic as the *jiazhang* could not catch up with the growing complexity of the organizational structure.

Fang/Jia-zu *'s interests over* jia *'s interests*

One of the major puzzles throughout our research on FBL was that Fong, on the one hand, genuinely believed that he sacrificed a lot for the company and strived to be a responsible boss who took care of the welfare of the employees. From our interactions with the employees and what we observed through our fieldwork, Fong was really concerned about his employees and dedicated all his time and energy to the company. On the other hand, what Fong did – from speculating obsessively in the property market, through borrowing money excessively to misappropriating company funds for his own use – obviously damaged the interests of the company and other shareholders. How can we make sense of this paradox?

We argue that the answer lies in the Chinese family ethic that gives priority to the interests of *fang/jia-zu* rather than those of *jia*. Recall that *fang/jia-zu* is a genealogical concept denoting the status of son/father, while *jia* refers to a co-residential group which functions to organize the domestic life of the group including *jiaye*. While the continuity of *jia* is important because it serves as an organizational and financial means to perpetuate that of *fang/jia-zu*, the continuity of the latter is more important than that of the former for several reasons. First, a *jia*, as mentioned in Chapter 7, will vanish anyway on the occasion of *feng jia* (division of *jia*) in which each son will establish a new *jia* and the original *jia* will be terminated, which is also to say that the termination of the original *jia* is a natural consequence of the division of *jia*. The division of *fang/jia-zu*, however, represents a totally different social process in which each generation of the patrilineal kin set is *genealogically* divided into *fang*s in relation to their father's *jia-zu* according to the number of sons; but the original *jia-zu* does *not* vanish. Second and more importantly, the continuity of *fang/jia-zu*, as mentioned in Chapter 7, symbolizes the eternity of the life. It follows that the continuity of *jia* will be sacrificed for the sake of that of *fang/jia-zu* if necessary.

In light of the earlier discussion, we can see that the native concepts of *fang/jia-zu* and *jia* produce a hierarchical relationship between the *jiazhang* and his *fang/jia-zu* members, *jia* members who are non-*fang/jia-zu* affiliates, and non-*jia* members in Chinese family businesses including Fong's FBL. First of all, Fong was concerned more about the interests of FBL (his *jia*) including those of the *fang/jia-zu* and non-*fang/jia-zu* members than those of other non-*jia* stakeholders including minority shareholders of the company. These non-*jia* stakeholders were perceived as outsiders. Fong did not bother to think about how his actions might affect their interests or if he was accountable to them. During our fieldwork, we never heard Fong mention anything about the shareholders, who supposedly shared with him the ownership of the company, but we repeatedly came across various occasions where Fong stressed his responsibility towards his own family (*fang/jia-zu* members) and employees (non-*fang/jia-zu* members of *jia*). It is therefore not wrong to agree with Fong that he did devote himself wholeheartedly to the prosperity of FBL and he was a responsible boss who had taken care of his employees.

Fong, however, tended to give priority to the interests of his *fang/jia-zu* rather than his *jia* and that is why he could risk the interests of FBL (his *jia*) for the sake of his *fang/jia-zu* by investing heavily in the property market or levying substantial loans on FBL, not to mention misappropriating FBL's financial resources for his own use or stealing money from the company, all of which would jeopardize the interests of FBL as a whole including those of its minority shareholders, its employees, and other stakeholders. We shall argue in the concluding chapter that this is the overriding problem of Chinese family businesses.

Conclusion

In this chapter, we have focused on examining the two major crises that the Fong family and FBL had undergone during the decade between 1998 and 2008 which led to the financial predicament of the company, the bankruptcy of Fong, the change of company leadership, the prosecution of Fong, Jackson and the senior management of FBL and their imprisonment. In the first section of the chapter, we have outlined the key events leading up to the financial crisis of the company and of Fong. We then turned to the court case and explained why Fong and Jackson were convicted for charges related to bribery, embezzlement, and defrauding the IRD.

In the second part of the chapter, we first pointed out the close relationship between the two major crises, showing how and why the financial crisis of the Fong family and FBL should be understood in relation to Fong's obsession with real estate, the formation of the speculative culture in Hong Kong, the cultural meaning of landed property in Chinese societies, and more fundamentally, Fong's running of FBL as his own *jia*. The fact that Fong ran FBL as his own *jia* helps explain why the monopoly of corporate power by Fong was never contested and why the discretionary power granted to FBL's employees was easily abused by some major members of the management team.

Finally, we identified the major puzzle throughout our research on FBL that while Fong had devoted himself wholeheartedly to the prosperity of FBL and had taken good care of its employees since the inception of the company, he, however, continuously committed serious mistakes that were proved to risk the continuity of FBL. We argued that the paradox itself in fact showed that Fong prioritized the interests of his *fang/jia-zu* over those of FBL (his *jia*), which we are convinced is the major problem of Chinese family businesses.

This long chapter also provided the historical context against which the reform of FBL initiated by Fong's daughter-in-law, Emma, after she took over the management of the company should be understood. After Fong and Jackson were sent to prison, the company was passed to Emma, Jackson's wife. Emma bore heavy responsibility to rescue the crippling company. Changes were urgently required to rebuild and transform the company. What Emma first did was to recruit a group of professional managers to run FBL. Upon their arrival, these professional managers introduced the so-called modern management which is one-to-one opposite to Fong's '*jan cing mei* management' regime. In other words, the historical context outlined in this chapter and Fong's '*jan cing mei* management' in Chapter 7 are the two important contexts against which the professionalization of FBL should be understood. We shall explore the process of professionalization of FBL in the coming chapters.

Notes

1 Negative equity refers to the financial situation when the current value of an asset used to secure a mortgage is less than the amount of the outstanding balance on the mortgage. It becomes an immediate problem for people who want to sell their properties or to remortgage.
2 JOI is a pseudonym.
3 Both Zebra and Tsang King Pang are pseudonyms.
4 Icrop is a pseudonym.
5 To protect the privacy of our informants and the people involved in the court case, pseudonyms are assigned for all defendants and witnesses in the court case. All the discussions concerning the details of the court case are based on the judgement documents of the Court (Reasons for verdict and Reasons for sentence) and relevant news reports on the court case. We do not intend and are not in the position to validate the details of the court case, the charges and the judgement as stated in the judgement documents.
6 The Independent Commission Against Corruption (Hong Kong) was established in 1974.
7 NER is a pseudonym.
8 Jackson is a devoted Christian. We shall return to this in Chapter 9 and Chapter 10.
9 MJS is a pseudonym.

9 The transformers and the transformation

On the day of judgement of his court case, reckoning that he would be found guilty of the charges, Jackson Fong resigned as the chairman of the company. Emma Fong, his wife, took up the position. Another defendant of the case, Otto Schneider, the then CEO of the company, also resigned. He was replaced by Desmond Chen, a long-time friend of Jackson. Emma was charged with the heavy responsibility of safeguarding the collapsing company during the absence of her husband and father-in-law. One year later, Emma, with the help of Desmond, succeeded in getting the approval of the Hong Kong Stock Exchange to resume trading of the shares of the company, which had been suspended for more than three years since the ICAC charged Fong and other related parties. Since 2010, the company has undergone a transformation led by a group of professional managers recruited by Emma. These professional managers, who had extensive experience working in large, modern enterprises before joining FBL, played a major and active role in introducing professional management to, fostering organizational reform in, and rebranding the company.

In this chapter, we aim to examine the nature and content of the transformation of the company. We will show that the transformation itself amounts to the professionalization of FBL that introduces 'modern' management to the company. The 'modern' management constitutes a point-to-point opposite to Fong's *jan cing mei* management regime outlined in Chapter 7. We will further argue that the professionalization measures especially the Vision, Mission, and Value (VMV) campaign initiated by Emma and her management team should be seen as discursive practices that function to foster a perspective among the employees of FBL which see the relationship between the modern management and Fong's *jan cing mei* regime not as two equal and different management systems but a hierarchical one, with the former being good, modern, progressive, rational, scientific, democratic, and efficient and the latter bad, old-fashion, backward, irrational, intuitional, feudal, and inefficient. The transformation is therefore political; it is a politics between the modern management and Fong's *jan cing mei* regime. Underlying this politics is a more complex micro-political dynamics among the owners, the professional managers, and the *lou san zi* that, as will be demonstrated in the next chapter, had facilitated the transformation at the beginning, and made the transformation a failure in the end.

The guardian angel

When Jackson foresaw the coming of the final storm that would eventually uproot his life, he entrusted the company to Emma, his wife and his soul mate, as the two are both devoted Christians. Emma was suddenly enthroned to lead and save the crumbling empire. She *alone* certainly could not save the company. She needed help, and Desmond was the only person whom she could turn to when she took up the chairwoman position as most senior executives had already left the company at the time of the crisis. Desmond's father was Fong's friend, so Desmond and the Fong siblings got to know each other when they were teenagers. Desmond was the classmate of Joseph, Fong's oldest son, in the secondary school in Hong Kong. Desmond was then sent abroad to study in the United States. When he was studying in the university, according to Desmond, he encouraged Jackson to join him and guided Jackson through his Christian journey. When they were both in the United States, Desmond became Jackson's spiritual mentor in the Christian belief for a period. The Christian bond between them has since remained strong.

After graduation, Desmond set up his own information technology company in the United States. He returned to Hong Kong when his father fell sick. Jackson met Desmond again in 2005 at Desmond's wedding and invited him to join FBL. At that time, Desmond was just shopping around to figure out his next career move. He explained to us why he accepted Jackson's offer:

> Jackson didn't understand why I just did something 'virtual'. He asked me to try to do some 'tangible' businesses and invited me to join FBL. At that time, I was interested in learning more about customer experience; and the profit margin of retail is very high, I was quite interested in learning more about that too. But I didn't have any retail experience, so I suggested to Jackson that I would just work four days a month to see how it went, a bit like a consultant.

On the fifth day of Desmond's work, Jackson and Fong were arrested by the ICAC. Desmond told us that it was quite a drama:

> I just started [to work in FBL] and then the incident took place. It's me who got to the bank to get the money and bail them out. They couldn't use their own money at that time. It was the first time that I made it to the headline of the Apple Daily,[1] well, under such an occasion [Desmond was laughing]. I didn't expect that of course.

Desmond was later appointed to oversee the operation of the showrooms, the problematic business that triggered off the whole court case as mentioned in the previous chapter. When Jackson and Fong were found guilty, the company faced enormous problems and its reputation was severely damaged. Desmond did not follow other senior executives to leave the company; instead, he chose to stay and take up the position of CEO to assist Emma. Desmond explained his decision to us:

Many people thought that I should leave [at that time] to save my own reputation. After all, I just joined the company. I did seriously think about that,
frankly. However, I thought that I should stay, especially during such a difficult time, to keep the Fong family company. I thought I would be like a
guardian angel to the family, in a Christian sense. In Christianity, the concept
of *tung hang* (walking together) is very important. Jackson invited me to join
the company because he cared for me in the first place. I couldn't abandon
them when they desperately needed me. After discussing with my family, I
decided to stay.

Christianity plays an important role in motivating Desmond to stay with the company and the Fong family. He emphasized his role as a guardian angel to the Fong
family and his mission to support and save the crumbling family. The similar,
if not the same, rhetoric and emphasis on the religious faith and the mission of
salvation, as we shall demonstrate in the next chapter, occurred again and again
in the transformation of FBL. Let us turn to the measures adopted by Emma and
Desmond to manage the immediate crisis first.

Crisis management

The most urgent tasks for Emma and Desmond were to convince the authorities
to resume the trading of FBL shares in the Hong Kong Stock Exchange and to
rebuild the reputation of the company. To achieve that, they had to demonstrate
that they would adequately address the problems identified in the court case.
Since the showroom business of FBL was the focus of the court case, Emma and
Desmond had to tackle the problems of the showrooms at once.

Desmond told us that in order to demonstrate to the public that the company
tried to improve the operation of the showroom business, they emphasized the
principle of 'whiter than white' to enhance the corporate governance. He explained
the principle to us:

> The operation of the showrooms is extremely complicated and involves a lot
> of hidden deals and cash payments. In other words, it's very difficult to trace
> the transaction records. In fact, the problems are industry-wide instead of
> FBL-specific. Our aim was to make sure that everything would strictly fol-
> low the regulations and as clear as a crystal so that the company would not
> get into any troubles again.

A series of measures were taken to achieve that goal. Desmond requested all the
travel agents to sign a contract with FBL, which clearly listed all the details of the
collaboration. If a travel agent refused to sign the contract, FBL would not work
with the agency anymore. 'We might actually lose half of our partners,' Desmond
said. 'But it was a price that we had to pay.' The company also reduced the ratio of
cash transactions involved in the operation of showrooms to minimum. Most of the
payments by the company would be settled by auto pay or cheque instead of cash.

In fact, the company focused on improving not simply the showroom operation but the overall corporate governance. For instance, in addition to the external auditor, the company also set up an internal audit team and employed an additional independent auditor to keep track of the accounting records. According to Desmond, the new composition of the core management was also a bonus point to gain the trust of the authorities and the public, as he told us:

> We [referring to Emma and himself], were all outsiders. We just joined the management. It would be easier for us, the fresh faces, to gain the trust of others since we could convince them that the company would now be different from the past.

In short, the new leadership of the company attempted to construct a new image of FBL by appointing 'outsiders' and fresh faces in the senior management team and demonstrating a new style of corporate governance. All these attempts aimed to water down the old association between the company and the patriarchal line of the Fong family, at least in the public eye.[2] The awareness of the new leadership to distance the company from the Fong family at that time, as we shall demonstrate, is also an important factor contributing to the transformation of FBL.

In 2009, the trading of FBL shares was finally resumed. At this point, Emma had completed the first major assignment left by her husband. Challenges, however, remained as the company still struggled to clear the stigma and rebuild its image.

Rebuilding FBL

As the company had overcome the immediate problem, Desmond, who had been appointed as the Deputy Chairman of the company, turned to devote more time and energy to developing his own social enterprises and business. In early 2010, Desmond resigned from the CEO position. Emma then became both the CEO and Chairwoman of the company. Desmond's resignation, according to Emma, was in fact a result of the negotiation between the two, as she said:

> Our styles are just very different. I'd say I am a down-to-earth person, but Desmond is more unsettling. He loves to try many different things. It's hard to keep him in one place. He could not focus on dealing with the business of FBL only. When I took up the CEO position from him, my workload was the same. I mean, I had to shoulder his work even before he resigned from the position.

With Desmond's withdrawal from the day-to-day operation of the company,[3] Emma desperately needed someone to help her manage the company. She, the new leader, had to look for a person and a team that she could work with and that could help achieve her goal. On the one hand, she had to build a new FBL image with new personnel, style, and way of doing business to rebuild the confidence of the public. On the other hand, and in fact more importantly, Emma had to help Jackson to maintain FBL on his behalf during his 'vacation'.[4]

Encountering the angel

But who could help Emma to maintain the company? Emma told us that, at the beginning, she just wanted to find someone to fill Desmond's position to oversee the sales of the company. She did not have any particular candidate in mind neither had she thought about reforming the company. She just shopped around to meet with different potential candidates and got different new ideas through the process, until she met Chris Tse who is also a devoted Christian.

Chris is widely known and respected in the local marketing field. Starting as a marketing executive in TTI[5] in 1990, Chris was promoted to the position of General Manager when he was only 29 years old. In 2000, Chris joined the Hong Kong Tourism Board (HKTB) to oversee its destination marketing. In 2007, he became the Managing Director of Cards and Unsecured Loans for an international bank, WOB.[6] He was taking a career break when Emma approached him. When Emma met Chris and discussed the situation of the company with him, Chris suggested to her that the company should focus on sales and marketing. The idea to drive the company through sales and marketing, according to Emma, was new to FBL. She explained to us why she was willing to adopt Chris's idea:

> I thought Chris [his expertise and idea] might help us [FBL]. We [FBL] had been quiet for a long time after 1997. We hadn't launched any TV commercials since then. We were afraid that the public had already forgotten us. Branding is very important to Jackson. He really wants to create a new image for FBL. I thought Chris might help us achieve the goal. I thought we could give it a try.

Emma's decision to recruit Chris was daring as FBL had never employed a senior executive who had no prior experience in the jewellery industry to oversee the daily operation of the company. When we asked Emma why she trusted Chris, she explained:

> because he's noticeable! I think there are several reasons. First, he's someone who has 'experiences.' I mean he has gone through ups and downs in his life, like FBL [and the Fong family].[7] He can better understand our situation. His past experiences and achievements are also impressive. His devotion to the Christian faith is also important to me. I hope that the top management team of the company has a Christian background, as I want to put Christian values into the company.

Chris appeared to be the right man at the right time for Emma and FBL. Emma appointed Chris as the COO of the company in March 2010 when Jackson was still serving his sentence. From that time, Chris took the lead to reform and rebrand the company.

Reforming the company

When he joined FBL, Chris was very clear about his goals: to help the company to reform the organizational structure and to improve the brand image. Between 2010 and 2011 alone, Chris created three new departments as he had to build up a new team to support the marketing and branding revision of the company. Through his recommendations, Emma recruited several senior executives, who had no prior experience in the jewellery industry, to join the company. The recruitment of non-jewellery people has since become a new 'tradition' at FBL.

When Emma recruited Chris, she set a precedent in employing a senior executive from outside the jewellery industry. Most if not all of the senior managerial positions of the company in recent years have been filled by people who did not have a jewellery background. Emma explained her rationale to us:

> I preferred those who are not from the jewellery industry. As we want to do something new, it'd be good for us to recruit some outsiders. We've got a lot of jewellery people already and very often they cannot catch up with the latest market trend. To differentiate ourselves from the competitors, I think we need to borrow the wisdom from other industries. That's why I think it's important to have a diverse pool of talents.

In fact, one of the most noticeable aspects of the transformation of FBL is the recruitment of senior executives who 'have been specifically educated to be managers rather than experts in whatever the company's particular products or markets' (Schein, 1995, p. 234, cited in Hall and Nordqvist, 2008, p. 54). The recruitment of professional managers can be seen as one step towards the professionalization of family business (Hall and Nordqvist, 2008, p. 54).

Introduction of modern management structure

Another step towards professionalization, as Hall and Nordqvist (2008, p. 54) quoting Songini (2006) argued, 'is to change the informal atmosphere of the organization by introducing more formalized systems, meaning, among other things, increased use of quantitative and systematic information collection in the organization'.

Strategic planning

Having gotten the green light from Emma, Chris took the lead to create new positions and departments and referred his former colleagues to join the company. The first new department that Chris created was Strategic Planning. He believed that in order to formulate a good marketing strategy, it is important to have the support of fact-based analysis. In other words, branding and marketing, in Chris's view, must be supported by scientific research. Chris explained his rationale to us:

> It's basically a package of doing branding and marketing. You can't simply rely on your gut feeling to do marketing. I am not a 'figures' guy, so I especially need help from those who can do marketing research.

According to Chris, having a strategic planning department is common in big corporations but not in smaller-scale companies such as FBL. The company had never had such a department, as Chris told us:

> The main difficulty is that the boss and even the Human Resources Department did not understand the function of the [Strategic Planning] department very clearly. The HR department asked me to help with the interview as they didn't even know the exact job specifications and functions.

Chris however still tried very hard to convince Emma to set up this department as he believed that the department would be essential to the building of a marketing environment. He also believed that the department could help the company formulate the medium to long-term planning. Emma was convinced by Chris's idea partly because, as she told us, she is a 'figures' person, who believes in figures and facts-based analysis.

Chris eventually recruited Kevin Wu, his former colleague at TTI to head the new Strategic Planning department in May 2010. Kevin was a graduate of a local university in Hong Kong. He also holds a master's degree from the United States. Before joining FBL, he had worked in various banks. He got to know Chris when he worked in TTI and HKTB. He told us that when Chris approached him, he was taking a long break:

> I had been unemployed for a year [laughing]. I had been thinking about retiring. I said yes to Chris because I thought maybe I could contribute to the company.

Emma told us that she would really like to recruit Kevin after learning that he's a 'figures' guy:

> I think that our company didn't have many figures guys, I really wanted to get one. At the beginning, the department focused on doing marketing research to support the branding and marketing of the company. But I wanted to make full use of Kevin's potential. So, I tuned him to drive towards the strategic planning part. The department is now able to help with the overall planning of the company.

Group marketing

After setting up the Strategic Planning department, Chris then attempted to get the 'real' work started. He wanted to set up another new department, which would be responsible for the corporate-level marketing. The goal Chris had was to transform FBL into an international jewellery brand, something beyond a traditional Chinese goldsmith company. Chris elaborated on the concept of group marketing to us:

> In the past, the company certainly had marketing people, but the marketing was very much limited to the frontline operational level. If we wanted to build a brand, we definitely needed macro-level branding. I am talking about

creating a group image, not simply about printing some coupons or putting up some print advertisements.

Chris recruited Kayden Ma, his former mentee at TTI, in August 2010 to build a group marketing team. He explained his choice:

> Since we want to make FBL look more modern and stylish, we want someone who has fashion sense, you know, someone who can appreciate beautiful things. Kayden is quite a trendy person. He's that sort of person who loves to shop at Lane Crawford,[8] for example.

Kayden majored in Marketing when he was an undergraduate student at a local university in Hong Kong; he also got an MBA degree at the same university. After graduation, Kayden worked as a Management Trainee at TTI, where he first met Chris. Referred by Chris, Kayden also worked at the HKTB for a while. Prior to joining FBL, Kayden had worked in a major information and communications technology company in Hong Kong.

The major difficulty in setting up the new department, according to Chris, was that the company simply had very little budget for campaigns. In fact, when Kayden first joined the company, he was the only person in the new department, as Kayden told us:

> Before I joined FBL, I had led a team of around ten people. When I first joined FBL, we even didn't have the Group Marketing Department – it was just something like Strategic Marketing. It was basically a one-man band, I had to develop my team from scratch.

When we asked Kayden why he was willing to join FBL, he told us that he was touched by the sincerity of Emma:

> I remember that Emma wrote a very long reply to my thank you letter after the interview. I think that she's passionate and sincere and she really appreciates talents. She really wants to make some changes and she understands very clearly that she needs outside help. She can respect the values of an individual. I think we share similar ideas, like doing some international crossover campaigns.

Kayden emphasized that one important motivation for him to join FBL is that he saw the potential in the company:

> When I told people that I was going to join FBL, nine out of ten said that I was just an idiot [because of the bad reputation of the company]. When I was young, I just wanted to work for the coolest brands in the world. However, when I become older, I become more concerned about proving my leadership. I want to help a potential brand, to make it better. I think FBL really has potential. I am very much convinced.

Chris, Kayden emphasized, was also an important factor. He trusted Chris's choice. In a similar vein, Emma also trusted Chris's recommendation:

> At that time, we wanted to launch digital marketing, so we wanted someone who is energetic and has fresh ideas. Kayden has a lot of good ideas. We didn't have the same kind of person in the company. It's good to bring some new elements into the company.

Human resources

Around the same time, Chris referred Maria Cheung, another former colleague of his to oversee the Human Resources Department of FBL. Maria had extensive managerial experience and had worked in various big corporations in different fields such as telecommunications and banking before joining FBL. Not unlike Kevin, according to Maria, she was taking a break and thinking of getting retired when Chris approached her:

> At the beginning, Chris just asked for some referrals from me. He said that the company had been shopping around for a director for the HR department for quite a long time. I referred some candidates to them, but they still couldn't find the right person. Chris then asked if I myself would be interested in taking up the position. He said the company culture would suit me. I was not that interested, but out of courtesy, I still agreed to meet Emma.

Maria told us that after some conversations with Emma, she thought that FBL might suit her character, and her experience would help the company. We asked Maria to further elaborate. She told us that she was convinced by Emma's passion:

> Emma told me that she would like to transform the company. She told me she wanted to bring in good practices. I told her my ideas and she thought they were great. I think she really had a vision for the future of the company. She also talked very openly about the court case. She also told me that the company culture and structure were very simple. I would just report to her directly. It's a bonus point indeed. I hated the politics of the big corporation.

Maria did not forget to emphasize that Chris was also a key factor, as she told us:

> Chris played a very important role. I trust Chris. He gave me the confidence that the company has potential. As he's there, I guess FBL can't really be a terrible place.

Retail marketing

When Chris was creating the Group Marketing department, he already had in mind the idea of setting up a Retail Marketing department along with Group Marketing.

He said that it was getting more difficult to convince the boss to create another new department, but he still thought that it was necessary to do so. The major goal Chris had was to integrate the retail marketing of Hong Kong and China for the company and to develop a coherent policy and strategy. He explained to us:

> We also needed macro-and group-level coordination of marketing in retail. Retail and group marketing work hand in hand. Customer relationship management is very important. We had to change the mentality of our staff. In the past, they just worked on their own without paying attention to the central or group concept.

Chris recruited Ryan Leung, again, one of his former colleagues from TTI, to take up the new position in August 2011. Chris got to know Ryan in the early 1990s when Ryan joined TTI as a summer intern. Ryan specializes in marketing. In addition to TTI, Ryan also worked for other large corporations. Before joining FBL, he was responsible for developing digital marketing for the HKTB.

Ryan told us that at the beginning he had reservations about joining FBL as he had a stable job in the HKTB. The scale of FBL was also relatively small compared to the companies where he had worked. It was not an easy decision, according to Ryan. We asked Ryan why he was willing to 'take the risk'. Not unlike Kayden and Maria, Ryan also mentioned that Chris was an important factor. He had confidence in working and getting along with Chris. More fundamentally, as he told us, he was motivated by a sense of mission:

> I think the company desperately needed help. They needed new blood to revitalize everything. You have a feeling that you can help the company in need, and they appreciate your value too. We also share common values, like the emphasis on crossover and breaking the old way of doing business in the jewellery industry and perceiving FBL as a brand not just a jewellery company. They emphasized that they wanted non-jewellery people. They also wanted someone to develop the Chinese market. I thought that would be a good chance for me to gain some exposures.

Showroom as an alternative channel

The last senior executive whom Chris recruited is Aaron Chow, who was appointed as the Director of Showrooms in 2014. As mentioned earlier in the chapter, Desmond had overseen the showrooms since the court case incident until he gradually withdrew from the day-to-day operation of FBL. Chris told us that they did not just want to find someone to replace Desmond but to transform the showroom business:

> It's not hard to find a director for the showroom. The key point is that we want to transform the whole business. We need to look for someone who is tough enough to break the tradition.

Chris's goal was to transform the showroom into one of the 'alternate channels' of the company. He explained to us why he wanted someone who had experience in running businesses on different platforms to take the leadership:

> We [the showroom business] are facing cutthroat competitions. The show-room business was our cash cow in the past, but today it has to become something more 'progressive', like an alternative channel. Otherwise it is not sustainable. We emphasize that FBL is a brand, not simply a retail outlet. We can sell FBL, the brand, through diverse channels and the showroom is one of them.

'Aaron is a tough guy,' said Chris. 'He's a good candidate to drive the changes in the showroom.' Among the people he referred to FBL, Chris has known Aaron for the longest period. Aaron was a Marketing graduate of a local university in Hong Kong. His first employer was a foreign tobacco company. Then he worked in TTI for ten years, where he met Chris. He also worked for one of the property giants in Hong Kong. Through the recommendation of Chris, he also worked in HKTB and WOB previously. In the HKTB, according to Aaron, his major duty was be the bridge between the government and the industry. Through this experience, he became familiar with the taxi, jewellery, and watch industries.

Aaron did not tell us in detail why he decided to join FBL, but Chris, again was apparently one of the major reasons, as Aaron told us:

> I joined FBL because of Chris's recommendation. He asked me to help the company to add value. I got to know Chris back in 1991 when I was still working at TTI. He suddenly became my boss one day. We worked closely together. Then he referred me to HKTB and to WOB. After Chris left WOB, I took up the job in a joint venture between a company and WOB. After completing my job there, I joined Chris in FBL.

The modern organizational and managerial approach

The team-building process reflects Chris's vision of a modern organizational and managerial approach. He told us that he is well-trained in organizational restructuring:

> I got a lot of training in this area, haha. The companies I had worked for before went through rounds of organizational restructuring. I was known as an 'o-chart god' among my colleagues [laughing].

'In the past, the company didn't even have a proper organizational chart,' Chris said. The major problem with the organization of FBL, according to Chris, was that the division of labour was unclear and job functions were not well defined, one of the major features that characterized Fong's *jan cing mei* management regime as mentioned in Chapter 7. As a result, the efficiency was extremely low. Chris explained the situation to us:

> For instance, we visited a retail branch one day and spotted some problems with the images in the store. We asked the store manager to fix the problem. She referred us to the marketing team. The marketing team then referred us to a staff in another department. The staff then told us that he was just responsible for photo shooting and told us we should go to the Interior Design Department instead. It's just one among many examples. Very often we can't find the one who is accountable to a particular job and project.

To solve the problems with the organizational structure of FBL, Chris attempted to formalize and institutionalize the organizational structure of the company so that the report line and job functions could be more clearly defined.

Following the practice of many big, modern companies, Chris attempted to introduce a matrix cum cluster organizational approach to FBL. Following this approach, Chris divided the business of the company into different clusters, such as 'Showroom and Alternative Channels', 'China Retail', and 'Hong Kong and Overseas Retail'. The centre would provide corporate expertise to support these clusters and enhance the sense of business ownership of each cluster. At the same time, localized and functional expertise were also provided to help achieve a balance between control and efficiency.

The sales and operation of China Retail at FBL, according to Ryan, for instance, had undergone drastic localization to emphasize local team-building:

> It's about a sense of responsibility and ownership. The heads of the sales operation have become the regional general managers, who have the responsibility to oversee the whole operation. The purchase of products has also been localized. The company has now set up a 'buyer' system. The buyers are the representatives of a particular region of sales unit. They will be responsible for 'ordering' the products for their own region. The purchase of the products is no longer decided by the Hong Kong headquarters so as to take care of the regional taste. At the same time, the local sales units have to take the responsibility for their own decisions.

The corporate management committee

Most of these organizational changes had taken place *before* September 2011 when Jackson and Fong finally re-joined the company. Jackson was employed as Chief Merchandising Officer while Fong was employed as an adviser to the company under the title 'Founder'. After Jackson returned, the company established a Corporate Management Committee (CMC) to support the new organizational and managerial approach.

The CMC was established as the top management team of the company and was designed to share the function of the CEO and represent different business clusters and functions. The members of the CMC included Emma, Desmond, Chris,

Jackson, Henry (CFO), and Maria. According to Maria, the CMC was responsible for setting the corporate strategies and making important decisions. The members of the CMC would discuss and communicate with each other on various issues and try to reach a consensus. When the committee failed to reach a consensus, the CEO would have the final say.

The establishment of the CMC was to further align FBL with a modern corporate framework. A very crucial element of a modern corporation, according to Kevin, is that the decision-making process should not be concentrated in the hands of one or two figures of the company; instead it should be facilitated by a team. A 'modern corporation is not a personal but a collective concept,' emphasized Kevin.

To summarize, the new organizational structure of FBL was directed towards a matrix and cluster approach with the support of a top management team represented by the CMC. The new structure attempted to ensure that the decision-making power would not be concentrated solely in the hands of the owners but shared among the professional managers. On the other hand, the job functions and reporting of the employees would be more clearly defined through the organizational change. Through the organizational restructuring, the professional managerial class of FBL, with Chris at the core, has been fostering the modern management system in the company.

VMV and corporate culture building

The CMC, modelled after large corporations, also took the lead in implementing a series of corporate culture building activities through the establishment of a special taskforce. In 2012, after some long discussions, the CMC and other senior executives formulated the Vision and Mission of the company. The CMC also picked a set of five core values that best represented the corporate culture, namely, caring and respect, integrity, quality service, accountability, and long-term thinking. The formulation of the Vision, Mission, and Value (VMV), according to Maria, was extremely important to the company as she told us:

> Corporate culture is very important, I think. It helps the company to differentiate itself from the competitors. We also want to build up solidarity. We should not focus on the monetary benefit only. It's important to emphasize the corporate values and cultures too.

The VMV, according to Jackson, also included some Christian elements:

> I think that a leader of a company is like a preacher. Religion is about sharing the good things with others and touching them. We are Christians, we think that our religious faith is something good, so we would also like to share it with our employees.

The company adopted a top-down approach to promote the concept of VMV among the employees. The VMV would be introduced to all new employees of the company during the orientation session. In addition, a special taskforce was set up in the summer of 2013 to enhance the knowledge and identification of the employees of FBL with the corporate values. The taskforce received a budget from the company and reported to the CMC directly. It was composed of 14 employees from different departments. According to the chairman of the taskforce, the members of the taskforce belonged to the rank of officer/manager. Basically, different departments had to send their own representatives to join the taskforce.

During the first meeting of the taskforce, Emma was present to introduce the VMV to the members. The major responsibility of the taskforce was to promote the VMV in an 18-month timeframe. The taskforce had to meet regularly to discuss the plan for the promotion. They spent around three months to promote each of the five values. In addition to designing the activities, the members of the taskforce were also responsible for facilitating and promoting the activities especially in their own departments.

The active participation of the top management was one of the major characteristics of the implementation of the VMV scheme. The CMC members took the initiative to be the delegates of the five core values and convened the VMV taskforce: Maria was Ms. Caring and Respect, Henry Mr. Integrity, Jackson Mr. Quality Service, Chris Mr. Accountability, and Desmond Mr. Long-term Thinking. And Emma was the representative of the whole VMV. In fact, the top management team tried very hard to engage in the VMV activities. They surprised the employees very often by making unannounced appearances in the activities. The following brief field note written by Chau, one of the authors of the book, demonstrates the participation of the top management in the VMV promotion:

> It's around 8:30 a.m., I arrive at the [office] lobby a little earlier than I usually do. I didn't have enough sleep the day before, so I feel like my mind is away. When I try to go through the entrance gate, the clatter of the people catches my attention. I haven't paid any attention to my surroundings as I just keep looking at the floor. 'What's going on,' I say to myself. I raise my head a bit and I see Emma standing in front of the staircase. There are a couple of staff there too. 'Good morning,' Emma said while distributing something to me. I just realize that I have walked close enough to her to catch her attention. I haven't become fully awake. I can only greet her back after a couple of seconds. When I am walking up, I look back and see the stunned faces of employees getting to work. No one will expect your boss to wait at the lobby of the office to say good morning to you, obviously. I take a look of what I have got from Emma as I head back to my desk. It's a VMV newsletter. I then realize the staff downstairs are members of the VMV committee. People are discussing this the whole morning, especially those who are late for work. 'Damn it, I have been caught by Emma,' one of them says.

The field note mentioned earlier illustrates how the top management of FBL attempted to promote a new corporate culture in the company. Not just Emma, but other members of the CMC actively engaged in different VMV activities. In the process, they intentionally created an easy-to-approach image.

The organizational change and recruitment of new blood at FBL also reflected the emphasis of the company on branding and marketing. In fact, the desire of Emma and Jackson to rebuild the image of FBL and transform the company into a modern and international brand is the major reason that Chris was recruited in the first place, as branding and marketing was his main field of expertise.

(Re)branding FBL

Chris played a key role in formulating the new branding and marketing strategies of the company. To get rid of the stigma of the company, Chris had to reposition and redefine FBL to regain the support of customers. After communicating with Emma, Chris proposed the new brand concept of 'Trendsetting Craftsmanship'. According to Chris, 'trendsetting' focused on the trendy and modern aspect of the company while 'craftsmanship' highlighted tradition and technique; the concept reflected the aspiration of the company to blend tradition and modernity. He explained to us the process of looking for a brand concept:

> I spent a lot of time discussing with Emma. It [the concept] is a product of rounds of discussion and brainstorming. I asked her several questions, like, 'What shall the brand represent?' 'What is the DNA of FBL? 'What does FBL represent?' It is important that we have to ask ourselves who we are. The very first step for any branding and marketing campaign is that we have to create a concept and identity.

Chris told us that he first came up with the concept of 'craftsmanship':

> My idea is that while other big jewellery companies were founded as a trading and retailing house, FBL was founded as a workshop and a production house. Thus, FBL should emphasize its tradition in craftsmanship to differentiate itself from the competitors.

'Craftsmanship' alone however, according to Chris, was not strong enough to stand as a core positioning of the brand:

> It [craftsmanship] is not innovative enough. I then proposed to add some international and fashion elements to emphasize the modern side of the company. We finally have the 'trendsetting' part.

Chris told us that in fact Jackson did not accept the concept at the beginning:

> Emma accepted the concept very quickly, but Jackson needed time to consider. He was alright with the emphasis on craftsmanship, but he was not so sure about the 'trendsetting' part. He thought that jewellery should be something timeless instead of trendy or fashionable. At first, Jackson's mind set was pretty much production-oriented. He put a lot of emphasis on the quality of products.

To reach a consensus, Chris suggested that Jackson represent 'craftsmanship' while Emma the 'trendsetting' dimension. The new positioning of the company was announced in early 2011 even though Jackson still had some reservations. After the success of several marketing campaigns built around the concept, according to Chris, Jackson was gradually convinced. The Vision and Mission of the company, as decided by the CMC, indeed reflected the new brand concept of the company by emphasizing 'global styles' and 'international lifestyles'. The vision was designated so as to

> provide a total styling solution that demonstrates and perfects one's style and taste through the daily wearing of 'Fine Jewellery Accessories' of global styles which makes one appreciate and actualize his/her true-self.

In order to achieve the vision, the mission of the company was set to

> offer a variety of fine jewellery accessories that satisfy the specific needs of different target segments, and to bring international lifestyles to China & beyond.

Rebranding love

After drawing up the new brand concept, Chris and his team then started to work on a series of branding and marketing campaigns to deliver the brand identity to the public. In 2012, the company launched a 3.5-minute TV commercial. FBL had not launched any TV commercials since 1997. This commercial had a special meaning to the company as it signalled to the market the 'full come-back' of the company.

FBL's new TV commercial was meant to illustrate the new positioning of the company as 'the artisan of love'. In the commercial we see the female protagonist becoming deaf after a car accident, and then trying to avoid meeting her boyfriend, who is a pianist, as she thinks that she is no longer a good match for him. Later, the boyfriend asks her out and she realizes that he has learned sign language in order to communicate with her. They arrive at a performance hall and the boyfriend performs a song, which he had spent the past months writing especially for her. She can 'listen' to the song by feeling the vibration of the piano and recalls their memories. After performing the song, her boyfriend then proposes to her.

The key message of the commercial, according to Chris, is that love is not always an easy process; one has to go through a lot of difficulties and must persevere in the process. This is in fact a way of FBL to try to differentiate itself from the competitors, as Chris explains to us:

> As you know, all jewellery companies feature love in their advertisements. How can we stand out? What story can we tell? Very often, in the jewellery advertisements, love is portrayed as something happy, sweet and perfect. We want to depict a different image of love, one that reflects the reality. Love is not just about those joyful moments, there are also pains and suffering.

What's important is to persevere, not to give up despite all the difficulties. Honestly, Mr. Fong didn't like it [the commercial] at the beginning. There's a car crash, blood and all those 'bad' things. It's just counterintuitive to him. They [traditional jewellers] didn't do things in that way. But that's exactly what we want. We want to reveal the real story of love.

The commercial, according to Chris, was intended to represent the story of Emma and Jackson as well as the company. He wanted to present to the customers the idea that despite the low tide, the company still persevered; and the Fong family also kept each other company and underwent the crisis hand in hand. In other words, to position FBL as 'the artisan of love' was an attempt by the company to promote the love story between Emma and Jackson and to underline the efforts of the company to overcome its difficulties.

The production of the commercial also represented the attempt by the company to internationalize. The company recruited a Japanese director to shoot the commercial in Taiwan. The girlfriend and boyfriend in the commercial are Taiwanese and Japanese respectively. Chris told us his intention:

I guess you don't think it's [the commercial] very Hong Kong, right? We don't want to create a very local feeling. People tend to associate local Hong Kong jewellery companies with traditional Chinese goldsmiths. This is not something we want.

According to Chris, they did not want the market to interpret FBL only as a local Hong Kong brand; they wanted to appeal to a wider audience in Asia, at least.

In 2014, FBL launched another campaign to further promote its brand image of 'artisan of love'. This time, instead of emphasizing the perseverance in love, the company attempted to highlight the appreciation of love. Chris explained his idea:

After the success of the first commercial, we continued to explore a new way to tell the story of love. Then we came up with this idea. Very often, when we send a gift to another person, it's because I want to express my love to you, right? I want to deliver the message: I do love you. It's all about me, about my perspective. But how about you and your love? Very often, we just take the love and care of another person for granted. We seldom express our gratitude for others' love. That's why we came up with this campaign, to tell people to be thankful for love.

FBL launched a twin TV commercial featuring the perspectives of the boyfriend and the girlfriend respectively. The story of the commercials is simple. It portrays the daily life of a couple and features the monologue of the boyfriend/girlfriend thanking his/her other half.

These campaigns demonstrate how Chris and his team attempted to create an emotional touch for the FBL brand through a portrayal of love stories in an unconventional way.

Trendsetting crossovers

In addition to emotional storytelling centring around the theme of love, Chris and his team also emphasize the concept of crossover to differentiate FBL from its competitors. The company launched a series of crossover marketing campaigns to collaborate with different artists from different places.

The first such campaign was launched in April 2011, when FBL collaborated with a micro-sculpture artist to organize an exhibition in one of the major shopping malls in Hong Kong. The exhibition featured a piece of micro-sculpture entitled 'created by the artist' on a one-karat diamond. The main purpose of the function was to promote FBL's newly launched 100-facet diamond products. The exhibition, according to Chris, had a very good reception:

> It's an idea proposed by our PR agency. We thought it's quite interesting and it would help promote the idea of craftsmanship. We didn't have the budget to do a TV commercial in the early period, so we could only work on some marketing campaigns. TVB[9] covered the exhibition as well. It's been a long time since FBL got such high-profile media coverage.

In the exhibition, the visitors could use a microscope to view the art pieces while checking out the diamonds at the same time. The exhibition was also held in Shanghai in May of the same year.

In the next year, FBL launched another crossover campaign attempting to blend fashion and jewellery together. Through a collaboration with a Hong Kong raised and New York based fashion designer, FBL was able to make a name on the runway at New York Fashion Week. The designer and FBL tried to collaborate by using the same motif, the Chinese Five Elements,[10] to design the jewellery and the fashion for the show. The designer was responsible for the design. The jewellery design team of FBL in turn helped to modify the design fit for actual jewellery production.

At the beginning, the designer was not willing to collaborate with FBL. It was Kayden who initiated the project. He spent almost half a year persuading the designer to join the project. Kayden told us how he won the support of the designer at the end:

> I think it's important to create a win-win situation. We wanted to gain international exposure and give the brand a more stylish image. The designer, on the other hand, hoped to enhance her exposure in China. The collaboration helped both sides. In an international fashion show, jewellery usually just plays a minor role. In this collaboration, jewellery and fashion were put on the same level. I think it's worthwhile.

Chris also agreed that the campaign was a successful one, as he said:

> We have become the first local Hong Kong jewellery company to appear at an international fashion show. It's cool. It's a big step for us to become an international brand. We ran the show again in Beijing a year later.

After collaborating with a sculptor and fashion designer, FBL collaborated with a painter in 2014 to launch another crossover marketing campaign. The company collaborated with a Malaysian painter to showcase some modern paintings combining a new set of jewellery designed by FBL with other materials such as feathers, pins and artificial flowers. Chris explained the collaboration to us:

> The artist is known as a painter who can paint without a paintbrush. She uses various daily materials to create her paintings. We like her works. The purpose of the campaign is to position FBL as a brand which appreciates the value of arts.

They held a jewellery art exhibition in Beijing. FBL also arranged jewellery masters to demonstrate the process of jewellery making in the venue to illustrate the 'craftsmanship' of the company.

The rationale behind these crossover marketing campaigns was to deliver a message to the consumers that FBL represents trendsetting craftsmanship. It is not a coincidence that FBL chose to collaborate with artists. First, their artworks represent craftsmanship. Second, by collaborating with artists, the company attempted to demonstrate that it knows how to value art and has good taste. The artists chosen, we want to emphasize, have an international outlook and their artworks are known for their trendy and unconventional style. This, again, aligned with the new brand emphasis on being international and stylish.

The efforts of Chris and his team to rebuild the brand image of FBL seemed to pay off. Chris was proud of the achievement, as he told us during an interview in 2015:

> When I joined FBL, the brand recall rate was just around 40 per cent. Now, it has reached around 80 per cent. People had almost forgotten the company, but now we have come back, and people are aware of it. We have a very high brand efficiency ratio. You know, we've only got a very tiny budget, compared to what I used to have in those big companies.

The achievement by Chris was also recognized by the company. In 2013, Chris was promoted to Deputy CEO (Commercial). In the same year, FBL also designated Jackson as Deputy CEO (Supplies) and Desmond as Chief Corporate Development Officer.

Conclusion

This chapter made several important observations that are relevant to the nature and content of the transformation of FBL. First, the on-going transformation can be seen as an effort by Chris and his team to introduce to FBL modern management through professionalization which consists of three major steps. The first step was to recruit professional managers who are 'traditionally depicted as someone with formal management education . . . and the ability to take a universal, that is, noncontextual and objective, impersonal and nonemotional approach to the job' (Hall and Nordqvist, 2008, p. 54). The second step was to introduce a new management system that emphasizes rationalization and formalization of the corporate structure, professionalization of each functional unit of the organization, transparency and democratization of the decision-making process, decision-making based on scientific research, and the improvement of the corporate governance. The final step was to develop business strategies that stress the importance of brand-building and marketing.

All of this constitutes a point-to-point opposite to Fong's *jan cing mei* management regime. While Fong, as an entrepreneur, dominated all the decision-making processes inside the company, the new management promoted collective decision-making practices by professional managers; while Fong tended to ignore the organizational chart and relied only on his *lou san zi* to get things done, the new management upheld the principle of 'the right man in the right place', emphasizing rational division of labour, clear job demarcation, job assignments according to a clear command chain, and sophisticated professional managerial control; and while Fong used a low-pricing strategy to sell his products, the new management emphasized 'Trendsetting Craftsmanship' as the core concept of FBL's corporate brand and the modern marketing strategies to promote the brand.

Second, while Fong treasured and encouraged *jan cing mei* embedded in the interpersonal relationships between the staff and himself and among the staff, the new management stressed the importance of general core values as we can see from the VMV campaign. Jackson, Emma, and their newly recruited professional managers understood that the new management system could not be successful if the employees, especially those *lou san zi*, would not change their mindset developed in the previous *jan cing mei* regime. The new management team therefore decided to impose on their employees 'a particular way of seeing and being' (Comaroff and Comaroff, 1989, p. 267) through the VMV campaign. The new management system, therefore, cannot be understood simply as a new institutional arrangement *only* because it is also a discursive practice that fosters what Stanley Deetz (1992, p. 122) calls 'a point of view or manner of paying attention' among the staff. As Deetz (1992, p. 122; italics original) explained it through an example:

> If presented with a *cat, dog, tree,* and *squirrel* and asked which one is different, we can strike the difference along multiple thematic lines, such as plant/animal, wild/domestic, like/not like, in my yard/not in my yard, and so forth. As a thematic line becomes a focus, it can be extended into an endless horizon of other applications, other moments of decision, considerations of what can be done with it, questions like whether it feels pain and excludes other experiences and considerations. The thematic line can be said to be an articulation (to foreshadow a more recent term) of that experience, a particular way experience is centered and put together. Every experience can be thematized in multiple ways. Certain thematic structures are used over and over again and can be said to become sedimented and thus make it difficult to see the multiple thematic opportunities

By the same token, the new management system represents a thematic line which constructed and articulated the difference between the new management and Fong's *jan cing mei* regime as one between good/bad, modern/old-fashion, progressive/backward, rational/irrational, scientific/intuitional, democratic/feudal, efficient/inefficient, and so on, in the course of which the relationship between the new management and Fong's *jan cing mei* regime was converted from a relationship between two equal but different management systems into a hierarchical one.

Understood as such, we can consider the VMV campaign, targeting the *lou san zi*, as a way, to paraphrase Jean Comaroff and John Comaroff (1991, p. 4), 'to colonize their consciousness with the axioms and aesthetics of an alien culture'. The 'alien culture' in the context of FBL must mean both the new management system and the set of five core values promoted by the VMV campaign, which is also to say that the transformation is at once ideological and institutional, symbolic and material.

It follows that the transformation process itself is political. We have to add hastily that the political struggle was not just between the new management system and Fong's *jan cing mei* regime; it was underlined by a more complex micro-political dynamic. The dynamic, as will be shown in the next chapter, includes the relationship among the owner (Jackson and Emma), the professional managers (Chris and his management team), and the *lou san zi*. The relationship, however, is very complex because each of these three major players cannot be perceived as a homogenous group and therefore the members of each group did not always act in the same way. As will be demonstrated in next chapter, some professional managers would try to sympathize with the *lou san zi*, while others tended to maintain a harsh attitude towards the latter; on the other hand, some *lou san zi* would try to build a friendly relationship with the professional managers, while others resisted the latter's domination outright. To make the situation more complex, the owners would try to side with one group in one circumstance and switch their position to side with the other group on other occasions. More importantly, Jackson and Emma did not always agree with each other. When disagreements between them arose, each of them would seek the support of different groups by establishing temporary allies with the group from which they sought support. In short, the forms and characters of the circumstances is crucial because the major players would alter their goals, strategies, and actions according to the circumstances, which in turn changed the forms and characters of the interaction among the major players, and as a result of which the consequences of the interaction would change correspondingly. We argue in the next chapter that it is this complex micro-political dynamic that had made the transformation possible at the beginning; but when the circumstances change, it is the same dynamic that rendered the transformation a failure in the end.

Notes

1 *Apple Daily* is one of the major newspapers in Hong Kong. The arrest of Fong and Jackson became headlines in the major newspapers. Desmond was photographed together with Fong.

2 One may immediately point out that Emma is also a member of the Fong family. How-ever, she is not the daughter of Fong; she only married into the Fong family. In this sense, she is still able to claim and emphasize her outsider status, at least partially.

3 At the time of writing, Desmond is still the Non-Executive Director and Deputy Chairman of FBL.

4 Within the company context, the employees and even Emma herself referred to the imprisonment of Fong and Jackson as a 'vacation' to down play the nature of the event.

5 TTI is a pseudonym. It is one of the largest telecommunications companies in Hong Kong. During the colonial era, it was a prestigious company and a dominant player in the market.

6 WOB is a pseudonym.

7 We will describe Chris's personal story in detail in Chapter 10.

8 Lane Crawford is a well-known retail company in Hong Kong selling luxury goods from different international brands.

9 Television Broadcasts Limited, established in 1967, is the major television broadcasting company in Hong Kong.

10 The five elements are wood, fire, earth, metal, and water.

10 The eternal return of the Chinese boss

As demonstrated in Chapter 9, FBL had undergone a transformation in which modern management was introduced by a group of newly recruited professional managers who had no prior experience in the jewellery industry. Within a couple of years, the company seemed to be successfully transforming from a traditional Chinese family into a modern corporation. The transformation, however, deteriorated very quickly. Chris and his team started to resign from 2016 and almost all the newly recruited professional managers left the company in the following two years. The crucial questions then are: what made the transformation possible in the first place? And what rendered the transformation a failure in the end?

We argue that the transformation itself should be seen as a social process in which Jackson, Emma, the professional managers, and the *lou san zi* interacted with each other to produce the consequences of the transformation. We have to stress that the nature, form, and character of such an interaction were ever-changing because they all depended on the goals, strategies, and actions of each player involved, which varied with circumstances. The consequence of the interaction therefore was contingent on specific circumstances. Analytically, attention should thus be paid to the goals, strategies, actions of each player involved, *and* the circumstances which motivated them. Methodologically, we should study the interaction among Jackson, Emma, Chris and his team, and *lou san zi* in the total social context of different circumstances. This naturally requires our analysis to have a longer temporal span to capture the process of the interaction.

This chapter therefore starts from the first circumstance in which Emma took over FBL after the arrest of her husband and her father-in-law. We will examine why Emma was forced to recruit professional managers outside the company to help her transform FBL; how Jackson's aspirations helped shape the form and character of the transformation; and why Chris and his professional managers were willing to join FBL. We argue that Emma's motivations and Jackson's aspirations helped explain why Chris and his team were able to gain the trust of the Fong couple to carry out a number of reforms in the company in the first place.

In the second part of this chapter, we will identify two forms of politics underlying the transformation process. The first is the politics between the *lou san zi* and the professional managers; the other among Chris, Emma, and Jackson. We will show how these two forms of politics shape the consequences of the reform.

In the last part of this chapter, we will show how a new circumstance (the second circumstance) has changed the goals, strategies, and actions of the major players including Emma, Jackson, Chris and his professional team, and the *lou san zi* which in turn altered the form and character of the interaction among the major players; and how the new form and character of the interaction led to Chris's resignation. Finally, we will examine why Jackson as the *jiazhang* regained control of the company, or to be more accurate, the *jia*.

The first circumstance: the crisis

The first circumstance at issue was the unexpected Independent Commission Against Corruption (ICAC) prosecution and the imprisonment of Fong and Jackson. The event had several consequences that directly and indirectly contributed to the inception of the transformation of the company. First, it led to a leadership vacuum. The founder, the chairman, and the CEO of the company were all gone together with most of the company's senior executives. The company and Emma desperately needed to scout new people to support the operation. Second, it created an urgent need for the company to reform and rebuild its image. Henry Ng, the then CFO, believed that the crisis was a good thing for FBL. He explained his view to us:

> That [the crisis] helped remove a lot of obstacles. When you want to reform something, there is always resistance, of course. Then you could remind the people about the court case, "You see, it's not me who wanted to create troubles. We have to change, we have to do this, otherwise we will undergo the same thing again." The crises basically gave impetus to the transformation. Even the owners understood that they had to do something.

For Emma, the coming of Chris and his team helped consolidate her leadership in the company. What mattered to her, during the early period of her chairmanship, was to rally support. Imagine Emma's position in the company. She did not have any trustworthy ally in the company. Her husband was still in prison; Desmond was rather unsettling; the *lou san zi* in the company had a lot more experience in the industry than she did; and she shared with neither the class nor educational background, ideas of where the company should go from that time on with them.

In addition, Emma did not have a lot of top-level managerial experiences before taking up the chairwoman position. As one interviewee told us:

> When she first started [as a chairman], she had very little knowledge of the industry and did not really know how to lead and manage the company. She had to rely on us [the professional managers].

More importantly, Emma was more comfortable working with the professional managers instead of the *lou san zi* because of their similar backgrounds. Emma was born into a middle-class family in Hong Kong in the early 1970s. Like Jackson, Emma was also educated in the United States. After finishing secondary school in Hong Kong, she attended grade 12 at a high school in the United States. She then went on to major in Computer Engineering at a university. She met Jackson at a church event as the two attended the same university. The two devoted Christians soon fell in love with each other. The couple married in 1996 in Hong Kong. It is thus not a surprise that Emma felt at ease with Chris, who shares a similar background with her (we will turn to Chris's personal story later). Both came from a middle-class family, received education overseas, had exposure in large corporations, and shared the same religious beliefs.

Emma's intention to recruit professional managers is also related to her devotion to Jackson, her husband. After she married Jackson, Emma worked for several multinational corporations (MNCs) before joining FBL in 2002. Emma decided to join FBL because she wanted to help shoulder Jackson's burden. When she took up the chairmanship from Jackson, Emma's goal was very clear. She was determined to look after the company on behalf of her husband until he came back. She could not let the company fall and die. She had to be tough as Jackson relied on her. As she told us:

> After the sentence, I got to visit Jackson in prison during the weekend before going to work. Jackson simply asked me, 'Why are you here? Go back to work, help me look after the company!' I was quite hurt at that moment, frankly. But I understood Jackson's feelings.

Emma repeatedly emphasized during the interviews with the media and with us that everything she did for FBL, she did it because of her love for her husband. She joined the company and became the chairwoman simply because she loves her husband so much that she wants to help her husband to realize his dream.

Emma thus regards herself as a proxy, if not an extension, of her husband, especially when he was absent. It is of the utmost importance for her to live up to the expectations of Jackson. To be a good wife in this context is to help look after the company for her husband. To fulfil her role as a good wife, Emma then had to save the company, to manage the crises and to realize Jackson's aspiration. We therefore cannot understand the transformation that took place under Emma's leadership without understanding that she was working as a 'proxy' for Jackson.

Jackson's aspiration

Jackson's aspiration was to transform FBL into an international brand such as Cartier and Tiffany. To understand why Jackson came up with such an aspiration, we must trace his biographical experience. Jackson has a strong sense of ownership of FBL. As the successor and the new *jiazhang* (head of the family) of the family's business, Jackson believes that he bears the sole and heavy responsibility to preserve the family legacy.

Religion also plays a crucial role in shaping Jackson's aspiration. Jackson is a devoted Christian. Christianity affects his personal values and business ideologies considerably. He was eager to share his faith with us:

> I got to know God because of my siblings. Joseph became a Christian a year before he went to the United States. Daisy later said that she felt that she constantly had the experience of a ghost pressing on the bed. Joseph brought her to the church, she then also became a Christian! Later, Joseph asked me to join a summer camp organized by the church. At first, I told myself that I would not 'fall' into Christianity. Never. But eventually I got to believe God as well. I had not predicted that at all.

Jackson had originally been given a chance to pursue a doctoral degree in the United States, but he decided to return to Hong Kong to help with the family business. When Jackson joined FBL in 1994, Daisy, his sister, had already been working in the company to take care of the business in China. Jackson was appointed as the Executive Director and assigned to manage the retail operation in Hong Kong. 'At the beginning, I didn't even know how to "use" a secretary,' Jackson said. 'I worked from 8:00 a.m. to 12:00 a.m. every day.'

Service-centred retail culture

Although the business of FBL was booming when Jackson joined the company, he clearly had other thoughts on his mind. Jackson believed that the major problem of FBL was that the company, not unlike other local jewellery and goldsmith companies, did not care about branding and innovation. He told us his ideas at that time:

> The jewellery and goldsmith stores were making good money back then. But they didn't pay attention to the details nor the need of the customers. The industry was very traditional. I just thought that this way of running a business was not sustainable. We couldn't go on like that forever. We had to make some changes.

The first thing Jackson did to change the company was to introduce the culture of 'customer-service' to the retail operation of FBL in Hong Kong. In order to build a service-centred culture among the frontline staff, Jackson contacted a consultancy to provide various customer-service-related trainings to the employees. He also took a lead in establishing a training department in the company. According to Zoe Tang who joined FBL in the late 1980s, Jackson also actively looked for new blood to help improve the service in the retail operation. He set up the new position of 'Regional Manager' and recruited experienced salespeople to take up the posts to help monitor the progress of the stores in adopting the new 'culture'. Jackson also placed a strong emphasis on the various 'service awards' in the industry, encouraging and training the frontline staff to participate in the competitions.

Jackson's goal was to convince the frontline staff that business and customer service are intertwined, and customer service shall become the core of FBL retail operation. Jackson wanted to make customer service the trademark that differentiates FBL from its competitors.

Brand building: from Fong Bou Lung to FBL

Jackson further introduced many different changes into the company during his chairmanship. He changed the official name of the company from pure Chinese into a mixture of Chinese and English. The aim of the change was to give the brand a more Western, if not international, appeal. The company was no longer referred to as 'Fong Bou Lung' in Chinese characters but as 'FBL' in three English letters. The English form, according to Jackson, could be better understood and memorized by non-Chinese speakers. He also chose the colour grape as the corporate hue to represent vibrancy and a balance between modern and tradition.

Second, Jackson changed the layout of the retail stores to provide a better shopping experience for his customers. He explained his idea to us:

> The interior layout of local jewellery and goldsmith companies was like a racecourse for horse racing. The showcases were either arranged in a 'U' or 'I I' shape.[1] It is not a very good design. The customers would feel enormous pressure as all the attention of the staff was directed to them.

Jackson attempted to convert all the FBL retail stores into boutique shops built around the modern, or to be more accurate, Western design motif. According to Tam Chi Chong, who joined FBL in the early 1990s as a salesperson, the new version of the store layout design was the work of a Western designer employed by Jackson. The signage, exterior walls, and facades of the stores have all been replaced. Inside the stores, showcases, according to Jackson's concept, have been arranged in clusters instead of the traditional 'U' or 'I I' shapes to create a more spacious atmosphere. Jackson also created a new set of in-store graphics featuring Western models exclusively. By the end of the financial year 2006–2007, 85 per cent of the FBL retail outlets in Hong Kong and all of those in China had been 'upgraded' to Jackson's version of modern, boutique stores.

These changes demonstrate that in Jackson's mind, to be modern and international is to be Western or at least to look Western. This would differentiate FBL, as Jackson believes, from its competitors. We would like to point out that Jackson's reform should also be understood as his attempt to differentiate himself from his father, who never talked about Western design, branding or customer service and experience. Jackson's attempt, however, was disrupted by the court case and the ensuing events. His aspiration had to be realized by Emma during his absence. That is also why Emma was willing to recruit professional managers to help realize Jackson's dreams after the imprisonment of Fong and Jackson.

A more compelling reason for Emma to seek outside help was that the recruitment of the professional managers, who were fresh to the jewellery industry, helped create a new corporate image that enabled FBL to dissociate itself from the scandal. In other words, the professionalization of FBL was a strategic move that the Fong couple took to rebuild their reputation and FBL's brand rather than an endeavour to introduce professional management to the company.

What about the professional managers? Why were they willing to join the company? As we have previously mentioned, one common factor that brought Chris, the leader of the professional managers, together with Emma and Jackson was Christianity.

Christianity as a common identity

It is not exaggerating to say that Christian faith motivated Chris to join FBL. Chris was born into a middle-class family in Hong Kong in the mid-1960s. Not unlike Jackson, Emma, and Desmond, Chris received his tertiary education abroad. As we have shown in the previous chapter, Chris's career went relatively smoothly. However, in 2008, when the economy was heavily damaged by the financial tsunami, Chris was laid off by WOB, the company he was working for at that time. He told us how he felt at that moment:

> I just couldn't help asking God: 'God, are you kidding me? Why such a joke?' I just kept wandering in Causeway Bay. I didn't know what to do. I didn't want to talk to anyone. Then a melody suddenly came into my mind. It's a gospel song that I wrote. The title is *What Matters?* I didn't know why but then I felt really calm. When I returned home, a reporter called me to confirm if I had been sacked. I simply said yes. You know, I really didn't have any mood to think and talk about it at that time. On the next day, to my great surprise, I found my story covered in the newspaper. I didn't know why but the reporter wrote that I would become a gospel singer. It was clearly a beautiful mistake, maybe it's a message from God.

Chris indeed devoted himself wholly to gospel singing after he left WOB. At that time, he did not have any specific plan or intention to dive into the commercial world again. When Emma invited him to join FBL, Chris declined the invitation because he was not really interested in retail or the jewellery business. In addition, Chris had never worked in a local Chinese family firm. More importantly, he enjoyed making gospel music and was not willing to give it up. The final reason was that the reputation of FBL was not good at all and he was concerned about the negative impact on his own portfolio.

After meeting Emma several times, Chris, however, changed his mind and decided to join the company. He told us what happened:

> A former colleague of mine recommended me to Emma. He told me that Emma wanted to find someone to help her with the operation of the company. Out of courtesy, I agreed to meet Emma and to learn more about FBL. Emma was very sincere and left a very good impression on me. However, I still did

not plan to join the company after meeting her twice. Then, on an evening after practising spiritual formation, I came across a book titled *The Purpose Driven Life*. I didn't know why but I just started to read it. The book inspired me to reflect on my life journey so far. I thought that there must be some purposes for my past career achievement. I then had the idea that maybe I could fulfil my purpose by becoming a CEO and a gospel singer at the same time. It's something new and inspirational. At that point, I began to reconsider Emma's offer. I told myself: 'If Emma is willing to disclose the details of the court case with me frankly, then I will give it a try.' During the third meeting with Emma, I had the feeling that she had nothing to hide from me. I thought maybe that was a chance for me to devote.

The decision to join FBL was regarded by Chris as a kind of calling as he believed that he could help the Fong family and FBL. As he told us:

> Honestly, companies like Cartier or Tiffany won't need me, but FBL will. Emma wants to transform the company while keeping the family tradition. She doesn't want FBL to be like a traditional and typical family business. That's why she wants people like me to help remake the brand.

We can see that Chris decided to join the company because he thought that, like a guardian angel, his expertise and experience could help save the Fong family and FBL through which he was able to derive a meaning for his life. Chris repeatedly emphasized that it was important for him to do something that he found meaningful, and this is inspired by his Christian faith. Note that Desmond, another devoted Christian, also used the same metaphor to explain his decision to stay with the Fong family and the company after the crisis, as we have demonstrated in Chapter 9. To help the company and the family in need was very much like a religious dedication, if not a mission, to them.

Emma was also a major reason why Chris was willing to join FBL. According to Chris, Emma's trust and passion really touched him and they shared similar beliefs and visions in the transformation of the company. Chris explained to us:

> Both Emma and I believe in transferrable skills. I position myself as a 'general manager'. Although I didn't have any experience in the jewellery industry, I believe that my experience in other industries is still highly useful. And it's important that Emma is convinced by that as well. I understand that it's not easy to implement reform and introduce something new to a family business. In fact, it's very risky, from Emma's perspective, to invite me to join the company. Emma has confidence in my expertise and value.

Another reason is that the company enabled him to strike a balance between religion and work and, in fact, to blend his religious faith with work. Recall that when Emma approached Chris, he dedicated all his time to gospel singing. He was not willing to give up his service to God. Emma and Jackson not just allowed but even encouraged Chris to continue making gospel music. They actively supported, for instance, Chris's personal concert by buying the tickets and distributing them to the employees. They also arranged to play Chris's songs in the office during breaks. Ryan Leung, who is also a Christian, also told us that he appreciated the support of the company of the Christian belief:

> It's good that the bosses are Christian. I feel like we have common values. There are very few companies that can integrate religious belief with the business operation. They try to instil Christian values in the business. For instance, we don't sell Buddhist products.

Christianity also helped to enhance the bonding among the top management of the company. In fact, all but one CMC members are Christian. During the interviews with them, they invariably said that they felt a click with Emma and had a feeling that they shared similar religious values. However, Christianity *alone* cannot fully explain the professional managers' motivation to join FBL. Then what was the most fundamental motivation that convinced Chris and his team to 'downgrade' themselves to join the company? The saviour ideology, we contend, is the answer.

The professional managers as saviours

The new senior executives including Chris primarily perceived themselves as saviours to the company and the Fong family. They invariably pointed out the gap between their previous companies and FBL in terms of the size, reputation, exposure, and work environment. The message is very clear: joining FBL must mean that they had to downgrade themselves from an international level to a local level; from a big, modern company to a small, Chinese family firm; and from a professional setting to a nonprofessional environment. They however still decided to join the company because they believed that their experiences, exposure, and expertise would be valuable to this struggling company. They reiterated in the interviews that they would like to *help* the Fong family and the company. In other words, they considered themselves the saviour to the company and the Fong family.

More importantly, FBL gave them the chance to take up a higher position within the corporate hierarchy, to have more discretion and to make more impactful differences. Note that these professional managers did not belong to the top management in those large corporations they had worked for. However, when they joined FBL, they became the VIPs as they were regarded as 'professionals'. Chris, for example, became one of the most powerful figures in FBL overseeing virtually every aspect of the operation of the company.

The transformation process however was not a smooth one. As explained in Chapter 9, there were two major areas of reforms carried out by Chris and his team. The first area was related to brand building in which Chris helped formulate and implement a comprehensive brand revitalization strategy. The second area was related to corporate management. Chris introduced 'modern' management into FBL by implementing organizational reform and recruiting professional managers to join the company. Chris's efforts to introduce modern management to FBL challenged not just the previous business strategy and orientation of the company but also the way of doing business, the management of employees as well as the work environment and atmosphere under Fong's *jan cing mei* regime. Tension inevitably arose under such context. One of the major frictions caused by the transformation was the confrontation between the professional managerial class and the *lou san zi.*

Battles between the manager and the lou san zi

We have to point out that at the beginning both the professional managers and the *lou san zi* did not see themselves as a social group, not to mention sharing the same collective identity. We argue that it is the specific historical situation which gave rise to their group consciousness. Under the new organizational chart, the professional managers occupied all the top management positions; they had more corporate power, higher social status, and better salaries than *the lou san zi*, which is also to say that there was social, political, and economic inequality between the two groups within the company. This structural inequality required meaningful signification and cultural legitimation. The professional managers, as the superior group, attempted to protect their privileges by denying the worthiness of the *lou san zi*'s experience in the industry. The most effective way to do so was to emphasize, if not exaggerate, the values of their professionalism in modern management.

The superiority of the professional managers was also strengthened by their middle-class background and the positive images associated with it. The professional managers are all highly educated and had management experiences in large modern corporations in different fields, such as banking, finance, telecommunication, and tourism. They identified themselves *and* are regarded by others as 'middle-class professionals'. Many of them grew up in middle-class families and considered themselves as belonging to the middle class. As pointed out by Tai-lok Lui (2003, p. 172; italics ours), '[i]n the eyes of the local people, middle-class professionals, administrators, and managers are *successful* individuals who are able to capitalize on new opportunities open to them in the process of economic development'.

The superiority of the professional managers was further justified on some putative cultural grounds. The middle-class professional 'was closely linked with the Western world in terms of *cultural outlooks* and professional training' (Lui, 2003, pp. 174–175; italics ours). They work in multinational companies as professional managers, speak good English, always follow an executive dress code, and maintain a middle-class lifestyle, all of which made FBL look like a 'backward', if not primitive, company. The location and work environment of FBL, for instance, were regarded as unsatisfactory by the professional managers. The company is located in a remote industrial area while the newly recruited professional managers used to go to work in Central or Causeway Bay,[2] the major commercial centres in Hong Kong. As one interviewee told us:

> I had never gone to the headquarters of FBL before the first day of my work. It's so hard to find the location. I drove around for a long time. . . . There is no window in our office, maybe because of the security reason. I really have the feeling that I am trapped inside an industrial building.

There were also other work-related practices which appeared to be weird in the eyes of the professional managers. For instance, employees of FBL are required to punch in and punch out. At 9:00 a.m., 1:00 p.m., 2:00 p.m. and 6:00 p.m., there is a bell ringing to remind the employees to start and end their work. The interviewee said that he found the arrangement totally strange:

> It's really like a factory. I think they have been using these for a long time since the company was still a workshop.

In addition, Chinese is the major medium of communication in the company. However, many of the professional managers did not even know how to type Chinese, not to mention that they had to learn to use Chinese frequently to communicate with the employees. Besides, the work environment was quite casual, as the interviewee noted:

> I am quite surprised that only I and another colleague wear formal dressing here. Only we two wear suits.

What the interviewee found most difficult to adjust with was the arrangement of business trips, as he told us:

> I could only take an economy-class flight for a business trip to New York. It is the style of the company and the owners. Jackson and Emma also only take an economy-class flight. I remember that when I first went on a business trip to China, the staff helped me book a hotel. The room condition and the surrounding environment were just terrible. The staff told me they always reserved the same hotel. I thought the room only cost around $300 a night. The concept of 'executives' does not really exist in the company.

All these examples in fact reveal that the professional managers, consciously or unconsciously, regarded themselves as superior in their relations to the *lou san zi* and even the owner.

   More importantly, the middle-class professional managers 'believe in personal efforts to achieve success and accept the rules of fierce races for a higher status based upon competition, fairness in ensuring the more capable to earn more, and equality of opportunities rather than outcomes' (Lui, 2003, p. 172). Lui concluded that to the middle-class people in Hong Kong, '[s]uccess is dependent on individual efforts, either through the acquisition of formal qualifications or through hard work' (Lui, 2003, p. 173). In other words, the middle-class professional managers emphasize the importance of continuous self-improvement through education and hard work, and by extension, they are more than willing to help others to improve themselves. The subjectivity of the middle-class managers was further framed by a kind of 'saviour ideology' through the Christian discourse in this particular context: not unlike God who sends his only son, Jesus, to save the sinful men through Jesus's death and resurrection, the newly recruited professional managers also joined FBL to save the company, the Fong family, and the *lou san zi* by 'sacrificing' themselves, such as by suffering from the 'backwardness' of the company, as we have mentioned earlier.

The saviour ideology then led the professional managers to perceive themselves as coaches and the *lou san zi* (and even the owners, as we shall demonstrate later) as trainees who had to learn the 'professional' way of doing business and managing the company, which further reinforced the saviour ideology of the professional managers. In the event, the relationship between the professional managers and the *lou san zi* was converted into a hierarchical one with the former being regarded as superior and thus desirable and the latter inferior and thus undesirable.

Most of the *lou san zi*, by contrast, share a similar class background with Fong, coming from lower class families. They generally have a lower educational level than the professional managerial class but have worked in the jewellery industry for a long period of time. They have a local cultural outlook; they neither speak English nor uphold a cosmopolitan consumption taste.

The superiority of the professional managers then legitimated their power, status, and economic privileges, while it concomitantly negated similar entitlements to the *lou san zi* on putative cultural grounds, class background, and the images and lifestyles associated with it.

The *lou san zi* reacted with a reciprocal denial of the values of the professional managers by emphasizing their industry know-how and experience, which the professional managers lacked. Some of the *lou san zi* we interviewed explicitly expressed that they were not convinced by the new management style introduced by the professional managers. The major reason, as those *lou san zi* claimed, is that the professional managers do not have any experience in the jewellery industry. One of the interviewees, for instance, challenged the competency of the professional managers:

> Among the top management, only Mr. Fong really 'knows' the jewellery industry. The others simply don't have any experience in the industry. How can they lead the company? I am not convinced.

Many of the *lou san zi* simply did not agree that the managerial skills of Chris's team are transferrable and applicable in the jewellery industry. They cast doubts on the competency of the professional managerial class. To the *lou san zi*, the professional managerial class was just a group of *outsiders*, who were highly educated but out of touch with the real world of the jewellery industry and were therefore not qualified to 'supervise' them.

In addition, the *lou san zi* were not impressed by the 'scientific' turn. They tended to trust their own instincts and experience in the industry. One of them, for instance, had reservations about the overemphasis on statistics and research, as he told us:

> As early as in 1997, the then CEO of FBL said that the company had a 'product disaster'. Later the company introduced the supply chain management system recommended by a consultancy. They [the consultants] collected the information and confirmed that we really had the so-called product disaster. But you know what? The system showed that we were selling karat-gold products, but in fact we were selling platinum-gold products.

The point that this *lou san zi* wanted to make is that statistics are static while the real business operation is something always on the move. 'We wanted to be a trendsetter, but the consultant just asked us to use the statistics of yesterday to deal with the issues today. It didn't work out,' he added. The *lou san zi* tended to improvise when coping with the contingencies instead of planning ahead based on scientific research, which was pretty much in line with Fong's own style.

The *lou san zi's* distrust of the statistics and research was *interpreted* by one of the professional managers as a proof of their unwillingness to make a change. He told us that many of the *lou san zi* in the showrooms were not prepared to change their mentality:

> They [the *lou san zi*] don't understand why they have to change. They believe that they did well in the past even without conducting any data analysis or research. In fact, they probably failed to capture all the profit potentials when the tourism industry was booming. I mean, when the economy was good, it's just easy to earn money. However, when the market is back to the normal state, as what we are facing now, it's when the real warfare begins. We have to change to survive.

The mentality, the professional manager noted, was fundamentally rooted in the corporate culture under Fong's *jan cing mei* regime:

> In the past, this company did not really focus on business continuity. The staff have not been used to doing any planning either. They do not tend to plan. Their mentality is to deal with things only when they turn bad. It really requires a lot of time and effort to change the culture.

We argue that it was this marked opposition between the professional managers and the *lou san zi* that helped create the communal self-definition, the collective social identities for the professional managers and the *lou san zi* as social groups. The formation of the professional managers and the *lou san zi* as two independent and interdependent social groups should be seen as a function of the specific circumstance: the structural inequality between them within the company. In other words, the emergence of the professional managers and the *lou san zi* as social groups and the awakening of group consciousness are the product of historical processes which structured the relations of inequality between them.

Interestingly, the collective identity of the professional managers and the *lou san zi*, once formed, was objectified as a social 'principle' by which the interaction between the professional managers and the *lou san zi* was regulated. The professional managers attempted to impose the standard and practice of professional management on the *lou san zi*. For example, the decision-making, the professional managers argued, must be supported by statistics and scientific research as assumed in professional management. They further argued that it is important to justify and back up a decision with facts, measurable outcomes, and a trackable plan.

Given their subordinated position, the *lou san zi* adopted an avoidance strategy. They tried not to work with the professional managers by confining themselves to work for Jackson directly or by delaying the compliance demanded by the professional managers through the typical argument: whenever the *lou san zi* were required by the professional managers to follow the professional management practices, they always replied that they had to seek approval from Jackson first. When we revisited the script of the interviews conducted with the *lou san zi*, we noted that none them of ever mentioned a single incident in which they worked closely with the professional managers, not to mention any interaction with the professional managers outside the company.

Despite the avoidance strategy, the *lou san zi* lost the flexibility they once enjoyed in the battles between professionalism and experience. The organizational reforms introduced by Chris led to the formalization of division of labour in the company. There were more explicit rules, regulations, and more visible boundaries. A number of *lou san zi* resigned because they could not adapt to the new management style and environment. Lee Wing Tat, the former Senior Manager of the Showroom, is one of the prime examples (we mentioned his story in Chapter 5). Fong was sad about his resignation, as he told us:

> He [Wing Tat] has worked for the company for so many years. He does not get along with the new head. He came to see me when he left. He told me, 'I am really sorry, Mr. Fong. I am forced to do this. I will go to work for another jewellery company. Please forgive me.' I understand his difficulties. He has worked for us for so long.

Fong also lamented the loss of *jan cing mei* as a result of the increasing 'modernization' of the company. Recall the story of Fun, the old office attendant of the company, mentioned in Chapter 7. Fong was upset by her situation, as he told us:

> She has been working for the company for several decades. She now turns 70, and the HR [Human Resources Department] said that we can't continue to

employ her because of the labour regulation. [Fong sighs] She's a very miserable lady, she lives alone. . . . Why can't we be more flexible?

Eventually Fun had to leave the company. 'Mr. Fong is a very nice guy. Sometimes he even helps me to take the rubbish to the collection point. He is a very good boss,' Fun once said.

The third zone

The relationship between the professional managers and the *lou san zi*, however, cannot be captured in the simple equation of domination and resistance because there was always a third zone where the complexity of the political dynamics between the two groups was played out. Despite the common background of the professional managers, they were hardly a homogenous group. Some of them did attempt to resolve the tug of war between the professional managerial class and the *lou san zi* by emphasizing mutual respect and frequent communication. Kayden Ma, for instance, shared how he gained the support of the *lou san zi* to contribute to the marketing campaigns:

> It is not easy to launch marketing campaigns in this company. Many people here have been 'still' for a long time; even if your own motor is fast, they just can't follow. The hardest thing is to mobilize people to work towards the same goal. However, after launching some events, some old staff cried. I really didn't expect the reaction. They were very touched by the success of the events. They thought that FBL is finally back.

More and more *lou san zi* were willing to help out actively in the events, according to Kayden, as they had been convinced by the effect of the new initiatives. Stanley Lee, who joined the company in the 2010s, also told us that it is important to let the *lou san zi* experience the success and failure by themselves:

> When I first joined the company, I noticed that the staff tended to stick with what they had been doing. For example, when we open new stores now, we need lots of figures and statistics. They didn't understand why they have to prepare the data, they thought that they didn't need them in the past. My strategy was to let them get their way first and taste the feeling of making mistakes. After learning the lessons, they then started to follow my suggestions.

Stanley also emphasized his role as a mediator between the top management and the *lou san zi*:

> Old staff are not good at articulating their thoughts. I will try to help them deliver their messages to the boss. They will be happy if their ideas are heard and adopted.

Ryan concurred that it is important to foster the knowledge transfer between the *lou san zi* and the professional managerial class:

> They [the *lou san zi*] have a lot of knowledge of jewellery, but the knowledge is all inside their heads. They don't know how to present the knowledge in a systematic and comprehensible way. I love to talk to them and ask them to explain and elaborate. It's like doing translation. We can learn a lot from them if we are patient enough.

All of this effort made by some professional managers, however, cannot be understood as indicating that the professional management class recognized the equal status of the *lou san zi* and the *jan cing mei* management style. The former still believed that their professional management – with an emphasis on the organizational formality, scientific research and planning, modern managerial knowledge and skills – was far superior to the latter's *jan cing mei* management style characterized by flexibility, improvisation, and industry know-how. As a result, they still firmly believed that the *jan cing mei* management style should be replaced by their professional management.

Of course, not all the *lou san zi* resisted the professional managers; some *lou san zi* were eager to cooperate with the professional managers. For example, one *lou san zi* working in the marketing department always adopted a supportive stance towards the professional managers' new marketing campaigns. She even asked for more marketing campaigns from the professional managers because she believed that the new marketing campaigns were effective in promoting the products of the company.

The decisive factor in winning this battle is the stance of the Fong couple, especially Jackson, who considered himself to be the *jiazhang*, because they had the ultimate authority in deciding which side could win. At the beginning of the reforms, Jackson and Emma supported the professional managers for various reasons described earlier. However, while the professional managers were pushing through the reforms, Jackson and Emma started to show reservations on some measures Chris wanted to introduce to the company, which further led to tension between the professional managers and the owners of the company.

Battles between the manager and the owner

As mentioned in Chapter 9, Chris joined the company in 2010 when Jackson was still in prison. Chris gained Emma's trust quickly and formulated the new branding strategies and initiated organizational reforms. However, the situation was different when Jackson finished serving his sentence and re-joined the company as Deputy CEO (Supplies). Everybody in the company understood that the real boss had now come back, and his return disrupted the power balance established since Emma had taken over the chairmanship of the company. As we pointed out earlier, Emma was just a proxy chairman who took up the position to fulfil, primarily, her responsibility as Jackson's wife. According to one interviewee, Emma gradually receded to enable Jackson to play a more central role in decision-making:

> Emma always sides with Jackson in the meetings. She never opposes or challenges him, at least in public. I think Jackson already took charge of the company around 2013. I would say Emma was already under Jackson [in terms of power] around 2015, as far as I can recall.

Chris faced the real challenge when he now had to work with Jackson who was eager to take control of the company again. The major problem, as Chris told us, was that Jackson was not clear about Chris's role and the division of labour between the owner and the professional manager:

> Jackson didn't think that one has to distinguish the role between the manager and the owner. He thought that he was the boss of the company so naturally he would take charge of the operation of the company. He didn't really think in terms of modern management. That's why he didn't understand my role in the company. For instance, he didn't understand why I had to question and involve myself in so many things. He might just wonder, 'Why couldn't you just take the orders from me?'

Jackson's confusion about the role of the professional managerial class in the company, Chris believes, is rooted in his lack of understanding of modern management and of the experience of working in a modern corporation. Chris further elaborated:

> In a big corporation, many things are well-understood between the decision-makers and the managers. Here, you have to explain and educate the boss. You have to convince him that what you do will create values. One obvious problem here is that the boss emphasizes immediate monetary return. The effects of the branding and marketing campaigns, however, take time to be realized. You need to have a long-term instead of short-term thinking. Again, we have to explain this logic to the boss.

We would like to add that Jackson, not unlike his father, considered himself to be the *jiazhang* of the *jia* (FBL). He expects that his staff are to serve his needs and take his orders. We will turn to this later.

Attempts to resolve the conflicts

Chris attempted to resolve the tension that had arisen by taking the initiative to communicate with Jackson, as he told us:

> After Jackson returned to the company, we flew to the United States together for a photo shoot. During the trip, Emma, Jackson, and I had in-depth

conversations. I had the chance to share my thoughts with them. I explained to Jackson that I am just a custodian of the company. My main responsibility is to help them transform FBL into a brand with values and provide my advice and expertise in the process. I also explained to him the difference between the owner and the custodian.

One major message that Chris attempted to deliver to Jackson was that he was just a custodian. By emphasizing his role as custodian, Chris attempted to convince Jackson that he had no interest in 'taking over' the family business from Jackson. His active involvement in the daily operation of the company, as Chris attempted to illustrate, was part of his duty as a professional manager. Chris also wanted to emphasize that his primary role as a custodian was to help the company to realize its full potential. He was there to help Jackson with his expertise and experience and to realize his dream to turn FBL into a brand.

Chris's efforts seemed to pay off. According to Chris, he gradually gained the trust of Jackson after the business trip to the United States, as Jackson had a deeper understanding of his role. In fact, Chris even played the role of mediator between Emma and Jackson especially when the couple had conflicting views, as he told us:

> On the management level, Emma and I are more like-minded. Emma is logical and has experience working in MNCs. She is familiar with business planning tools such as KPI [key performance indicator]. Emma is very concerned about budgets. Jackson doesn't really understand these kinds of things. On the other hand, I share Jackson's ideas and beliefs. Jackson and I love creativity. We find a lot in common in terms of branding, corporate identity building and CSR [corporate social responsibility]. As a middle man, I could actually help the couple to better communicate with each other.

Reflecting on his own experience in FBL, Chris emphasized that trust-building was an ongoing process and could not be achieved through one or two events. He told us that it took a lot of patience for him to gain Jackson's trust:

> I have tried to do things step by step. I mean you need to get some concrete results of your work before you can ask for more resources from the boss. I would not demand many things at one time. I would also try to explain the rationale behind my demand and communicate with them patiently.

There was no doubt that Jackson appreciated Chris's values and entrusted the revitalization to his hands, at least for a brief period. One should not forget that Chris's promotions and many of his initiatives were approved and endorsed by Jackson after he regained control of the company. It seemed that Chris had successfully resolved the tension between the owner and the manager by forging a close partnership with the owner-couple. The fundamental conflict between the professional managers and the owner-couple in FBL however remained intact.

When new circumstances arose, the confrontation between the two groups eventually led to the end of the partnership.

The second circumstance: the decline of FBL's business

To the surprise of many, Chris resigned within a year after he was appointed as a new executive director of FBL in 2015. Chris's resignation seemed to be abrupt. Why could the trio of Chris, Emma, and Jackson no longer work, even after several years of negotiation and communication? To answer this question, one must pay attention to the fact that by the time Chris resigned, the circumstances had already changed in terms of the broader business environment, the transformation of the company, and the mentality of the owner.

The jewellery industry in Hong Kong, after enjoying a boom in the early 2000s, had begun experiencing a significant downturn since 2015. FBL was not immune from the broader decline of the industry. Perplexed by the worsening business performance, according to one of the interviewees, Jackson and Emma lost their patience with the reforms:

> I think we [the industry] underwent the golden period between 2011 and 2013. The business turned bad in 2015. The bosses started to lose their patience. They thought that we [the professional managers] could not help them capture profit. They wanted some quick solutions. The financial situation of the company also went bad. They had to fire people.

Another interviewee also told us that the business downturn had put the bosses and the company under great pressure since 2015:

> The business performance of the company was bad. And honestly, the cost of the company increased sharply as a result of the recruitment of many new professional managers. The high staffing cost on the one hand and the decreasing profit on the other created huge pressure for the bosses.

The downturn of the business, the increase in staff cost, and the lack of immediate monetary return all prompted Jackson and Emma to cast doubt on the value of the transformation and, fundamentally, of the expensive professional managers.

At the same time, FBL was no longer the same company as it was in 2010 when Chris first joined FBL. It was no longer a company in crisis, still haunted by the memory of the court case. After years of efforts to revitalize the brand, FBL had largely succeeded in establishing a new brand image and brushing off the taint of the scandal in 2015. FBL's success in eliminating the state of emergency, however, also meant that Chris and his team were no longer as desirable as in the past. As we mentioned earlier, Jackson and Emma needed the fresh faces of the professional managerial class to help distance the company from the Fong family and the court case scandal. After the company was put back on track, the indispensability of the team of outsider-transformers was severely undermined.

The revitalization of FBL also boosted the confidence of Emma and Jackson to run the company in their own ways. The change in Emma, according to one interviewee, was obvious, as he told us, 'she [Emma] gained more and more confidence especially after getting so many entrepreneurial awards'. Jackson also restored his power and leadership in the company. The growing confidence of the Fong couple had disrupted the power balance between themselves and the professional managers and, as the former became less reliant on the latter to 'save' the company.

To make the situation more complex, according to our interviewees, Emma started to argue with Jackson about different issues. The difference in opinion between the Fong couple was partly due to the different personalities of Emma and Jackson. While Emma is very rational in calculating profit and loss, Jackson appears to be somewhat emotional. If he finds something interesting, he does not care about the cost. Recall that Jackson oversees the product supply of FBL. According to our interviewees, Jackson always chose to ignore the budget allocated to his department by the Board headed by Emma and went ahead with the purchase of expensive jewellery material, claiming that he was the only person in FBL who knew the industry well. On some occasions, Emma would try to stop her husband ending up in some fights; but on other occasions, Emma would just give in to avoid further conflicts. On most occasions, Emma and Jackson would seek Chris's support separately. As the person who was stuck in the middle, Chris was put in a very difficult position. Chris always ended up offending both, which further damaged the trust between him and the Fong couple.

The trust among the trio of Emma, Jackson, and Chris was further undermined by the appointment of a new professional manager, Crystal Fong, in July 2015. Crystal was recruited to replace Henry, who had resigned as the CFO of the company. Prior to joining FBL, Crystal had worked in the real estate industry. She was the CFO of Zenville[3] and the executive director of Man Kwong Properties.[4] These two companies, we have to emphasize, are also Chinese family firms.

Crystal gained the trust of Emma and Jackson quickly and was soon appointed as Deputy Chairman of the company. Chris was disgruntled by the dominance of Crystal in the company, as he told us:

> In the later period [shortly before Chris resigned], the top management meetings only included me, Emma, Jackson and Crystal since the other members had left. She [Crystal]'s not just a 'yes' woman; she also carried out Jackson and Emma's decisions to a far greater extent, cutting budgets and firing people ruthlessly, for instance.

The downslide of the business, the growing impatience of the Fong couple with Chris and his team, the growing ego of the owners, and the shift in favour of a new professional manager contributed to the increasingly estranged relationship between the owner and the original professional managerial class. Maria was among the first to leave.[5] Chris followed suit. The resignation of Chris triggered a chain effect leading to the resignation of the rest of team members, one by one

(Aaron in early 2017; Kevin and Ryan in 2018). Some left rather calmly while others left feeling disappointed and disillusioned. Chris was particularly disheartened by the final outcome of the transformation.

From collective decision-making to individual decision-making

The professional managers were particularly frustrated by the fact that the collective decision-making process, which was institutionalized by the establishment of the corporate management committee (CMC), gradually returned to the previous format in which the owners monopolized the decision-making power within the company. According to the interviewees, Jackson became dominant in the top management meetings and would not listen to any disagreeing voices. One of the interviewees simply could not stand Jackson's dominant attitude:

> Jackson is a very dominant person. You can't challenge him. Very often, he just bypassed everyone else to make a decision. He just wants you to follow his orders. It's basically like: 'Don't ask, just do whatever I tell you.' He just wanted a 'yes' man.

The reason behind Jackson's dominance, if not arrogance, lies in his belief that, according to the interviewees, he is superior to the professional managers in terms of his industrial know-how, the same mentality which was widely shared among the *lou san zi* mentioned earlier. Another interviewee also explained the reason why it was hard to work with Jackson:

> Everything changed after Jackson came back. In the past, we could always share and discuss different views. Jackson thought that he's very familiar with the industry, no one should challenge him. He's way too dominant in the meetings. We weren't able to make an informed decision.

The appointment of Crystal, according to an interviewee, aggravated the collective decision-making process, as he told us:

> She's basically a 'yes' woman. She just did what Jackson and Emma asked her to do. Emma sided with Crystal very often. I was basically alone there in the meetings. It was not possible to have any rational discussions, not to mention debates. The company just became a one-man company again, like it used to be.

Another interviewee added that Jackson's arrogance was related to something more fundamental: the *jiazhang* mentality of Jackson:

> Jackson always thought that he was much more capable than others to run FBL. Others simply didn't understand or care as much as he did. For instance, he thought that others were not as concerned about the financial situation of the company as he was just because he, not others, is the boss. He didn't

really trust us fundamentally. The distrust was intensified when the business went down.

Jackson's *jiazhang* mentality, according to another interviewee, also led to his disrespectful attitude towards his employees:

> He always tried to demonstrate his ability and never failed to deliver the message that he was the boss of the company and would have the final, if not absolute, say. He would be really disrespectful to others in the meetings, giving people hard feelings. Other colleagues loved to describe him as an 'artist' because he's capricious and emotional. He just wanted to do whatever he felt like, because he's the boss.

Ignorance of the organizational chart

The *jiazhang* mentality of Jackson also led him to disregard the corporate structure, according to the interviewees. One interviewee pointed out that the Fong couple always ignored the formal division of labour: 'They just transferred the managers to take up different tasks which were beyond their expertise.' The major reason why one of our interviewees left FBL was that he was assigned a wide range of tasks that he could not handle. By the time he resigned, the interviewee was not only in charge of his own department but involved in the operation of three other departments. He told us that the workload was simply too much:

> I am personally fine with taking up different tasks. I mean we are generalists, so we are able to take up different roles. The problem is that we have to be resourcefully supported. If you don't give me resources but expect me to produce the same output, sorry I just can't do that. That's why I think I really can't contribute much to the company anymore.

One interviewee also confirmed Jackson's ignorance of the corporate structure and norms as he wanted to keep everything firmly under his own control:

> In the early stage, Jackson basically focused on the Chinese market. Later, he started to get involved in other stuff including my department. He said one day that he would find someone else from outside to help with some functions of my department. I was shocked. I mean I was just being notified. He didn't follow the normal procedure. He would also challenge anyone from any department in the email directly, in the capacity of Deputy CEO in Supplies.

Jackson's disregard for the formal corporate structure and procedure, in one interviewee's view, was due to his *jiazhang* mentality, on the one hand, and his lack of understanding of modern management on the other:

> He doesn't have enough knowledge of modern management. He doesn't think in terms of a big, corporate picture. He cares about the details, so he

wants to control everything. He doesn't need a management team to help him, he just needs some yes men to execute his orders. Because he can't see the big picture and can't articulate his ideas, he changes his decisions from time to time.

The primacy of familial interests over corporate interests

The professional managers were also displeased with the fact that the Fong couple placed personal/familial interest over corporate interest. They would just do something, one interviewee noted, that they personally wanted without considering if that would suit the overall interest of the company:

> One good example is their decision to sponsor Jack Lam's[6] concert. It has nothing to do with the music of Jack, whether it's good or bad. The problem is that Jack obviously does not fit the brand image of 'trendsetting craftsmanship'. I mean he's sort of old-fashioned. They [the Fong couple] wanted to sponsor his concert because they wanted to preserve Cantonese music. I mean that's completely fine if they did it with their own money. But we are talking about the corporate sponsorship.

Another interviewee was not surprised by Jackson and Emma's decision to sponsor the concert at all:

> They [the Fong couple] don't distinguish the private from the corporate. Well, I would just say one's personal taste shouldn't represent the company without thorough and careful discussion among senior executives.

The company was still run like a *jia* as if it belonged to the Fong family *only*. One of our interviewees gave another example:

> They [the Fong couple] would love to bring their kids along when they visited the stores. They would ask their kids to comment on the display and the kids would directly point out things that they disliked in front of the branch manager. I don't think that's a good practice. They don't draw a line between the private sphere and the corporate sphere.

The family rather than the company, as the interviewee contended, was always placed in a higher priority by the Fong couple. The interviewee told us:

> Emma treated me well. The problem is that she would never say no to Jackson. She's very traditional. I mean it's of utmost importance for her to maintain her relationship with Jackson and to play the role of a good wife. To her, family is always more important than the company.

From the perspective of the professional managerial class, the lack of trust, if not blatant disrespect, of their expertise, the disregard of the corporate norms and rules by the Fong couple, and their the emphasis on the personal/familial interest over the corporate interest were the major reasons leading to their resignations. The professional managers were bitter about the unhappy ending and felt betrayed by the hypocrisy of the Fong couple.

We would like to add hastily that the things Jackson did and that the professional managers complained about are in fact due to the fact that Jackson, not unlike his father, considered the company to be his *jia* and himself as the *jiazhang*, and ran the company in the way his father did in the past. We will return to this in a moment.

From VIPs to fallen angels

The professional managers' saviour ideology is also an important reason behind their negative sentiment towards Emma and Jackson. As mentioned earlier, the professional managers perceived themselves primarily as saviours of the company. They repeatedly emphasized that they would like to 'help' the Fong family by aiding the Fong couple to transform the family business into a modern corporation. Their discourses of why they were willing to join the company revealed a sense of superiority.

The sense of superiority was further sustained by their pride and belief in their professionalism. They emphasized the need to 'educate' the *lou san zi* and even the boss regarding the idea of modern management; they also demanded 'respect' and 'gratefulness' from the boss for their way of doing things, because, from their perspective, they had expertise in modern management. It is the 'manager's burden' to enlighten the company, the *lou san zi*, and the owners with the knowledge of modern management to help them move forward.

The sense of superiority made the professional managers regard themselves as VIP experts recruited by FBL. They assumed and more importantly expected that their expertise would be highly valued and that their opinions should be held in a high regard. They even perceived themselves as being on equal terms with the owners as the latter needed the help and guidance from the former.

Their pride, however, was shattered when they discovered later that the owners did not pay due respect to them, ignored their norms and rules, and only wanted them to be 'yes' men. They also found that their positions could be easily replaced by other newcomers. They thought that they had been betrayed as they were willing to 'lower' themselves to join this crumpling company in the first place and had made so much effort to transform the company. Their dedication, however, was not appreciated by the owners.

They were especially hurt when the owners did not even attempt to ask them to stay when they resigned. One interviewee told us that he decided to resign when he realized that he was no longer needed:

> My budget had been cut. Eventually, there's no budget for my team. I couldn't do anything; it was meaningless to stay. I've got no more value in the company. If they don't need me, I will just walk away. I wanted to leave before our relationship further deteriorated. They didn't ask me to stay.

Another interviewee also told us that the bosses did not try to keep him:

> I decided to resign to avoid further conflicts. I no longer understood my role in the company. With or without me was the same. They didn't ask me to stay.

We can now see that the professional managers chose to resign primarily because they thought that the owners had gradually changed their attitude towards them and their reform. From their perspective, the Fong couple were very respectful to them and had treasured their values at the beginning; their attitudes however had now completely changed. Chris was still emotional when he talked about his decision to resign. He told us that he indeed felt hurt because Jackson and Emma destroyed the mutual trust among the three in particular and did not adhere to the Christian values in general. Chris and his team members therefore had no alternative but chose to leave the company like a fallen angel.

We have analyzed in this section the tension between the professional managers and the Fong couple from the perspective of the professional managers. The tension, according to some professional managers, lay in the conflicting views of the role of the manager vis-à-vis the owner. The professional managers believed that the power of the owner should be restrained by the corporate structure while the Fong couple put the personal/familial interest over the corporate interest. The former also thought that the managers should participate in the decision-making process while the latter just wanted the managers to follow and implement their decisions. The tension between the two groups escalated when the industry experienced a downturn along with the appointment of a new CFO. The professional managers felt bitter because they believed that they were no longer respected or appreciated by the owners. They also felt betrayed as they thought that the Fong couple had changed their attitudes towards them.

But from the perspective of the Fong couple, the professional managers simply could not understand Jackson's *jiazhang* mentality and his way of running FBL as his *jia*.

The eternal return of the jiazhang

Jackson was very often described by our interviewees as someone full of contradictions. The first set of contradictions, as reported by our interviewees, was the one between his passion and action. Almost everyone, including the professional managers, *lou san zi*, and even Fong, shared the view that Jackson and Emma were extremely hardworking and strived to make FBL a better company. What they did, however, did not always serve the best interests of the company. Another set of contradictions is between Jackson's idealism and his impatience. Making profits, according to our interviewees, was not Jackson's only goal. 'Jackson always emphasized that we should not focus on making money only,' one of them said. Another interviewee elaborated on his interpretation of Jackson's mentality:

They don't aim at making a lot of money. Unlike Fong, they don't want to make a quick buck. They want something 'higher'. They want to achieve some ideals in their mind. But what exactly is the ideal? I am not sure. It seems that they changed their ideals from time to time.

On the other hand, the Fong couple was impatient with the lack of immediate results from the reforms led by Chris's team.

We have to understand all these contradictions in terms of Jackson's complicated and contradictory subjectivities constructed in different contexts. The first context is Jackson's position in his family. As we have already mentioned, Jackson is not Fong's eldest son; his performance at school was not as good as that of his siblings. He also had a very strong father who proved himself a successful entrepreneur. All of this gives Jackson great pressure not only to prove but also justify himself as a proper successor to his father. He therefore must show that he is not only different from but also better than his father.

We have already pointed out that Jackson wanted to create an ideal FBL that is distinct from the FBL founded by his father. One strategy for him was to emphasize Western design, branding, and customer service and experience, to which Fong paid no attention at all. Another strategy was to deemphasize what Fong emphasized, such as the 'all-for-money-making' mentality. It was then not a surprise to see that the Fong couple loved to talk about 'values' – religious values, corporate values, brand values, common values, etc. – to distinguish themselves from Fong who is characterized by the *faat cin hon* mentality. By adding 'values' to the company, Jackson attempted to demonstrate that he elevated the status of FBL to a 'modern' company. However, as our interviewees said, Jackson did not have a very clear picture in mind for what the ideal FBL should look like. He could only articulate the picture in some abstract terms such as 'taste', 'design' and 'international'. After all, what the transformation is does not matter, what matters is that it is different from his father's FBL.

In other words, the transformation of the company is just a means for Jackson to create his ideal image of FBL that helps him distinguish himself from his father. Jackson, like Fong, perceives FBL primarily as a *jiaye*, the family business of the Fong family. He has never wanted a fundamental reform which would challenge his role as the *jiazhang* in the family business and the very nature of FBL as his *jia*. To recruit Chris and the other professional managers was just a strategic move in the first place. Jackson did not intend to give up his power to the professional managers. Instead, he just wanted the professional managers to help him, as the *jiazhang*, to achieve his ideal, which is also to say that although Jackson had been trying his best to distinguish himself from his father, he ironically had the same *jiazhang* mentality as Fong.

As we discussed in Chapter 7, Fong could be perceived as a founder-chief in a *bong paai* company in which he was the unchallengeable centre, the sole decision-maker and the sole arbitrator. This explains why Fong regarded himself as inseparable from FBL. FBL the company was Fong the individual. Jackson, as Fong's son and successor, also regarded himself as the chief of the company, whose authority could not be challenged. Jackson believed that the company belonged to the Fong family, if not him, even though the company is a public company. It follows logically that he would not understand why the professional managers refused to take his orders in the name of protecting the interest of the company. According to Jackson's *jiazhang* mentality, one could not be loyal to the company (*jia*) without being loyal to the *jiazhang*. The sharing of power between the owner and the managers also sounded culturally ungrammatical to Jackson. Why would he have to share his own *jiaye* with outsiders? As we have already pointed out in Chapter 7, those who are closest to the founder-chief enjoy a sense of superiority over others. However, the followers do not actually own the power, they just *borrow* the power from the chief to exercise authority over others. The chief never shares power. In other words, the employees can never expect to gain an equal footing with the *jiazhang*.

The major problem with Chris and the other professional managers is that they did not understand the mentality of the *jiazhang*. One interviewee, who had worked previously in companies with a single controlling shareholder, succinctly pointed out this problem:

> The majority of them [referring to Chris and other team members] didn't have experience in dealing with a single boss. I mean they worked for big corporations without a dominant controlling shareholder. You can say that basically the 'bosses' that you deal with are just employees like you. The salaried boss is not the same as the boss in a Chinese family business like this [FBL]. It's true that they worked for the companies, not for the bosses.

It may also explain why Crystal quickly replaced Chris to become the new right-hand woman to the Fong couple as she had a lot of experience in dealing with bosses-as-owners. We were not able to conduct an interview with Crystal. However, we were able to get a sense of her attitude towards her bosses through some newspaper reports. For instance, Crystal was once interviewed by reporters when she accompanied Emma to attend a press conference. She told the reporters jokingly:

> She's [referring to Emma] our princess. We are just maidservants; you know those who fan behind. We shouldn't steal the show, but we can't embarrass our princess either. (our translation)

In another interview, Crystal shared her career experience and her philosophy in dealing with different bosses (our translation):

> You have to respect him [the boss]. He must possess certain wisdom, experience and insights that you don't have. I don't rule out that the majority of his decision will be correct. After all, he's in the industry for so long, he must possess more knowledge than we do. . . . You see I am doing fairly well right, so I think I am getting the right way. Every boss has his own character and

temper. You have to treat them like clients. When you have to work with your clients, of course it's you who have to make the compromise, not the other way around. I think that's a normal logic. And, of course, you won't set your clients up either, right?

Crystal demonstrated that she clearly understood her role and position vis-à-vis the Chinese boss: she is neither a VIP consultant nor an expert – she is just appointed to be the 'maidservant' of the prince and the princess. Unlike Chris and his team, Crystal not only possesses professional expertise and work experience in large companies but also understands the mentality of the Chinese boss.

Conclusion

The purpose of this chapter is to argue that the professionalization of FBL initiated by Emma is a very complex social process in which major players including Emma, Jackson, Chris and his team, *and* the *lou san zi* interact with each other to produce the effect of the professionalization. We showed that such an interaction was underlined by two forms of politics. The first one is the politics between the *lou san zi* and the professional managers which itself is also very complex. We cannot assume that the collective identity of these two groups exists from the beginning because the collective consciousness of the professional managers and the *lou san zi* as social groups emerged as a response to the structural inequality between them resulting from the introduction of professional management to the company. The collective identity, once formed, had become an 'independent variable' that shaped the goals, strategies, and actions of the professional managers and the *lou san zi*.

More importantly, we showed that neither the professional managers nor the *lou san zi* as social groups are homogeneous. The former had different views on their relations with the latter, while the latter adopted different attitudes towards the former. To make the situation more complex, some of the long-serving employees chose to make alliances with the professional managers, while some others were determined to resist the management system introduced by the professional managers. Some of the professional managers tried to find a way to encourage the *lou san zi* to accept the new management system, while some others were inclined to ignore the voices and feelings of the *lou san zi* and directly imposed their views on the latter.

The second form of politics is the one between the professional managerial class and the Fong couple. We showed that the politics was a result of the difference in expectations. The professional managerial class expected an active role in the decision-making process, respect from the boss and emphasis on the corporate interest over the individual benefit. From the perspective of the Fong couple, the professional managerial class failed to understand Jackson's *jiazhang* mentality. Jackson is like Fong who perceives himself as the chief of the *bong paai* company seeking absolute loyalty and obedience from the employees. He has never intended to have a fundamental transformation that would challenge the very nature of his position as the *jiazhang* of the company (*jia*). The persistence of the *jiazhang* mentality is the key to understanding the unhappy ending of the professional managerial class at FBL.

We also demonstrated the importance of studying the transformation of the company in specific circumstances. Chris and his team once gained the trust of the Fong couple to carry out a number of reforms in the company; but the same team of people lost the trust of the owners and were not given any resources to carry out the transformation under changing circumstances. In the new circumstances in which the industry was declining, the boss was getting impatient; the company had already rebuilt its reputation and a new CFO was recruited; and the politics between the professional managerial class and the Fong couple was intensified – all of this eventually led to the disbandment of the transformers.

Notes

1 Refer to Figure 6.1 in Chapter 6.
2 Working in Central in particular symbolizes one's standing as a white-collar professional as Central is where the headquarters of multinational companies and finance and professional services companies are located.
3 Zenville is a pseudonym. It is a listed property development company on the Stock Exchange of Hong Kong.
4 Man Kwong Properties is a pseudonym. It is one of the major property developers in Hong Kong.
5 Maria resigned in early 2016. Henry had resigned earlier than Maria in 2015. Henry's case is ambivalent here. On the one hand, he was not a member of the team of transformers recruited by Chris. Henry joined FBL in the early 2000s. On the other hand, he is a professional manager like Chris.
6 Jack Lam is a pseudonym. Born in the mid-1950s, Jack is a DJ and folksong singer in Hong Kong.

11 Conclusion[1]

The general contribution of this book is to communicate to our colleagues in mainstream-US-dominated management sciences that business activities, not unlike other human phenomena, are meaningfully constituted and therefore should be understood culturally. To understand business activities culturally is to situate them in a cultural context because the meaning of business activities is the significance the property of business activities acquires from the context in which they take place. Our study of Fong as an entrepreneur, his Chinese family firm, and the professionalization of the company testifies to the importance of contexts in understanding business and the value of ethnography which can help capture the meaning of human phenomena because ethnographic research is a commitment to the contextualization of human phenomena.

We proposed in this book that entrepreneurship as a business activity refers to the difference-making that acquires significance and importance in the socio-cultural context in which it occurs. Both the difference-making and the socio-cultural context are necessary to entrepreneurship, but neither of them can determine its total effect. For the properties of difference-makings cannot determine their significance and importance, while the socio-cultural context cannot specify the form or character of the entrepreneurial pursuit. Entrepreneurship is the result of the mediations between the difference-making and the socio-cultural context.

As we have demonstrated in the book, Fong's entrepreneurial pursuit was driven by the logic of production maximization, which was motivated by his distinctive *faat cin hon* driven pragmatism and *gau geong* mentality nurtured from his unique biographical background and experiences during his formative years (Chapter 3). But the transformation of Fong's company from a manufacturer to a retailer in the local jewellery industry is an *unintended* and *unexpected* consequence (Chapter 4–6). For Fong's intention cannot determine the significance of his entrepreneurial pursuit because the latter emerges from what Sahlins calls 'conjunctural situations' (Smith, 2002, p. 288). Fong was put in a conjunctural position that amplified the historical effect of Fong's pursuits in the jewellery industry, which Fong had not planned. That is to say, the socio-economic context of Hong Kong is also a necessary condition for Fong's entrepreneurial process.

We, however, are not saying that entrepreneurship is simply determined by the environment because the broader production-to-service transformation of the Hong Kong economy cannot dictate Fong's entrepreneurial pursuit. Fong's motives for profit-maximization likewise cannot be reduced to the wider socio-economic factors because they were also informed by Fong's own biographical background and the experiences he had during his formative years.

What marks our anthropological idea of entrepreneurship is that the cause of entrepreneurship cannot be monogenic but what Jon Remme (2014, pp. 413–414) called polygenic, by which he meant that 'the effect is produced by many causal factors that alone cannot produce the effect but which all are conductive to it'. Entrepreneurship is not caused by either individual pursuits or the socio-cultural contexts where such pursuits take place but the way the two mediate with each other. In other words, neither individual pursuits nor the socio-cultural contexts *alone* can cause entrepreneurship.

We are not suggesting that scholars of mainstream-US-dominated management sciences seriously believe that social phenomena can be explained by a single factor. But very few of them actually attempt to explain and illustrate the actual process of mediations involved in entrepreneurship.

Entrepreneurship is contextually relative

The polygenic causality of entrepreneurship has an important implication: entrepreneurship cannot be essentialized; it instead is contextually relative. In the corporate context, Fong is an entrepreneur because what he did could cause changes to his company. In the industrial context, Fong is known as an entrepreneur because he successfully transformed his company from a jewellery workshop into a retail chain, which made a difference to the industry. At the societal level, Fong simply followed the general developmental path of Hong Kong from a manufacturing- to a service-economy and he thus cannot be considered to be an entrepreneur because he does not make a difference to the local economy. In short, entrepreneurship is contextually relative.

If entrepreneurship is contingent on contexts, it cannot be defined *sui geris*. Entrepreneurship can only be determined *retrospectively*. That is why Fong would not know the outcome of his entrepreneurial pursuits because he would not know *a priori* that his difference-making in itself could acquire significance from the socio-cultural context, not to mention that he could not know whether what he was doing was entrepreneurial or not.

Of course, to the person who makes differences, the entrepreneurial pursuit, at least at the experiential level, is a *forward-looking* process in which he or she 'discovers', 'evaluates', and 'exploits' the 'opportunity' to seek profit. In other words, entrepreneurship is a dual process, the study of which must pay attention to how the entrepreneur moves his or her pursuit forward (forward-looking process) and how the pursuit is mediated by the socio-cultural context in which the pursuit occurs and acquires its significance (retrospectively constituted).

Individual and corporate entrepreneurship

The fact that the determination of entrepreneurship is relative to contexts also means that the historical effects of entrepreneurial pursuits vary with contexts. In the context of the local jewellery industry in Hong Kong, the historical effects of Fong's entrepreneurial process can be described as what Sahlins calls 'revolutionary change' that changes or 'reverses' course (Smith, 2002, p. 287). Fong's forward integration of production and circulation was indeed very rare, if not unique, in the jewellery industry in Hong Kong. Most of the jewellery workshops tended to remain in the manufacturing sector. On the other hand, all major players in the jewellery retail market, except Fong's company, started out as retail outlets. They would attempt to achieve backward integration after they had accumulated sufficient capital to claim control over the suppliers. The major reason Fong is considered to be a legendary figure in the industry is that he broke down the barrier between the manufacturing and the retail sectors. Fong was among the few entrepreneurs who operated a showroom in Hung Hom. After Fong's success in his showroom business, other entrepreneurs followed suit to establish jewellery showrooms in the same area where Fong's showroom was located, which transformed the area into a major cluster of jewellery showrooms in Hong Kong specifically catering to tourist groups (Chapter 5).

Fong also revolutionized the local jewellery industry by fostering the massification of the jewellery industry (Chapter 6). He was the first major jeweller to popularize the use of sales campaigns in the industry. Instead of marketing the glamour and grandeur of the jewellery products like other jewellery retailers, Fong instead focused on underscoring the price worthiness of his products. Fong played an important role in transforming the public perception of jewellery from an untouchable luxury to an everyday necessity.

However, when we situate Fong's case in the broader Hong Kong context, the development of his company can only be described as following a 'developmental change' which, according to Sahlins, refers to the change that 'continues a given course of development' (Smith, 2002, p. 287). In contrast to the revolutionary change, it is evolutionary by nature. The development of FBL simply followed the broader economic transformation of Hong Kong, capitalizing the opportunities created by the rise of the manufacturing sector, the tourism industry, and the retail market. While Fong made significant differences to the local jewellery industry, he did not have an equal impact on the Hong Kong economy.

The previously mentioned different modes of historical changes determine the types of historical subject for Fong's entrepreneurial process. At the industrial level, Fong is identified as the historical subject of the entrepreneurial process, while FBL, his company, is made the historical subject at the societal level. The difference in historical subject in these two levels can be attributed to the nature of historical changes. As mentioned earlier, what Fong did at the industrial level was revolutionary; while at the societal level, Fong's entrepreneurship only caused evolutionary changes. As Sahlins (2004, p. 127) effectively argues, the historical subject is defined by the mode of historical changes the subject caused.

Revolutionary changes are usually attributed to one single individual, while evolutionary changes relate to collectives. In other words, the historical subject causing revolutionary changes always refers to some individuals, while in the case of evolutionary changes, some collectives are often held responsible. The former is an example of what some scholars in mainstream-US-dominated management sciences call individual entrepreneurship; the latter of corporate entrepreneurship (Sharma and Chrisman, 1999). We are making an unconventional argument here: what distinguishes individual from corporate entrepreneurship is not dependent on whether it is the individual or the existing organization which initiates the entrepreneurial pursuit but on the mode of historical changes caused by the pursuit.

Professionalization of family business as a social process of being-and-becoming

The polygenic causality of entrepreneurship as a business phenomenon suggests that academic attention should be paid to what Comaroff (2010, p. 530) called 'being-and-becoming' which 'is the mapping of those processes by which social realities are realized, objects are objectified, materialities materialized, essences essentialized, by which abstractions – biography, community, culture, economy, ethnicity, gender, generation, identity, nationality, race, society – congeal synoptically from the innumerable acts, events, and significations that constitute them.' Following Comaroff, we did not take any abstraction such as 'professional managers' or 'long-serving employees' for granted when we investigated the professionalization of FBL. We have tried to trace the historical processes in which the categories of 'professional managers' or 'long-serving employees' 'are pragmatically produced, socially construed, and naturalized' (Comaroff, 2010, p. 530). As we have demonstrated in Chapter 10, the group consciousness of the professional managers and the *lou san zi* emerged from their structural inequality. This structural inequality required meaningful signification and cultural legitimation. The professional managers, as the superior group, protected their privileges by denying the worthiness of the *lou san zi*'s experience in the industry. The *lou san zi* reacted with a reciprocal denial of the values of the professional managers. This marked opposition between the professional managers and the *lou san zi* helped to create the communal self-definition, the collective social identities for the professional managers and the *lou san zi* as social groups.

Once the collective identity of these two groups was formed, such collective identity was objectified as a social 'principle' by which the interaction between the professional managers and the *lou san zi* was regulated. Within the company, the professional managers attempted to impose the standard and practice of professional management on the *lou san zi*, while the *lou san zi* adopted an avoidance strategy whereby they tried not to work with the professional managers.

The relationship between the professional managers and the *lou san zi*, however, cannot be reduced to the simple formula of domination and resistance. For there was a third zone where the complexity of the political dynamics between the professional managers and the *lou san zi* was played out. Some professional managers attempted to resolve the tug of war between the professional managerial class and the *lou san zi* by emphasizing mutual respect and communications as a mediator, while some *lou san zi* were willing or even eager to cooperate with the professional managers.

The relationship between the owners and the professional managers is also very complex. The owners' attitudes towards the professional managers changed with the circumstances. When the company was in trouble after Jackson and Fong were put in prison, Emma showed her appreciation of the skill of the professional managers; she even made good use of Christianity to recruit them. All of this changed after the new circumstances emerged as the industry was declining. Both Emma and Jackson started to lose their patience. On the one hand, the professional managers seemed unable to accept the fact that Jackson understood FBL as his *jia* and saw himself as the *jiazhang*. On the other hand, Jackson was not satisfied with the fact that the professional managers did not treat him as the *jiazhang* or show their loyalty to him. The conflicts between the professional managerial class and the Fong couple escalated and eventually led to the resignation of the professional managers. We can see that the relationship between the family managers and the professional managers could be harmonious and co-operative or conflictual and rival; it all depends on the circumstantial context.

In short, the professionalization of the family business cannot be seen simply as an event in which the professional managers replace the family managers. Instead, it should be understood as a complex social process in which major players interact among themselves to produce the historical effect of professionalization according to their interests, motivations, and strategies which vary with circumstances.

Different cultures, different ideas of families; different ideas of families, different family firms

If human phenomena are culturally constituted according to a symbolic system which is not the only one possible, it is not that all cultures have families, but that all families have culture. We would like to add hastily that different ideas of families will have different impacts on family firms which will then display different configurations of management. As we have demonstrated in Chapter 7, the idea of Chinese families shapes the way Chinese pursue their business activities in two major ways. First, the Chinese family serves as the organizational format for the Chinese family firm. Chinese entrepreneurs tend to apply the kinship logic to his personal relationship with his employees, which further gives rise to three major characteristics of Chinese family firms: the general ignorance of the organizational chart, autonomy and agency of individual workers, and the emphasis on the holistic relations between employee and employer as well as among employees themselves. Second, the Chinese tend to give overriding importance to the genealogical aspect of the family (*fang/jia-zu*) and they are prepared to sacrifice the economic aspect of the family (*jia* or/and family firms) for the sake of its genealogical continuity, as demonstrated in the crises faced by the Fong family and the company (Chapter 8). The family firm for the Chinese is an instrument to enhance the *fang/jia-zu* interest.

The cultural specification of the family has one important methodological implication: in order to understand the *family business*, we need to understand the *family* first as the latter determines the organizational format, the management, and the value of the former. The same also goes to the study of family businesses in Japan, Korea, and other regions of the world. Unfortunately, as far as we know, scholars of mainstream-US-dominated management sciences seldom take seriously the fact that different cultures have different concepts of families and that, as a result, family businesses in different cultures exhibit very different forms of organizational behaviours. In short, the cultural context matters.

We are not sure whether the immediate goal of management science should be set to predict human behaviours without specifying the context in which the behaviours take place. The possible goals of the study of business, we believe, are to help practitioners of business to understand what certain behaviours mean in a particular context, why a certain person does not conform to the cultural system in a specific context, what would be the cultural consequences or effects of a certain management policy, and how people would behave in a certain context. All of this can be achieved only if we understand and study business culturally.

Note

1 Parts of the discussion of entrepreneurship here are taken from our forthcoming co-authored article titled 'Several Things that We Know about Creativity: History, Biography, and Affordance in Entrepreneurship' (Wong and Chau, forthcoming).

References

Abbott, A. (2001) *Time Matters: On Theory and Method*, Chicago & London: The University of Chicago Press.

Acevedo, A. (2012) 'Personalist Business Ethics and Humanistic Management: Insights from Jacques Maritain', *Journal of Business Ethics*, vol. 105, no. 2, pp. 197–219.

Achmad, T., Rusmin, Neilson, J. and Tower, G. (2009) 'The Iniquitous Influence of Family Ownership Structures on Corporate Performance', *Journal of Global Business Issues*, vol. 3, pp. 41–49.

Aoki, M. (1988) *Information, Incentives, and Bargaining in the Japanese Economy*, Cambridge: Cambridge University Press.

Bird, B., Welsch, H., Astrachan, J. H. and Pistrui, D. (2002) 'Family Business Research: The Evolution of an Academic Field', *Family Business Review*, vol. 15, no. 4, pp. 337–350.

Bloch, M. (1971) 'The Moral and Tactical Meaning of Kinship Terms', *Man*, vol. 6, no. 1, pp. 79–87.

Carney, M. and Davies, H. (1999) 'From Entrepot to Entrepot Via Merchant Manufacturing: Adaptive Mechanisms, Organizational Capabilities and the Structure of the Hong Kong Economy', *Asia Pacific Business review*, vol. 6, no. 1, pp. 13–32.

Chen, C. N. (1986) *Fang and Chia-Tsu: The Chinese Linship System in Rural Taiwan*, PhD thesis, New Haven, Department of Anthropology, Yale University.

Cheung, G. K. W. (2009) *Hong Kong's Watershed: The 1967 Riots*, Hong Kong: Hong Kong University Press.

Chiu, S. W. K. (1994) *The Politics of Laissez-Faire: Hong Kong's Strategy of Industrialization in Historical Perspective*, Hong Kong: Hong Kong Institute of Asia-Pacific Studies, Chinese University of Hong Kong.

Chiu, S. W. K., Ho, K. C. and Lui, T. L. (1997) *City-State in the Global Economy: Industrial Restructuring in Hong Kong and Singapore*, Boulder, CO: Westview Press.

Chrisman, J. J., Chua, J. H., Pearson, A. W. and Barnett, T. (2010) 'Family Involvement, Family Influence, and Family-Centered Non-Economic Goals in Small Firms', *Entrepreneurship Theory and Practice*, vol. 36, no. 2, pp. 267–293.

Chrisman, J. J., Chua, J. H. and Sharma, P. (2005) 'Trends and Directions in the Development of a Strategic Management Theory of the Family Firm', *Entrepreneurship Theory and Practice*, vol. 29, no. 5, pp. 555–575.

Chrisman, J. J., Kellermanns, F. W., Chan, K. C. and Liano, K. (2010) 'Intellectual Foundations of Current Research in Family Business: An Identification and Review of 25 Influential Articles', *Family Business Review*, vol. 23, no. 1, pp. 353–373.

Chu, Y. W. (1992) 'Informal Work in Hong Kong', *International Journal of Urban and Regional Research*, vol. 16, pp. 420–441.

Chua, J. H., Chrisman, J. J. and Bergiel, E. B. (2009) 'An Agency Theoretic Analysis of the Professionalized Family Firm', *Entrepreneurship Theory and Practice*, vol. 33, no. 2, pp. 355–372.

Chun, A. (1985) *Land Is to Live: A Study of the Concept of Tsu in a Hakka Chinese Village, New Territories, Hong Kong*, PhD thesis, Chicago, The University of Chicago.

Chun, A. (1996) 'Discourses of Identity in the Changing Spaces of Public Culture in Taiwan, Hong Kong and Singapore', *Theory, Culture & Society*, vol. 13, no. 1, pp. 51–75.

Comaroff, J. (2010) 'The End of Anthropology, Again: On the Future of an In/Discipline', *American Anthropologist*, vol. 112, no. 4, pp. 524–538.

Comaroff, J. and Comaroff, J. L. (1989) 'The Colonization of Consciousness in South Africa', *Economy and Society*, vol. 18, no. 3, pp. 267–296.

Comaroff, J. and Comaroff, J. L. (1991) *Of Revelation and Revolution, Volume 1: Christianity, Colonialism, and Consciousness in South Africa*, Chicago, IL: University of Chicago Press.

Cookson, A. (1983) 'Precious Stone Business: Jewellery orders increase', *The Hong Kong Industrial News*, June, p. 2.

Deetz, S. A. (1992) *Democracy in an Age of Corporate Colonization: Developments in Communication and the Politics of Everyday Life*, New York: State University of New York Press.

Denison, D., Lief, C. and Ward, J. L. (2004) 'Culture in Family-Owned Enterprises: Recognizing and Leveraging Unique Strengths', *Family Business Review*, vol. 17, no. 1, pp. 61–70.

Dyer, W. G. (1989) 'Integrating Professional Management into Family Owned Business', *Family Business Review*, vol. 2, no. 3, pp. 221–235.

Faure, D. (2003) *Colonialism and the Hong Kong Mentality*, Hong Kong: Hong Kong University Press.

Fei, X. T. (1992 [1947]) *From the Soil: The Foundations of Chinese Society*. (trans. G. G. Hamilton & Z. Wang), Berkeley: University of California Press.

Fung, K. V. (1982) *From Non-Intervention to Reluctant Interference: The Hong Kong Government Policy toward the Stock Market*, Master thesis, Hong Kong, The University of Hong Kong.

Galambos, L. (2010) 'The Role of Professionals in the Chandler Paradigm', *Industrial and Corporate Change*, vol. 19, no. 2, pp. 377–398.

Gallo, M. A., Tapies, J. and Cappuyns, K. (2004) 'Comparison of Family and Nonfamily Business: Financial Logic and Personal Preferences', *Family Business Review*, vol. 17, no. 4, pp. 303–318.

Gedajlovi, E., Lubatkin, M. H. and Schulze, W. S. (2004) 'Crossing the Threshold from Founder Management to Professional Management: A Governance Perspective', *Journal of Management Studies*, vol. 41, no. 5, pp. 899–912.

Geertz, C. (1973) *The Interpretation of Cultures*, New York: Basic Books.

Glasmeier, A. K. (1994) 'Flexibility and Adjustment: The Hong Kong Watch Industry and Global Change', *Growth and Change*, vol. 25, pp. 223–246.

Graeber, D. (2007) *Possibilities: Essays on Hierarchy, Rebellion, and Desire*, Oakland, CA & Edinburgh, UK: AK Press.

Graeber, D. (2014) 'On the Moral Grounds of Economic Relations: A Maussian Approach', *Journal of Classical Sociology*, vol. 14, no. 1, pp. 65–77.

Graeber, D. (2015) *The Utopia of Rules: On Technology, Stupidity, and the Secret Joys of Bureaucracy*, London: Melville House.

Gudmundson, D., Hartman, E. A. and Tower, C. B. (1999) 'Strategic Orientation: Differences between Family and Non-Family Firms', *Family Business Review*, vol. 12, no. 1, pp. 27–39.

Hall, A. and Nordqvist, M. (2008) 'Professional Management in Family Businesses: Toward an Extended Understanding', *Family Business Review*, vol. 21, no. 1, pp. 51–69.

Hamilton, G. G. and Kao, C. H. (2018) *Making Money: How Taiwanese Industrialists Embraced the Global Economy*, Stanford, CA: Stanford University Press.

Hong Kong Government (1950) *Annual Report on Hong Kong for the Year 1949*, Hong Kong: The Government of Hong Kong.

Hong Kong Government (1952) *Hong Kong Annual Report 1951*, Hong Kong: The Government of Hong Kong.

Hong Kong Government (1957) *Hong Kong Annual Report 1956*, Hong Kong: The Government of Hong Kong.

Hong Kong Government (1963) *Hong Kong: Report for the Year 1962*, Hong Kong: The Government of Hong Kong.

Hong Kong Standard [HKS] (1971) 'Imitation Jewellery Exports Get Boost', 31 May.

Hong Kong Standard [HKS] (1983) 'Jewellery Industry Slow to Capitalise on Existing Talent', 4 August.

Hong Kong Tourist Association (1959) *Report of the Board of Management of the Hong Kong Tourist Association*, Hong Kong: Hong Kong Tourist Association.

Hong Kong Tourist Association (1971) *Annual Report & Accounts 1970/71*, Hong Kong: Hong Kong Tourist Association.

Hong Kong Tourist Association (1990) *Annual Report 1989/90*, Hong Kong: Hong Kong Tourist Association.

Hong Kong Tourist Association (1991) *Annual Report 1990/91*, Hong Kong: Hong Kong Tourist Association.

Hong Kong Tourist Association (2001) *Annual Report 2000–2001*, Hong Kong: Hong Kong Tourist Association.

Hong Kong Trade Development Council [HKTDC] (1987) *Hong Kong's Jewellery Industry and Exports*, Hong Kong: Hong Kong Trade Development Council.

Ku, A. S. (2004) 'Immigration Policies, Discourses, and the Politics of Local Belonging in Hong Kong (1950–1980)', *Modern China*, vol. 30, no. 3, pp. 326–360.

Law, K. Y. and Lee, K. M. (2006) 'Citizenship, Economy and Social Exclusion of Mainland Chinese Immigrants in Hong Kong', *Journal of Contemporary Asia*, vol. 36, no. 2, pp. 217–242.

Lee, J. (1999) *Housing, Home Ownership and Social Change in Hong Kong*, Aldershot: Ashgate.

Lee, K. M. (1997) 'The Flexibility of the Hong Kong Manufacturing Sector', *China Information*, vol. 12, pp. 189–214.

Lee, M. K. (1998) 'Hong Kong Identity: Past and Present', in Wong, S. L. and Maruya, T. (eds.) *Hong Kong Economy and Society: Challenges in the New Era*, Tokyo: Institute of Developing Economies.

Littunen, H. (2003) 'Management Capabilities and Environmental Characteristics in the Critical Operational Phase of Entrepreneurship: A Comparison of Finnish Family and Nonfamily Firms', *Family Business Review*, vol. 16, no. 3, pp. 183–197.

Liu, C. S. (1999) *The Bursting of Hong Kong Property Bubble in 1997: Causes and Effects*, MA thesis, Hong Kong, The University of Hong Kong.

Louis, W. R. (1997) 'Hong Kong: The Critical Phase, 1945–1949', *The American Historical Review*, vol. 102, no. 4, pp. 1052–1084.

Lui, T. K. (2003) 'Rearguard Politics: Hong Kong's Middle Class', *The Developing Economies*, vol. 41, no. 2, pp. 161–183.

Lui, T. L. (1994) *Waged Work at Home: The Social Organization of Industrial Outwork in Hong Kong*, Aldershot, England & Hong Kong: Avebury.

Lui, T. L. (2001) 'The Malling of Hong Kong', in Mathews, G. and Lui, T. L. (eds.) *Consuming Hong Kong*, Hong Kong: Hong Kong University Press, pp. 23–45.

Lui, T. L. and Chiu, S. (1993) 'Industrial Restructuring and Labour-Market Adjustment under Positive Noninterventionism: The Case of Hong Kong', *Environment and Planning A*, vol. 25, pp. 63–79.

Lui, T. L. and Chiu, S. (1994) 'A Tale of Two Industries: The Restructuring of Hong Kong's Garment-Making and Electronics Industries', *Environment and Planning A*, vol. 26, pp. 53–70.

Lui, T. L. and Wong, T. W. P. (1994) *Chinese Entrepreneurship in Context*, Hong Kong: Hong Kong Institute of Asia-Pacific Studies, Chinese University of Hong Kong.

Madokoro, L. (2012) 'Borders Transformed: Sovereign Concerns, Population Movements and the Making of Territorial Frontiers in Hong Kong, 1949–1967', *Journal of Refugee Studies*, vol. 25, no. 3, pp. 407–427.

Madokoro, L. (2014) 'Surveying Hong Kong in the 1950s: Western Humanitarians and the "Problem" of Chinese Refugees', *Modern Asian Studies*, vol. 49, no. 2, pp. 493–524.

Mark, C. K. (2004) *Hong Kong and the Cold War: Anglo-American Relations 1949–1957*, Oxford, New York & Clarendon: Oxford University Press.

Mathews, G., Ma, E. K. W. and Lui, T. L. (2008) *Hong Kong, China: Learning to Belong to a Nation*, London & New York: Routledge.

Mizuoka, F. (2014) 'Contriving "Laissez-Faire": Conceptualising the British Colonial Rule of Hong Kong', *City, Culture and Society*, vol. 5, no. 1, pp. 23–32.

Montilla, D. (1970) 'HK Jewellery Exports Pick Up in Japan', *Hong Kong Standard*, 27 July.

Navarro, M. S. and Anson, S. G. (2009) 'Do Families Shape Corporate Governance Structures?', *Journal of Management & Organization*, vol. 15, no. 3, pp. 327–345.

Neubaum, D. O., Kammerlander, N. and Brigham, K. H. (2019) 'Capturing Family Firm Heterogeneity: How Taxonomies and Typologies Can Help the Field Move Forward', *Family Business Review*, vol. 32, no. 2, pp. 106–130.

Nicolaou, N. and Shane, S. (2014) 'Biology, Neuroscience, and Entrepreneurship', *Journal of Management Inquiry*, vol. 23, no. 1, pp. 98–100.

Nicolaou, N., Shane, S., Cherkas, L. and Spector, T. D. (2009) 'Opportunity Recognition and the Tendency to Be An Entrepreneur: A Bivariate Genetic Perspective', *Organizational Behavior and Human Decision Processes*, vol. 110, no. 2, pp. 108–117.

Nofal, M. A., Nicolaou, N., Symeonidou, N. and Shane, S. (2018) 'Biology and Management: A Review, Critique, and Research Agenda', *Journal of Management*, vol. 44, no. 1, pp. 7–31.

Okano, M. and Wong, H. W. (2004) 'Hong Kong's Guided Tours: Contexts of Tourism Image Construction before 1997', *Taiwan Journal of Anthropology*, vol. 2, no. 2, pp. 115–153.

Ortner, S. (1995) 'Resistance and the Problem of Ethnographic Refusal', *Comparative Studies in Society and History*, vol. 37, no. 1, pp. 173–193.

Oswald, S. L., Muse, L. A. and Rutherford, M. W. (2009) 'The Influence of Large Stake Family Control on Performance: Is It Agency or Entrenchment', *Journal of Small Business Management*, vol. 47, no. 1, pp. 116–135.

Parada, M. J., Norqvist, M. and Gimeno, A. (2010) 'Institutionalizing the Family Business: The Role of Professional Associations in Fostering a Change of Values', *Family Business Review*, vol. 23, no. 4, pp. 355–372.

Quaye, L., Nicolaou, N., Shane, S. and Mangino, M. (2012) 'A Discovery Genome-Wide Association Study of Entrepreneurship', *International Journal of Developmental Science*, vol. 6, no. 3–4, pp. 127–135.

Ram, M. and Holliday, R. (1993) 'Relative Merits: Family Culture and Kinship in Small Firms', *Sociology*, vol. 27, no. 4, pp. 629–648.

Rau, S. B., Schneider-Siebke, V. and Günther, C. (2019) 'Family Firm Values Explaining Family Firm Heterogeneity', *Family Business Review*, vol. 32, no. 2, pp. 195–215.

Redding, S. G. (1990) *The Spirit of Chinese Capitalism*, Berlin & New York: W. de Gruyter.

Remme, J. H. Z. (2014) 'A Dispositional Account of Causality: From Herbal Insecticides to Anthropological Theories on Emergence and Becoming', *Anthropological Theory*, vol. 14, no. 4, pp. 405–421.

Riedel, J. (1973) *The Hong Kong Model of Industrialization*, Kieler Diskussionsbeiträge, no. 29, Institut für Weltwirtschaft (IfW), Kiel.

Sahlins, M. (1976a) *Culture and Practical Reason*, Chicago & London: The University of Chicago Press.

Sahlins, M. (1976b) *Use and Abuse of Biology: An Anthropological Critique of Sociobiology*, Ann Arbor: The University of Michigan Press.

Sahlins, M. (1981) *Historical Metaphors and Mythical Realities: Structure in the Early History of the Sandwich Islands Kingdom*, Ann Arbor: University of Michigan.

Sahlins, M. (1985) *Islands of History*, Chicago & London: The University of Chicago Press.

Sahlins, M. (2000a) 'Sentimental Pessimism and Ethnographic Experience, or Why Culture Is Not a Disappearing "Object"', in Datson, L. (ed.) *Biographies of Scientific Objects*, Chicago: The University of Chicago Press, pp. 158–202.

Sahlins, M. (2000b) *Culture in Practice: Selected Essays*, New York: Zone Books.

Sahlins, M. (2004) *Apologies to Thucydides: Understanding History as Culture and Vice Versa*, Chicago: The Chicago University Press.

Sahlins, M. (2013) 'On the Culture of Material Value and the Cosmography of Riches', *HAU: Journal of Ethnographic Theory*, vol. 3, no. 2, pp. 161–195.

Sanchez-Ruiz, P., Daspit, J. J., Holt, D. T. and Rutherford, M. W. (2019) 'Family Social Capital in the Family Firm: A Taxonomic Classification, Relationships with Outcomes, and Directions for Advancement', *Family Business Review*, vol. 32, no. 2, pp. 131–153.

Sartre, J. P. (1963[1957]) *Search for a Method*. (trans. H. E. Barnes), New York: Alfred A. Knopf.

Scott, I. (1989) *Political Change and the Crisis of Legitimacy in Hong Kong*, Hong Kong: Oxford University Press.

Sewell, W. H. (2005) *Logics of History: Social Theory and Social Transformation*, Chicago: The University of Chicago Press.

Shane, S. (2000) 'Prior Knowledge and the Discovery of Entrepreneurial Opportunities', *Organization Science*, vol. 11, no. 4, pp. 448–469.

Shane, S. (2003) *A General Theory of Entrepreneurship: The Individual-Opportunity Nexus*, Cheltenham & Northampton, MA: Edward Elgar.

Shane, S. (2010) *Born Entrepreneurs, Born Leaders: How Your Genes Affect Your Work Life*, New York & Hong Kong: Oxford University Press.

Shane, S. (2012) 'Reflections on the 2010 AMR Decade Award: Delivering on the Promise of Entrepreneurship as a Field of Research', *The Academy of Management Review*, vol. 37, no. 1, pp. 10–20.

Shane, S. and Venkataraman, S. (2000) 'The Promise of Entrepreneurship as a Field of Research', *The Academy of Management Review*, vol. 25, no. 1, pp. 217–226.

Sharma, P. (2004) 'An Overview of the Field of Family Business Studies: Current Status and Directions for the Future', *Family Business Review*, vol. 17, no. 1, pp. 1–36.

Sharma, P. and Chrisman, J. J. (1999) 'Toward a Reconciliation of the Definitional Issues in the Field of Corporate Entrepreneurship', *Entrepreneurship Theory and Practice*, vol. 23, no. 3, pp. 11–27.

Sharma, P., Chrisman, J. J. and Chua, J. H. (1997) 'Strategic Management of the Family Business: Past Research and Future Challenge', *Family Business Review*, vol. 10, no. 1, pp. 1–35.

Shiga, S. (1967) *Chugoku Kazokuho no Genri [Principles of Chinese Family Law]*, Tokyo: Sobunsha.

Shiga, S. (1978) 'Family Property and the Law of Inheritance in Traditional China', in Buxbaum, D. C. (eds.) *Chinese Family Law and Social Change: In Historical and Comparative Perspective*, Seattle: University of Washington Press, pp. 109–150.

Smart, A. (2006) *The Shek Kip Mei Myth: Squatter, Fires and Colonial Rule in Hong Kong, 1950–1963*, Hong Kong: Hong Kong University Press.

Smith, A. T. (2002) 'Endangered Specificities: An Interview with Marshall Sahlins, 16 October 2001', *Journal of Social Archaeology*, vol. 2, no. 3, pp. 283–297.

South China Morning Post [SCMP] (1980) 'Spectacular Growth in Jewellery Trade', 20 September.

Stanley, L. J., Hernández-Linares, R., López-Fernández, M. C. and Kellermanns, F. W. (2019) 'A Typology of Family Firms: An Investigation of Entrepreneurial Orientation and Performance', *Family Business Review*, vol. 32, no. 2, pp. 174–194.

Steward, A. (2003) 'Help One Another, Use One Another: Toward an Anthropology of Family Business', *Entrepreneurship Theory and Practice*, vol. 27, no. 4, pp. 383–396.

Steward, A. and Hitt, M. A. (2012) 'Why Can't a Family Business Be More Like a Non-family Business? Modes of Professionalization in Family Firms', *Family Business Review*, vol. 25, no. 1, pp. 58–86.

Sutton, C. (2017) *Britain's Cold War in Cyprus and Hong Kong: A Conflict of Empires*, Cham: Palgrave Macmillan & Springer International Publishing.

Tsang, S. (2007) *A Modern History of Hong Kong*, London: I. B. Tauris.

Turner, M. and Ngan, I. (1995) *Hong Kong Sixties: Designing Identity*, Hong Kong: Hong Kong Arts Centre.

Venkataraman, S., Sarasvathy, S. D., Dew, N. and Forster, W. R. (2012) 'Reflections on the 2010 AMR Decade Award: Whither the Promise? Moving Forward with Entrepreneurship as a Science of the Artificial', *The Academy of Management Review*, vol. 37, no. 1, pp. 21–33.

von Kimakowitz, E., Pirson, M., Spitzeck, H., Dierksmeier, C. and Amann, W. (2010) *Humanistic Management in Practice*, New York: Palgrave Macmillan.

Westhead, P., Cowling, M. and Howorth, C. (2001) 'The Development of Family Companies: Management and Ownership Imperatives', *Family Business Review*, vol. 14, no. 4, pp. 369–385.

Whetstone, J. T. (2002) 'Personalism and Moral Leadership: The Servant Leader with a Transforming Vision', *Business Ethics: A European Review*, vol. 11, no. 4, pp. 385–392.

Whetstone, J. T. (2003) 'The Language of Managerial Excellence: Virtues as Understood and Applied', *Journal of Business Ethics*, vol. 44, no. 4, pp. 343–357.

Whitfield, A. J. (2001) *Hong Kong, Empire and the Anglo-American Alliance at War, 1941–1945*, Basingstoke, Hampshire & New York: Palgrave Macmillan.

Wong, H. W. (1999) *Japanese Bosses, Chinese Workers: Power and Control in a Hong Kong Megastore*, Richmond: Curzon Press.

Wong, H. W. (2006) 'Babaiban de jueqi yu xianggang shehui bianqian' [The Success of Yaohan and Hong Kong Social Changes], in Lee, P. T. (ed.) *Riben wenhua zai xianggang [Japanese Culture in Hong Kong]*, Hong Kong: The University of Hong Kong Press, pp. 151–173.

Wong, H. W. (2013) 'Understanding Management Philosophy as Hegemony or Ideology: Or, The First Step toward Business Anthropology', *Senri Ethnological Studies*, vol. 82, pp. 155–175.

Wong, H. W. (2015a) *Youqing yu sili: yi ge zai Xianggang de rizi baihuo gongsi zhi minzu-zhi [Friendship and Self-Interests: An Ethnography of a Japanese Department Store in Hong Kong]*, Taipei: Airiti Press.

Wong, H. W. (2015b) 'Jiang shangpin kua wenhua qianyi dangzuo lishi shijian yanjiu – dui Babaiban jinjun zhongguo Xianggang diqu anli de yixie pinglun' [Studying Cross-Cultural Migration of Cultural Goods as a historical Event: Reflections on Yaohan's Venture in Hong Kong], *Renleixue yanjiu [Anthropological Research]*, vol. 6, pp. 1–40.

Wong, H. W. (2017) 'What Is Chinese Kinship and What Is Not?', in Han, M., Hironao, K. and Wong, H. W. (eds.) *Family, Ethnicity, and State in Chinese Culture Under the Impact of Globalization*, Encino, CA: Bridge 21 Publications, pp. 83–104.

Wong, H. W. (forthcoming) 'It Is Not That All Cultures Have Business, But That All Business Has Culture', in Mir, R. and Fayard, A. L. (eds.) *Routledge Companion to Organizational Anthropology*.

Wong, H. W. and Chau, K. L. (forthcoming) 'Several Things that We Know about Creativity: History, Biography, and Affordance in Entrepreneurship'.

Wong, H. W. and Hui, C. H. (2005) 'Honkon ni okeru nihon no daishū bunka no bunka eikyō: nihon no poppumyūjikku to yaohan ni kan suru kēsu sutadi' [The Cultural Influences of Japanese Popular Culture in Hong Kong: The Case Studies of Yaohan and Japanese Pop Music], *Nihongaku kenkyū [Japanese Studies]*, vol. 15, pp. 182–197.

Wong, H. W. and Yau, H. Y. (2012) 'popyūkaruchā o tsūjite shutsugen shita 『Honkon-nin aidentiti 』' [The Emerging Hong Kong Identity by Way of Popular Culture] (trans. Y. Goto), in Wong, H. W., Tanikawa, T., Sudo, N. and Choo, K. (eds.) *Kontentsuka suru Higashi Ajia: taishū bunka, media, aidentiti [The Digitalization of East Asia: Popular Culture, Media and Identity]*, Tokyo: Seikyusha, pp. 101–128.

Wong, H. W. and Yau, H. Y. (2014) 'There Is No Simple Japanization, Creolization or Localization: Some Reflections on the Cross-Cultural Migration of Japanese Popular Culture to Hong Kong', in Wong, H. W. and Maegawa, K. (eds.) *Revisiting Colonial and Postcolonial: Anthropological Studies of the Cultural Interface*, Calif, US: Bridge 21 Publications, pp. 39–68.

Wong, H. W. and Yau, H. Y. (2015) 'The More I Shop at Yaohan, the More I Become a Heung Gong Yahn (Hongkongese): Japan and the Formation of a Hong Kong Identity', in Kirsch, G., Martinez, D. P. and White, M. (eds.) *Assembling Japan: Modernity, Technology and Global Culture*, Bern: Peter Lang, pp. 161–182.

Wong, H. W. and Yau, H. Y. (forthcoming) 'Transcending Expressivity and Instrumentality: Critical Studies of Chinese Friendship and Gift Giving'.

Wong, S. L. (1988) *Emigrant Entrepreneurs: Shanghai Industrialists in Hong Kong*, Hong Kong: Oxford University Press.

Wong, T. W. P. and Lui, T. L. (1992) *Reinstating Class: A Structural and Development Study of Hong Kong Society*, Hong Kong: Social Sciences Research Centre, University of Hong Kong.

Wong, W. C. G. (2010) Three Essays on Housing Market in Hong Kong: Implications for Public Policy and Macro Economy, PhD thesis, Hong Kong, Lingnan University.

Zhang, J. and Ma, H. (2009) 'Adoption of Professional Management in Chinese Family Business: A Multilevel Analysis of Impetuses and Impediments', *Asia Pacific Journal of Management*, vol. 26, no. 1, pp. 119–139.

Glossary

bong paai	幫派	Chinese gang
ch'i	氣	breath
chaxugeju	差序格局	differential mode of association
daa gam	打金	goldsmithing
daa gung zai	打工仔	wage earners
daai paai dong	大排檔	street food stall
faat cin hon	發錢寒	craze for money
fang	房	signifier of the status of son in relation to father
feng jia	分家	division of the *jia*
feng shui	風水	Chinese geomancy
gaam	減	reduction
gam pou	金鋪	goldsmith
gau geong	夠薑	bold
go	哥	elder brother
guohuo gongsi	國貨公司	Chinese department store
gwai	櫃	showcase
hang gaai	行街	middleman
jan cing	人情	human warmth
jan cing mei	人情味	taste of human warmth
jau	優	quality
jau tin jau dei	有田有地	having fields and lands
ji gwai	二櫃	second showcase
jia	家	co-resident, commensal group of household
jia-zu	家族	signifier of the status of father in relation to son
jiaye	家業	family business
jiazhang	家長	head of the household
kaifong	街坊	neighbour
kung fu	功夫	Chinese martial arts
kuo-fang	過房	change of membership from one *fang* to another fang
li	禮	ritual propriety
loeng	兩	Chinese *tael*
lou san zi	老臣子	long-serving employee

lung fung aak	龍鳳鈪	bangles of dragon and phoenix
mei gwai	尾櫃	last showcase
mui	妹	younger sister
neoi	囡	daughter
ngei	捱	extreme endurance
ngoi gwok jan	外國人	foreigner
pok	搏	proactive and risk-taking
qi	氣	breath
qilin	麒麟	Chinese unicorn
saam gwai	三櫃	third case
saan zai cong	山寨廠	cottage workshops
sai gam	西金	Western gold/jewellery
shingmuk	醒目	smartness
sifu	師傅	master
suk	叔	uncle
suk haak	熟客	regular customer
Tanka	蜑家	boat people
tau gwai	頭櫃	first showcase
tin	田	field
tongxiang	同鄉	people from the same origin
tsung-tsu	家族	genealogical aspect of Chinese family
t'ung ch'i	同氣	sharing the same essence
tung hang	同行	walking together
zai	仔	son
zap sang	執生	improvise
ze	姐	elder sister
zoeng gwai	掌櫃	shopkeeper
zu	族	sets of agnates and their wives
zuk gam	足金	pure gold
zyubou gam hong	珠寶金行	goldsmith and jewellery companies
zyubou hong	珠寶行	jewellery stores

Index

Printed in the United States
by Baker & Taylor Publisher Services